TRANSNATIONAL CORPORATIONS, ARMAMENTS AND DEVELOPMENT

TRANSNATIONAL CORPORATIONS, ARMAMENTS AND DEVELOPMENT

Helena Tuomi
and
Raimo Väyrynen

St. Martin's Press   **New York**

338,887
T 927

ISBN 0-312-81473-9

Library of Congress Cataloging in Publication Data

Tuomi, Helena.
    Transnational corporations, armaments and
development.

    Includes bibliographical references.
    1. Munitions.   2. International business
enterprises.   3. Underdeveloped areas--
Munitions.   I. Väyrynen, Raimo.   II. Title.
HD9743.A2T86 1981   338.8'87   81-18444
ISBN 0-312-81473-9   AACR2

Contents

Tables

ANNEX TABLES

Preface

This study was a contribution by Tampere Peace Research Instutute (TAPRI) to the United Nations study on the relationship between disarmament and development, which was initiated by the Special Session of the General Assembly on Disarmament held in 1978. We are very grateful to TAPRI for all cooperation during our research.

We are also very grateful to the Finnish Ministry for Foreign Affairs for a research grant which made this study possible. We also owe thanks to the Nordic Cooperation Committee for International Politics, including Conflict and Peace Research, which gave us additional financial support. As authors we want to thank all those whose comments and other contributions helped us during the work. All views expressed in this study are those of us alone; thus neither the Finnish Ministry for Foreign Affairs nor the Group of Governmental Experts at the UN are responsible for the contents.

The division of labour between the authors has been as follows: Helena Tuomi, the research fellow of this project, has written Chapters 1., 2., 3., 4.1., 5.1., 5.4., 5.5., 6.1., 6.2. and the summaries while Prof. Raimo Väyrynen has written Chapters 4.2., 4.3., 4.4., 5.2., 5.3., 6.3. and 6.4. As a result of a mutual comment procedure we share the responsibility for the whole text.

Armament process is an outcome of cooperation between governments, armies and armament industries. The roles of the political and military institutions have been subject to rather numerous studies, while the role and policy of the arms industry has often been neglected in research.

This study was commissioned by the UN Group of Governmental Experts in the spring of 1979, and the report was delivered to the Group in May 1980. Since then some minor changes have been made in the manuscript. Due to the short research period this report is of a preliminary character. Much more research and publicity on arms production and on its developmental impact are needed, if we want to understand the social and economic role played by the arms races.

We hope the study will contribute to a political and economic evaluation of the subject. We also hope it will help to generate future research and discussion in this important but, unfortunately, largely unknown field.

Tampere and Helsinki, July 1981

Helena Tuomi   Raimo Väyrynen

Summary of the study

The international system is characterized by the rivalry between East and West and the dominance of the military conception of security, which drives the arms race forwards. The continuous development of new military technologies is, however, a heavy economic burden for all countries participating in the arms race, and arms production is faced with a chronic structural crisis. Arms production thus takes place under contradictory circumstances: certain political and military pressures call for more efficient arms, while the economic and social realities call for a rapid decrease in military production.

The new arms technology is being developed by two powerful armament centres. In the West the leader is the United States, followed by France and the United Kingdom, which all have a strong, independent technology. In the East the armament centre is the Soviet Union, which also has a strong, independent technological capability. From these main centres new arms and armament technology are being transferred to other countries, which have adopted the same high-technology model of security.

Among arms supplying countries a second group can be identified. It consists of countries with a strong arms production, which is, however, dependent on foreign technology and possibly also financing. Countries like the Federal Republic of Germany, Italy or Czechoslovakia can be mentioned as examples.

Arms are being produced by corporations, characterised by their large size, specialized technological capability and extensive international operations. The Western arms producers can be considered transnational due to their large exports, common sales of licences, international co-production and investments in foreign arms industries as well as their international service networks. The socialist armament industry is also international in character, but in a different way: licensing, co-production and subcontracting take place mainly among the socialist countries while outside the socialist alliance export of finished weapons is the main form of operation.

Particularly in the 1970's many developing or semi-industrial countries have launched plans for indigenous military production. For new technology and financing they have turned to the transnational arms producers, which are in turn eager to participate because they compete for customers. Five case analyses show that for a developing country it is very difficult to achieve military self-reliance if the desired technology is complex. In aerospace production the bottlenecks are not so much the airframes but the most complex components like electronics, engines and armour for the weapon systems. Although some countries like India have already achieved a high degree of local manufacture in their military production they have not managed to produce the most complex parts.

The common view that indigenous military production by the LDCs would decrease arms imports, or that production of conventional weapons would be an alternative to the nuclear option, is not supported by empirical data. On the contrary LDC arms producers are also among the largest importers of arms. Furthermore, some countries with large arms imports and a strong policy of self-reliance in conventional arms are also trying to get nuclear capability. The conclusion is that once the high-technology military capability is sought, different armament options tend to complement rather than exclude each other.

Arms imports are the most common form of arms acquisition. Their economic effects include foreign debt, distortion of trade profile, reduced possibilities to import civilian goods, the use of scarce skilled personnel for the maintenance of weapons, and investments in infrastructure required by modern weapons. In some countries a strong militarization of the culture can be noted in connection with large imports of foreign arms.

The same economic effects are also observable in countries starting arms production, but the involvement of the economy in the global military structure is much more intensive. The scarce production resources are being used for military consumption, which tends to develop into an isolated enclave within the economy. The civilian spin-offs of military production tend to be negligible, due to the specialized nature of modern military technology. While the developing producer may become able to produce its own weapons, total independence is not achieved. Thus the experience of the indigenous armament programs tells of increasing independence in certain respects but increasing dependence on TNC-owned technology and critical parts. Studies of the Indian armament programs show that indigenous arms production may be more expensive than would be the import of similar arms from abroad. A high foreign exchange burden was also observed, due to the high costs of imported parts needed by local production.

The LDCs seek for more security with their indigenous arms production. Dependence on foreign technology, components and critical parts may cause new security problems, however, because in case of a military conflict there is no guarantee of foreign supplies. The cooperation of foreign personnel cannot be certain, either.

The LDCs cannot be sure that their military technology is up-to-date. The development of military electronics in particular makes the life of a weapons system very short unless retooling takes place at regular intervals. A further security risk is that the leading military TNCs today have huge data banks which contain most military secrets of the LDCs. In the case of a crisis the LDCs who buy arms or technology from the TNCs cannot be sure how this information is being used.

The economic burden of high-technology military imports, the even higher costs of indigenous production and the new types of security risks caused by foreign dependence, call for alternative solutions.

Essential components of such solutions are increased political settlements of both international and internal conflicts, consequent disarmament and efforts to find more suitable military technologies which correspond to the level of technology of the country concerned and do not risk the satisfaction of the basic needs of the population.

1 Introduction: dynamics of the international system, military technology and transnational armament industry

The ending of the arms race and the achievement of real disarmament are tasks of primary importance and urgency. To meet this historic challenge is in the political and economic interests of all the nations and peoples of the world as well as in the interests of ensuring their genuine security and peaceful future, states the Final Document of the 10th Special Session, devoted to disarmament.

Yet the global society has a long way to go to make these goals come true. The international system is characterized by a concentration of power, wealth and resources for a few industrialized countries in the northern hemisphere. Divided into East and West, the rich part of the world implements two competing development models, capitalism and socialism, which fortify their positions and rivalry with a continuous arms race although it constitutes an enormous burden and threat to both. It is the industrialized countries that have invented the present arms race, the deadly technology, because they have been unable to abandon the doctrine of the balance of military terror. It is precisely the doctrine of the balance of terror, based on the military conception of security, which creates the huge demand for military production and mobilizes scarce material and human resources for absurd waste. Even societies which are not directly involved in East-West competition deliver their raw materials and other resources to be used for military purposes in the North. Thus, in its present form the East-West competition has a militarizing impact on the whole international system. Those countries which follow the model shown by the leading Eastern and Western powers, or which come under their influence, are inclined to militarize, too, as long as the only conception of security is the military one.

One of the most dynamic features in the Northern development has been the growth of science and technology. This field - which as such represents human creativity and ambition - has been corrupted by the balance of terror machinery. The absurdity of military technology - above all capability to

1

destroy mankind - has also turned the traditional military conception of security upside down. What used to be security has turned into double insecurity: insecurity because of the enormous destruction potential and insecurity because of the waste of the scarce resources.

The arms race of the world is led by two powerful armament centres whose internal armament dynamics and continuous development of new arms technology - which aims at maximum performance of weapons - drives the arms race forward. At the same time the continuous development of destructive technology creates preconditions for the international diffusion of this technology.

There are, however, some differences between Eastern and Western arms technologies. The West has all the time been the technological leader, aiming at flexible, multipurpose and precise technology. The Soviet Union has lagged behind and has resorted to massive overproduction to be able to compete successfully in the arms race. The United States has tried to maintain its technological leadership with a strategic embargo, which continuously worries the Soviet Union.[1]

The main responsibility for the global process of militarization belongs to the industrialized countries in the East-West setting which have not been able to abandon the doctrine of balance of terror in international relations and consequently have been unwilling to stop the mobilization of scientific and technological resources for destructive purposes. To liberate mankind from this growing threat and waste would require an agreed alternative conception of security which abandons the balance of terror principle, takes into political control institutions working with outdated military and strategic ideas and introduces peaceful practices into the East-West rivalry.

The contradiction and rivalry between capitalism and socialism cannot be abolished. Yet this competition must be directed into peaceful areas; without such peaceful practices the arms race cannot be stopped and other countries will follow the arms race model provided by East and West.

Besides militarism, economic expansion is characteristic of the northern

2

industrialized countries, particularly of the leading capitalist countries which have experienced accumulation of wealth for 500 years and which have the longest industrial tradition. The great economic wealth accumulated by the industrial capitalist countries particularly after the industrial revolution has resulted in powerful innovative capacity and concentration of production into large units. National borders, particularly after World War II, became a limit for the large companies because for them growth and expansion are the way of life. The accumulation of profits in large companies forces them in to growth, and growth and expansion create new sources for profits. Besides the profit motive, other important factors encourage them to expand geographically or to diversify their products. Competition between the firms may be so fierce that without expansion many companies would not be able to survive. International and national economies suffer from cyclical crises caused by the ups and downs of raw material prices, overcapacity, inflation and depressions. The answer of the companies is, again, rationalization, geographical expansion, product diversification and related strategies to make the base of the company more resistant against the crises that appear regularly.

The international expansion of large companies after World War II started in America, which had not suffered from the war as much as Western Europe. But as soon as Europe had recovered from the war, and particularly after the European Economic Community had been created, European industries started to follow the American model of internationalization. The transnational corporation emerged in America and in Western Europe. Of course, there had been international companies before, but this time the internationalization was much more efficient because of the new communication and transport technology.

Military production did not stay outside the process of growth and expansion. Although the end of World War II had meant a decrease in military production, it became evident by the end of the 1940s that the Cold War had started between East and West. In the West, the policy of containment resulted in large transfers of arms, creation of military alliances and assistance programs. The armaments industries found new outlets in this process, which further accelerated during the Korean war. The origins of the post-war internationali-

3

zation of armament industries can thus be identified within this period: the large American transfers were followed by minority participations in the industries of the allied countries, and the revival of the industries of the allies with the help of American production licences, e.g. Starfighter.

It was a logical consequence of the U.S. leadership in the Western alliance and the dominance of its technology that the American arms industries were the first to become international. They penetrated Europe with minority holdings and technology agreements. But just as the European civilian industries became competitive in the 1960s, so too did the European military industries. After all, they did not start from zero after the war. The British had their strong shipbuilding industry with its colonial connections as well as a strong aircraft industry. The German military industry, which had shown its capacity in the 1930s, survived abroad while the was production in West Germany. After 1955 the industry was ready to start production again, and many designers returned to Germany.[2] Nor did French industry lag behind. De Gaulle's foreign policy in the 1960s, which emphasized a strong, independent France and which resulted in the French withdrawal from NATO's military activities, gave new impetus to weapons production and development of French technology. A final factor contributing to the growth of arms industries was the official policy of the European Community to create a competitive European armaments industry as a sign of an economically and politically viable Western Europe.

We have so far emphasized the role of the East-West conflict formation as the main international explanation for the growth of Western, as well as Eastern arms industries after the war. Yet it is also clear that there were internal forces which demanded growth of weapons production, or which, at least, had their strongest traditions in that field. If companies like Krupp or Vickers were used for technologically complex weapons production, they probably wanted to continue their activities rather than close down their military divisions. Institutions are very often conservative and inclined to follow their traditions even in new circumstances. Thus the war had ended but the war production continued. Perhaps it was in this way that the politicians determined why arms industries should grow - the reason being Cold War needs - while the industries themselves determined how the industry should grow and how new weapons should be developed.[3]

The Soviet Union assumed leadership in the socialist system. Being on the defensive after the start of the Cold War, it mobilized enough resources for a full-range military production apparatus. With a few years' time it started catching up with the Western leadership in all major weapons categories. The main difference between leading socialist and capitalist arms industries was - and is - that the profit motive and thus the drive for economic expansion is lacking in the socialist industries. Their growth is solely based on strategic and political considerations, which of course are also present in capitalist industries. The essential decision of the Soviet Union in the 1940s was to achieve arms technology similar to or comparable with what the West already had - in this sense the socialist countries followed the Western model of technology. The rules of the game were made by the West.

In the 1960s it became evident that there was an overproduction of weapons in the West: too many companies, too large output and production capacity. The political relations between East and West were improving in the 1960s and the Cold War was followed by increasing peaceful cooperation. The East-West relationship simply did not justify such a large production of weapons. It is interesting that it was precisely at that time in the 1960'swhen the export drive of Western arms industries started in the Third World and the American companies met European competition. As a hypothesis we might even suggest that it was the fear of diminishing demand and decline of the whole military sector that pushed the armaments industries into international expansion. As the European markets were full and production exceeded local demand, the industries turned to the Third World, where the amount of weapons was still limited and expanding markets could be forecasted. The industries were not left on their own in this process; on the contrary their home governments promoted new sales and arranged public funds for the purpose.[4]

The North-South relationship is the other major dimension in the international system. While the East-West formation is young in historical perspective - it is only 35 years since socialism became international - the North-South (which is actually West-South) formation is about 500 years old. But these two formations have different dynamics in the international system. The West always regarded itself as superior vis-à-vis the South and did not fear the South until 1973. For 500 years there was no arms race between West and South because the colonies could not arm themselves against their masters, and also after the collapse of colonialism the armament process was dominated and controlled by the West. The situation on the East-West axis, on the other hand, produced the arms race because the socialist development model and its international policies were regarded as a real threat to the domination of Western hegemony and the capitalist development model. On the psychological level the threat was perhaps comparable only to Attila and his Huns 1500 years ago.

The history of the West-South relationship is characterized by Western economic, cultural and military dominance. In the precolonial era there had already been extreme examples of the power of the firegun. The foundation of the first colonial settlements was often carried out with arms. Slaves were sometimes captured with arms e.g. to dig gold and precious metals for export to distant metropoles. The local elites could then import more arms to exploit population as well as to import luxury goods for elite consumption.[5]

In the colonial era the transfer of weapons to the colonies served to equip colonial armies. The functions of these armies were twofold: to secure colonial holdings and interests in competition with other colonial empires and to repress local resistance to colonial exploitation.[6] Independent, local armies did not exist in the colonies but the Western military doctrines and practices were imposed so intensively that their impact was visible long after the collapse of the colonial rule. The colonies also participated in large European war efforts. India, e.g., produced aircraft for the Allied Forces during World War II while the Japanese produced aircraft in Manchuria and Korea. Another military function of the colonies was to supply raw materials, food and even soldiers for the European belligerents. World War II also stimulated military production in Latin America. The embargo on military equipment made some countries, notably Argentina and Brazil, seek arms supplies of their own.[7]

The colonial system had a destructive impact on many essential social structures. Local cultures, national identity and integrity were damaged. The production structure was distorted because its main function had been to satisfy the needs of the metropolitan areas. The natural formation of national social classes was also disturbed because of the colonial ownership of production and the alliance of some local groups with the colonial masters. It was no wonder that after becoming independent the nation-building process often started in most confused circumstances and various groups tried to take advantage of the general uncertainty.

The Western policy of containment brought many Third World countries under Western military influence, particularly in the forward defence areas in Asia. The Western military and security assistance programs taught how to use modern weapons, who the enemies were, how to organize an army - according to Western models - and how to maintain social order. Not only national defence against international enemies but also counterinsurgency against local political opposition became the task of the armed forces. Because the Third World societies often lacked stable social institutions and organizations, the army came into focus. The theory of "the modernizing soldier" implied that besides the defence function the army would have a modernizing impact in different civilian sectors and would participate in various development projects.[8] This conception also legitimized the practice of the military regimes which are the most common form in the Third World today. Military organization thus replaced political representation in many countries.

The 1950s and 1960s were a period of intense power struggles and wars in the South. Military coups followed one another and foreign interventions were common, which indicated the police role of the North in the South.[9] Arms for these wars were supplied by the North. At the same time problems of underdevelopment became more severe than ever. On the other hand, the political cooperation of the developing countries made progress in for example the movement of the non-aligned countries and in the UN. The developing countries became very conscious of their common problems. It was understood that political independence must be followed by more economic independence. Finally some countries added the idea of military independence to their goals.

At the beginning of the 1970s the developing countries, acting as a large political front, launched their demand for a major reorganization of international economic relations, the New International Economic Order (NIEO). Another historical moment was the oil embargo launched by the Arab oil producing states in 1973. Both of these events threatened the traditional dominance of the industrialized countries for the first time in history.

Problems of development were much too difficult to be neglected, and a general consensus on the need for the NIEO was achieved. The consensus, however, works only on the surface. Under the surface there are different interpretations and political as well as military strategies, which often reflect the traditional Northern interests in the South. The negotiations regarding the implementation of the NIEO did not make much progress in the 1970s. At the same time a rapid reorganization of international economic and military relationships between North and South took place.

In the present context it is essential to note that the traditional power tools of the North, i.e. militarism and technology, came to play leading roles in the reorganization of North-South relationships in the 1970s. The guiding principle was to take advantage of the differences among the developing countries such as size, level of development, industrialization and raw material resources. A number of developing countries were identified as "regional influentials" where the new efforts were concentrated.

On the economic front, an intensified spread of Western technology took place in regionally influential countries. The main actors were the TNCs, which control and own Western technology. Many developing countries even competed in trying to attract the TNCs, because their faith in the superiority of TNC technology is just as firm as in the West. These developing countries opened their economies by e.g. founding free production zones, by offering cheap labour, infrastructure, and various economic incentives. The newly-rich oil producing states launched large investment plans, which also called for TNC participation. While the oil countries often started totally new production, the semi-industrialized countries often offered a subcontractor role for their industries. Both resource-rich countries as well as semi-industrial countries also represented new markets for the TNCs which have suffered from depression and declining demand in the West since 1973.

The result of these developments is that <u>differentiation</u> among the Third World countries has speeded up. On one side there are resource-rich and semi-industrial developing countries, many of which try to achieve growth with the assistance of the TNCs. The rest of the South are those LDCs who are poor or very poor and who have no clear-cut role in the new policies. It follows from the differentiation - if it is the intentional policy of the North - that the reorganization resembles the divide and rule policies of the historical empires. The policies of differentiation may result in political splits within the South which would then restore the traditional leadership of the North vis-a-vis the South.

Many ideologists in the North believe that there is an objective tendency in the North-South relationship towards a new division of labour. One of the many facets of this new division would be that the North (West) specializes in high-technology production like space systems, communication, production machinery, complex energy installations and so on. These would then be exchanged for less complex, labour-intensive industrial products of the South as well as raw materials, energy and tropical agricultural products. Although this conception of future development is called the <u>new international division of labour</u>[10] it is actually a continuation of the old colonial division of labour where - to mention Ricardo's classic example - "Portugal specializes in wines and Britain produces cotton with new machines". History has shown that Portugal suffered many problems because of this theory, as did the colonies.

It is interesting that the representatives of the TNCs in particular have expressed their faith in the emergence of the new division of labour.[11] Another interesting feature is that the "new division" became a slogan at the same time as the developing countries voiced their demands for the NIEO. It could therefore be suggested that the "new division of labour" concept was actually meant to be a TNC interpretation of the future NIEO. "The new division of labour" would increase the control of the TNCs over international economy and maintain their technological monopoly. While the NIEO aims at the economic independence of the LDCs, and at their increasing indigenous technology, the "new division of labour" increases their dependence on the TNCs and northern technology.

Complex military technology can fit very well into the concept of the new division of labour, since it is an area in which the West is specialized and which requires very qualified personnel, developed R&D apparatus, substantial funding and complex production machinery. If weapons and weapons technology are transferred on the basis of the "new division of labour", the result is the military-technological monopoly of the West.

The economic reorganization of the 1970's was accompanied by increased military transfers from the North to the South. The regional influentials became the focus of a rapid militarization process, whereby the leading Northern powers - and leading companies - offered them not only the latest weapons but also production technology.[12] The socialist countries supplied arms to countries which had chosen the socialist development model or were candidates for such a choice. The socialist countries, however, usually offer only arms and technical advice, not production technology, with the notable exception of India.

The growth of arms and technology transfers is not a general North-South process, however. Not all industrialized countries supply weapons, and only some of the LDCs buy them in large amounts.

Table 1.   Rank Order of Major Arms Suppliers to the LDCs in 1970-78
             ($ millions at constant 1975 prices)

Supplier	Value $ mn 1970-78	Per cent of world total
USA	21 528	39
USSR	17 250	32
France	6 208	11
UK	4 416	8
Italy	1 335	2.4
Third World	987	1.8
China	823	1.5
FRG	632	1.2
Other Western industrialized	395	0.7
Canada	313	0.6
Netherlands	304	0.6
Czechoslovakia	132	0.2
Other Eastern industrialized	66	0.1
Sweden	60	0.1
Japan	27	0.05
Switzerland	26	0.05
Total	54 537	100.00 %

Source: World Armaments and Disarmament. SIPRI Yearbook 1979,
            London 1979.

Note: The figures are SIPRI estimates for transfers of major weapons
            (aircraft, armoured vehicles, missiles, ships). The statistics
            include sales of production licences. Items may not add up to
            totals due to rounding.

The military capacity of the North is very strongly concentrated in a handful
of countries. They are the leading military spenders, and account for practically all military research and development. The new weapons technology
originates in these countries and is produced by large industries, of which
many have become transnational in the course of large sales and technology
transfers. The socialist industries are not transnational, but their international

operations are extensive, which makes their political and strategic impact comparable to that of Western industries.[13]

The Northern countries, of course, would not be able to supply large quantities of arms to the South without demand. The largest demand has existed in precisely those regional influential states which have become important in the general transformation of the North-South relationship. Argentina, Brazil, South Africa, Israel, Iran, India, South Korea as well as the oil producing states have received the largest amounts of modern weapons. But dependence on imports was not enough for them. In the 1970s they also made major efforts to develop their own arms industries as a sign of their military and economic self-reliance.

Wars are still very common in the South, and they reflect the general political instability of different Southern regions, as well as the perceived legitimacy of war and violence as methods of social and international action. The transfer of Northern military technology to areas where military tension is high no doubt functions as an alternative to direct Northern intervention.[14] The leading military powers no longer prefer to send soldiers; they prefer to send arms, technology and advisors to the local parties. Sometimes the same supplier delivers arms to both parties of a conflict, with the aim to create a military balance in a given area as well as to exercise control over the conflicting parties (e.g. U.S. arms supplies to Egypt and Israel and the Soviet effort to supply arms both to Somalia and Ethiopia).

Some arms transfers cannot be explained by war or threat of war. On the contrary, arms often flow to countries which have no international enemies. In such cases the social control function of arms becomes more important, as well as the prestige function of fortifying the regime, which is often composed of soldiers.

The foreign arms are not neutral pieces of technology. They can have an intense impact on importing societies. Being complicated weapons systems, they represent an industrial conception of warfare, the technology of which may exceed the technological level of the recipient. Arms may also strengthen some elite groups vis-à-vis the others, and the position of the regime against opposition.[15] On the international level, transfers of arms and technology have an impact on the whole structure of North-South relations.[16]

Arms production is a sector where political and economic interests are closely intertwined. In the socialist countries this relationship is - so to say -built into the structure of arms production. In the capitalist countries, too, arms production is a sector with the closest connections between political and economic interests; in other sectors these interests can very often be separated from one another. Many large arms companies are nationalized, evidence again of overlapping economic and political factors, but also private arms industries are dependent on supervision, regulation and financing by the state.[17] The relationship between political and economic interests is also visible in international arms transfers. Arms companies cannot export arms or technology without the permission of the state concerned. Arms transfers, then, have both economic and political effects. Finally, arms transfers cause changes in security structures both in internal, regional and - if they accumulate - in global contexts. The security effects also call for state supervision.

Because the role of the state authority is so crucial in arms production and arms trade - both in exports and in imports - it is logical that arms transfers are most often studied as political phenomena. Indeed, arms transfers are an essential part of international political and security structure and a part of foreign policies of the countries concerned. The emphasis on the political and security aspects of arms transfers has, however, often meant that the economic aspects of arms production and trade have been neglected.

The purpose of this study is therefore to describe and analyze the role of large armament industries in military transfers, and the impact of these transfers on recipient societies. The focus on the largest arms industries is, in our view, justified for several reasons. The first reason is the growing role of technology and the role of those who control and produce it - i.e. the industries. As a hypothesis it could be suggested that he who controls the design and production capacity of new military technology enjoys a privileged position as long as the arms race goes on. He may also have certain power advantages over those military and political authorities who try to supervise the development of new technology. The technological specialization also increases the power of producers over political and military authorities.

The second reason is the increasing commercialization of military relationships. As it is very expensive even for the leading industrial countries to develop and produce modern military technology, they have decreased the amount of military assistance and grants and increased the transfers paid by the recipient. Commercialization also implies that the armies of the supplying states do not participate directly in the military projects of the developing countries. Instead, they contract with specialized private or state-controlled companies, which do the job in a business-like manner. That is, the military tasks in the foreign countries are delegated to specialized companies.

The third reason for the focus on arms industries is that having grown into a giant and very specialized sector, they have become a strong interest group which is able to exercise influence and pressure on state policies.

The fourth reason is that the increasing internationalization of armament production is a relatively unknown process which has not been studied in detail. We do not have very much information about the companies themselves, how they occupy their markets, compete with each other or cooperate with their foreign partners. If the companies are allowed to internationalize freely and the process is unknown, their political control becomes very difficult. The result is a growing autonomy of arms industries.

Finally, the development impact of the internationalization of arms industries has not been studied sufficiently. Therefore we do not know whether the military transfers increase or decrease the development problems of the recipient countries. Neither do we know whether their goals of self-reliance and independence are promoted or hampered by military transfers.

2 Transnational armament industries: the cases of the aerospace, electronic and engine industry

2.1. Military Production in the Western Industrialized Countries

Military production in the industrialized Western countries is in principle subject to political control and regulation. If arms production grows, as has happened, into an enormous sector, this has happened on the basis of political will and legitimation.

On the other hand it is questionable whether ordinary citizens and taxpayers are informed about the quality and quantity of military production. Security matters, the arms race and the extreme sophistication of modern military technology easily escape broad political control, either for reasons of military secrecy or because of the inability to follow technological developments. As a result, decisions concerning the development and production of new arms are often made by a small specialized elite. The role of the taxpayer is a passive one: large public funds are allocated for the development and production of new weapons but very few taxpayers are able to evaluate the rationality of these allocations.

The first motives for indigenous arms production are national security needs and procurements for their own, national armies. On the other hand national defence needs are no longer the only motives for arms production - if they were no arms exports would take place. Large-scale arms production and international arms transfers are also maintained by the great industrialized powers to strengthen the international political and economic positions of the main producer countries.

In the 1970s the NATO countries spent on average 10-20 per cent of their military expenditure on major purchases of equipment:

Table 2.   Spending on Major Purchases of Equipment as a Percentage of Total Military Expenditure within NATO, 1972-77

	1972	1973	1974	1975	1976	1977
Belgium	11.4	8.4	8.8	9.1	11.1	10.3
Canada	6.1	7.3	5.9	6.3	8.0	9.1
Denmark	15.4	17.2	19.3	19.0	19.4	17.3
FRG	12.3	12.1	11.9	11.8	13.2	13.3
Italy	16.9	15.2	15.2	13.9	13.1	14.0
Luxembourg	1.5	1.3	2.4	1.0	3.4	2.9
Netherlands	10.7	11.2	13.2	15.6	15.2	18.2
Norway	11.8	11.7	13.4	14.4	13.3	16.6
Portugal	7.5	4.5	3.1	1.9	1.9	2.2
Turkey	4.9	5.0	3.0	..	..	..
UK	18.6	19.3	17.2	19.3	20.6	21.8
USA	21.6	18.9	18.1	17.5	18.5	20.8

Source: Report on European Armaments Procurement Cooperation. European Parliament, Political Affairs Committee, Document 83/78, 8 May 1978, p. 51.

Because the table only concerns major purchases, the real shares are higher. We can note a clear tendency in the table: the largest countries spend a higher share on procurements than smaller economies.

By utilizing the information on the relative share of the purchases of military equipment and on the total military budgets we can roughly calculate the absolute value of the purchases in the NATO countries. Following this simple method we came to the conclusion that in 1972 the total purchases were, at constant 1973 prices, $ 22.3 billion, in 1974 $ 18.4 billion and in 1977 $ 21.0 billion. The decline is probably due to the end of Vietnam War and the consequent decrease in U.S. military production. This is shown by the fact that in 1972 U.S. purchases were $ 17.8 billion, in 1974 only $ 14.0 billion, but increased then again to $ 15.9 billion in 1977. The same tendency appears in the purchase budgets of the other NATO members - varying from $ 4.5 billion, through $ 4.4 billion to $ 5.5 billion - which indicates that   military production has again started to increase in the NATO countries.

The procurement budgets of the NATO countries can also be analyzed with the aid of the data from UN sources, originally delivered by governments to the UN Secretary-General. According to this information national procurement budgets in selected capitalist countries are as follows:[1]

Table 3.   Procurement Funds of Selected Countries, 1971-77, in Billions of National Currencies at Current Prices

	1971	1972	1973	1974	1975	1976	1977
United States ($)	..	18.9	17.1	15.7	15.2	16.0	..
UK (£)	..	22.7	..	..	..	25.8	..
FRG (DM)	3.5	4.2	4.8	5.4	5.7	..	..
France (franc)	4.2	4.6	5.0	6.2	7.3	8.0	8.9
Sweden (kronor)	1.8	2.0	2.1	2.2	2.5	2.7	..
Japan (yen)	257.4	395.0	347.1	377.6	407.9	427.1	..
Norway (kroner)	1.5	1.6	1.7	1.8	2.1	2.4	..
Netherlands (guilders)	0.8	0.8	0.8	0.9	1.0	1.1	1.2

The reliability of the figures presented in this section is enhanced by the fact that two independent sources, a UN report and the NATO data on the major purchases of equipment lead to relatively similar estimates of resources devoted to the procurement of weapons and military technology.[2] The procurement funds have increased most rapidly in France, FRG and Japan, in this order. In 1980 the total value of the U.S. defence procurement amounts to $ 40 billion.[3]

The position of the leading arms producing countries can be studied by calculating the number of weapons systems they produce. With this method SIPRI listed the eight largest weapons producers as follows:

Table 4.   Eight Largest Industrialized Producers of Major Weapons, by
             Weapon Category

Figures are numbers of weapon types produced.

Producing country	Aircraft	Armoured vehicles	Missiles	Warships	Total
USA	91	16	41	33	181
USSR	40	8	34	30	112
France	36	9	28	23	96
UK	24	14	19	26	83
Italy	24	6	14	15	59
FR Germany	8	14	4	15	41
China	7	3	10	10	30
Sweden	10	1	6	6	23

Source: World Armaments and Disarmament, SIPRI Yearbook 1979,
            London 1979, p. 65.

In the industrialized part of the world, the USA is the dominant producer of weapons, followed by the Soviet Union. In Western Europe the FRG, France, Italy and the United Kingdom are also largely self-sufficient in all conventional weapons categories: combat aircraft, helicopters, tanks, military vehicles, missiles, warships, ammunition, small arms. They are able to obtain military equipment from their own industries. The smaller economies rely more on imported weapons and their own armament industry mostly produces small weapons, ammunition, or it participates as a subcontractor in bigger countries' weapons programmes.

To be ahead in the arms race and to continuously develop new technology requires enormous costs, however. The development of new weapons as well as their production has become very expensive. At the same time many countries try to stay in the production because of nationalist motives: an independent, technologically developed country just has to have indigenous production of major weapons. This contradiction between the nationalist considerations and economic realities of military production has led to a structural crisis in Western armament economy.[4] To be able to survive the factories must be merged into the largest possible units - this trend could be called the merger movement of Western arms industry. In most cases the merger process has taken place within national boundaries. The formation of British Aerospace as a merger of several aerospace producers is a good example. In one case, the German-Dutch VFW-Fokker, there was an attempt to move the merger across national boundaries. Recently this international undertaking was, however, split again into its national components and the merger movement will most probably now continue between German aircraft companies. The fate of VFW-Fokker shows that national considerations still play a leading role in armament industries.[5]

The fact that many Western governments keep their arms industries alive although most of them have continuous problems, has introduced one more competitive element in to defence business: competition between different producers is very fierce since many of them try to sell to the same customers. The penetration of American arms industries into Europe is an indication of this competition as well as "buy-European" or "buy-American" principles in procurements. In the Third World, the competition is most intense - which is shown by the rush of all Western arms producers to the Middle East after 1973.

The rush to new markets is one of the main methods of overcoming the structural difficulties of arms industries. Other solutions are joint procurement programmes, joint arms projects (e.g. MRCA, Alpha Jet, Jaguar, Euromissile), large international co-production schemes (F-16), standardization among the allies to avoid overlapping costs, international coordination of defence investments and so on. Within the arms industry the planning and regulation processes are in general easier than in civilian sectors; this is due to the strong role of the state on the industry as well as the dependence of the companies on state funding for R&D and state procurement. Thus, even Marcel Dassault in France - a private company which the experts have mentioned as a most successful enterprise from the business point of view - had to accept representatives from the state on its board.[6] In Western Europe restructuring of armament industries is not just ordinary economic rationalization; it is also a political effort which is connected to the idea of strong, independent Europe, not subordinated to anybody but an equal partner.[7]

The role of the arms industry in the West can be illustrated by relating the military output to the total output in the key branches. Unfortunately, empirical data are not easy to come by and so we must be satisfied with figures which are ten years old. It is probable that on the whole the share of military production has stayed the same within the last ten years.

Table 5.   The Military Share of the Total Annual Output in Selected Sectors in the United Kingdom, France and the Federal Republic of Germany in 1968-69, Millions of Dollars

Industry	United Kingdom		France		Fed.Rep. of Germany	
	Military output	Share per cent	Military output	Share per cent	Military output	Share per cent
Airframes, aero-engines, missiles	815	53	540	46	275	70-80
Shipbuilding	396	34	18	4	72	5-10
Motor vehicles	104	2	72	1	140	5-10
Electronics	100	9	396	45	317	5-10
Other	246	n.a.	162	n.a.	322	n.a.

Source: Report on European Armaments Procurement Cooperation. European Parliament, Political Affairs Committee, Document 83/78, 8 May 1978, p. 41.

As can be observed from the table, aerospace industry is in absolute terms the most important individual sector in the total defence industry. It is followed by electronics, the role of which has increased in all fields of armaments as well as in operational activities. The role of shipbuilding is related to geographic position, as can be seen in case of the UK.

2.2.   Transnational Aerospace Industry

The dominant position of the procurement of aircraft and missiles can be documented by the U.S. data which show that their share of the total military procurement was 50.8 per cent in the fiscal year 1971 and 52.4 per cent in 1975. The share of military electronics was on the other hand lower than expected; 6.1 per cent in 1971 and 5.6 per cent in 1975.[8] The figures in Chapter 2.3.2. also indicate that these percentages are much too low. Some characteristics of the aerospace industry in the United States and in Western Europe have been compiled in the following table in order to illustrate the relative significance of this central sector in the military industry as well as in the national economy in general:

Table 6.   Aerospace Industry in the West, 1973

	Total sales millions of U.S. dollars	Labour force thousands	Share of GNP per cent	Share of labour force in manufacturing industry, per cent
United States	23780	948	1.8	5.1
France	2330	106	1.0	1.8
United Kingdom	2290	206	1.1	2.7
Fed.Rep. of Germany	1400	53	0.4	0.7
Italy	600	30	0.4	1.3
Sweden	390	17	0.8	1.9
Holland	190	7	0.3	0.7
Belgium	100	4	0.2	0.4

Source: Manne Wängborg, The Use of Labour and Industry for Military Purposes: Some Figures, in Experiences in Disarmament. On Conversion of Military Industry and Closing of Military Bases, ed. by Peter Wallensteen, Uppsala 1978, pp. 168.

It is typical of military production that it is carried out by the same companies which are also large civilian producers. Only few companies rely on military production only and most aerospace, electronic, shipbuilding and car manufacturers absorb the military needs into their civilian production. From the social point of view this is good, because if military demand diminishes the companies can diversify into civilian directions. But from the research point of view the coexistence of civilian and military production is a problem because it becomes difficult to estimate accurately the extent of military production and foreign military operations.

It is also possible that the companies hide their military operations behind the civilian facade. This point is particularly relevant in large transnational corporations (TNCs), which can spread military technology abroad through their civilian organizations.

Although the aerospace industry has taken on an influential role in the armament production of the industrialized countries, we do not know very well what the producers are like. Therefore we will shortly describe the role of some leading companies in Chapters 2.2.1., 2.2.2. and 2.2.3. We will also describe briefly some company profiles because such basic data on leading armament industries are not easily available. We feel that it is not very informative to describe the international operations of armament industries unless we have some idea of what the companies are like. That is, we have to proceed from the basic units of the arms production process, the companies themselves.

We also feel that the concept of "transnational armament industry" cannot be taken as given, because the internationalization process in armament industries is not the same as in civil industries, because of security considerations. It is not self-evident that arms industries are transnational, and if they are, they are probably transnational in a special way. To approach this difficult problem, much more information of the companies should be publicly available than is now the case.

2.2.1.   The United States

The U.S. has traditionally been the dominant producer of both military and civilian aircraft. Its share of Western countries' aerospace sales was 73 per cent in 1972. In 1976 the share had decreased to 64.5 per cent. Although the U.S. still accounts for two-thirds of aerospace sales, its share has been slowly decreasing while the share of West European producers has grown from 20.9 per cent in 1972 to 28 per cent in 1976. In 1978 the U.S. total aerospace sales were over $ 37 billion.[9]

The U.S. is also the largest market for aircraft: 42 per cent of Western aircraft are sold in the U.S., 25 per cent in Europe and 33 per cent in other areas (1976). It is worth noting that the relative share of the developing countries has doubled between 1970-1976.[10]

Aerospace markets are dominated by military sales. In principal Western countries and Japan 60-90 per cent of aerospace sales were for military purposes in 1976. An exception to this trend is the Netherlands whose military market was only 10 per cent of the total sales.[11] It is fully justified to conclude that in aerospace industry the military sector can be considered the dog while civil aircraft is the tail - not vice versa. Military aerospace is also the technological leader in the industry; e.g. in the 1950s the development of American long-distance bombers formed the technological basis for the first generation of American jet passenger aircraft. The reasons for the U.S. leadership in military aerospace were - and are - the large funds for military research and development.

The Vietnam War was a major factor in the growth of U.S. aerospace companies. The employment of aerospace industry was 1.069.000 in 1970, but 898.000 in 1976 after the withdrawal of the U.S. from the war. At the end of the 1970s the aerospace industry again started to grow, due to increasing commercial and military orders as well as exports. The present employment in the industry is about 1.100.000, i.e. about the same as during the Vietnam War boom.[12]

All the largest aerospace companies are also among the largest contractors for the U.S. Department of Defence (DoD). Actually the share of DoD contracts in the total company sales can be used as a rough measure of the degree of militarization in the companies:

Table 7. The Largest U.S. Aerospace Companies and the Military Content of Production in 1978[a]

Company	Sales 1978 $ Mill.	Rank in Fortune 500	DoD Contracts 1978 $ Mill. [b]	Rank in top 100	DoD contracts as % of sales
United Technologies[e]	6 265	32	2 400	3	38.3
Rockwell International	5 833	37	890	11	15.3
Boeing	5 463	40	1 524	7	27.9
LTV[c]	5 261	42	384	28	7.3
McDonnell Douglas	4 130	63	2 863	2	69.3
Lockheed	3 496	81	2 226	4	63.7
Raytheon	3 239	88	1 307	9	40.4
Textron/Bell	3 231	89	868	12	26.9
General Dynamics	3 205	92	4 154	1	129.6
Northrop	1 830	160	586	15	32.0
Hughes Aircraft[d]	(1 800)	n.a.	1 489	8	(82.7)
Martin Marietta	1 758	165	539	19	30.7
Grumman	1 571	185	1 180	10	75.1
Cessna Aircraft	759	309			
Fairchild Industries	544	395	508	20	93.4
Beech Aircraft	528	404	98	78	18.6

Sources: The Fortune Directory of the 500 Largest U.S. Industrial Corporations, Fortune, May 7, 1979, pp. 268-295 and Aviation Week and Space Technology, Oct. 22, 1978. In addition TAPRI data files and company reports.

Notes: [a] Aircraft and missile producers only. Engine manufacturers are discussed in Chapter 2.4.

b)Funds allocated by the DoD for the company as <u>prime</u> contractor. Some of the money may go to subcontractors.

c)Military sales were about 9 per cent of LTV's turnover in 1975; the main business divisions are steel, meat and food.

d)Hughes is a private company which does not disclose its accounts. The turnover is taken from a company brochure <u>Hughes Aircraft Company</u>, according to which "1979 annual sales exceeded $ 1.8 billion". Foreign sales were said to be appr. 18 per cent of total sales.

e)Mainly Sikorsky and Pratt & Whitney divisions. See also Chapter 2.4.

According to the table the aerospace companies can be divided into two groups on the basis of their degree of militarization. The first group consists of companies whose military contracts account for more than half of the turnover: <u>McDonnell Douglas</u>, <u>Lockheed</u>, <u>General Dynamics</u>, <u>Hughes</u>, <u>Grumman</u> and <u>Fairchild Industries</u>. The military orientation of these companies can be summarized as follows:

<u>McDonnell Douglas</u>: large number of fighters, space programmes, missiles;

<u>Lockheed</u>: reconnaissance aircraft, antisubmarine and large transport aircraft, ballistic missiles, remotely piloted vehicles (RPVs), space systems;

<u>General Dynamics</u>: fighters, cruise missiles and other missiles, nuclear submarines, rockets;

<u>Hughes</u>: helicopters, missiles, space systems, radar, general defence electronics;

<u>Grumman</u>: navy-related aircraft, fighters, early warning aircraft, transport aircraft (see also Annex tables E and F for the military profiles of the companies).

For these companies it is not only typical that they have large military production in relative terms; another feature is that state funding is essential for their existence. It follows that the concept of "free enterprise" is not totally correct for this type of military producers.

A second group as far as the military content of companies is concerned, are companies where military contracts account for 25-50 per cent of the turnover. In 1978 such companies were United Technologies, Boeing, Raytheon, Textron (Bell), Northrop and Martin Marietta. The role of these companies in the military production can be summarized as follows:

> United Technologies: helicopters (Sikorsky), aircraft engines (Pratt & Whitney);
>
> Boeing: bombers, early warning aircraft, transport aircraft, helicopters, missiles, RPV's, space systems;
>
> Raytheon: missiles, defence communication and electronics;
>
> Textron: helicopters (Bell);
>
> Northrop: fighters, attack and reconnaissance aircraft, trainers;
>
> Martin Marietta: missiles, launch vehicles, space systems (see Annex tables E and F for further information on these companies).

The lower share of military production in these companies is mainly a result of two kinds of factor: either the companies have a diversified production profile (UTC, Boeing) or the company is in military-related business without that many DoD contracts. These explanations are also valid for the third group of companies (Rockwell, Beech, LTV), which have diversified into civilian fields. It is notable that small aircraft producers like Cessna and Beech are active in military sales without large state funds. Civil aircraft is their leading business but many small aircraft models are suitable for military counterinsurgency purposes.

Some aerospace companies are totally specialized in aviation. For example, Northrop, McDonnell Douglas, Boeing, Hughes, Beech can be almost totally identified with aerospace; also related activities like avionics and services usually have their own divisions within the company. On the other hand some firms have launched diversification strategies. General Dynamics, for instance, has diversified into shipbuilding, electronics, telecommunication, building materials, and mining. Rockwell International, a producer of military aircraft and missiles, purchased North American Collins Radio Company in 1973; in 1974 the company started manufacturing TV sets, and even began oil prospecting later on. It also started manufacturing automobile components and machinery for lumber work. In 1979 aerospace accounted for 29 per cent of Rockwell's turnover, and electronics (for the most part military) for 24 per cent.[13]

Some aerospace companies have been called "odd conglomerates" because the company participates in most unexpected activities.[14] Textron is the world's largest manufacturer of military helicopters, and receives 33 per cent of the turnover from Bell division. Apart from textiles - which give the company its name - the company produces almost any kind of consumer goods (like toys, zips, garden tools), industrial machinery and tools, and many metal components. The leading missile company Raytheon produces energy, household equipment, asphalt, textbooks and engineering. United Technologies produces elevators, wire and cables, air-conditioning, electronics, and automobile parts.

Some aerospace companies have actively started to mine their own raw materials: e.g. Martin Marietta is involved in bauxite mining in Africa. Many companies also produce their own components and services, thus making use of the benefits of vertical integration.

Aerospace is also a field which has attracted companies in other fields when they diversify and grow. Goodyear Aerospace (Goodyear Tire and Rubber), Aerojet General (General Tire & Rubber) and Ford Aerospace and Communications (Ford Motor) are examples of aerospace as a target in the diversification strategies.

The importance of military aircraft for U.S. international policies can be seen in the composition of foreign military sales (FMS). In 1977, when the value of the FMS program was $ 7.1 billion, aircraft was the largest single category accounting for one-third of total FMS:

Table 8.   Distribution of Transfers of Goods and Services under U.S.
            Military Agency Sales Contracts by Major Categories, Per Cent

	1972	1977
Aircraft	41	32
Misc. services	11	19
Vehicles	9	13
Construction	2	11
Missiles	12	10
Other equipment	7	7
Ammunition	10	5
Training	8	3
Total value of FMS	$ 1.16 Bill.	$ 7.08 Bill.

Source: Walter G. Kealy Jr. and Rodney D. Thorn, Military Transactions
           in the U.S. International Accounts, 1972-77, Survey of Current
           Business, Vol. 58, No. 5, May 1978, p. 23.

Taking into account that aerospace industry also provides the missiles and
aviation equipment (e.g. radar, navigation and communication systems), we
can conclude that at least half FMS is supplied by aerospace industry.[15]

Foreign military sales have concentrated in major aerospace producers. In
1978 the top exporters were:

Table 9.   Leading U.S. Military Aerospace Exporters (net value of military prime contract awards, FY 1978)

Firm and rank as DoD contractor	Principal item	FMS $ Mill.	Per cent of total FMS	Per cent of DoD contract awards
1. General Dynamics	F-16, missiles	1 476	25.6	7.0
2. Litton Industries	aerospace and naval electronics	524	9.1	2.6
3. Textron	helicopters	441	7.7	1.5
4. Lockheed	C-130 Hercules	297	5.2	3.7
5. McDonnell Douglas	F-14, F-15 aircraft	274	4.8	4.8
6. Raytheon	missiles	271	4.7	2.2
7. Northrop	aircraft	267	4.6	1.0
8. General Electric	engines	176	3.1	3.0
10. Hughes Aircraft	missiles, heli- copters	156	2.7	2.5
11. United Technologies	Sikorsky heli- copters, Pratt & Whitney engines	115	2.0	4.0
14. Grumman	F-14 Tomcat, early warning aircraft	70	1.2	2.0
	The share of the above companies from the total		70.7 %	34.3

Sources: Aviation Week & Space Technology, October 22, 1979 and Department of Defence. Washington Headquarters services, Directorate for Information Operations and Reports, May 15, 1978 (mimeo).

Note: Only Ret Ser Engineering (Rank 9), Vinnell Corp. and FMC managed to penetrate into the company of leading aerospace producers.

As can be noted the top aerospace firms accounted for 70.7 per cent of foreign military sales, while they received only 34.3 per cent of DoD contracts. Thus we can conclude that aerospace industries are more dominant in foreign military relations than in the total defence economy. We can also observe that foreign military sales are more concentrated than the DoD contract system in the largest companies. The dependence of aerospace companies on military exports can be measured by calculating the share of foreign military sales in the total value of DoD contract:

Table 10. Foreign Military Sales (FMS) as a Percentage of Total DoD Contracts in Leading U.S. Aerospace Companies 1976-78

Company	FMS/DoD contracts 1976, %	FMS/DoD contracts 1978, %	Change 1976-78 % units
General Dynamics	4.3	35.5	+ 31.2
Litton Industries	26.4	33.6	+ 7.2
Textron/Bell	30.0	50.9	+ 20.9
Lockheed	9.2	13.4	+ 4.2
McDonnell Douglas	19.5	9.6	- 9.9
Raytheon	27.9	20.7	- 7.2
Northrop	87.3	45.6	- 41.7
General Electric	18.4	9.8	- 8.6
Hughes	19.1	10.5	- 8.6
United Technologies	8.5	4.8	- 3.7
Grumman	30.9	5.9	- 25.0

Sources: Aviation Week & Space Technology, March 14, 1977 and October 22, 1979, and Foreign Military Sales. Top 25 Companies and Their Subsidiaries Ranked according to Net Value of Military Prime Contract Awards. Fiscal Years 1976, 1978. Department of Defence. Washington Headquarters Services. Directorate for Information Operations and Reports, May 15, 1978 (mimeo).

In 1976, Northrop was clearly the most export-dependent firm, followed by Grumman and Textron/Bell with a big difference. In 1978 the export leader is

Textron/Bell, followed by Northrop, <u>General Dynamics</u> and <u>Litton Industries</u>. Large single deals, like the sale of F-16, can rapidly change the shares. In general, the export market accounts for less than half the military sales of U.S. aerospace firms.

2.2.2.   Western Europe

The West European aerospace industry has been developed with the aim to become competitive with the American industry. In commercial aircraft the goal has not yet been achieved: in 1976 only 21 per cent of the aircraft used in Europe was constructed in Europe. Well-known examples like Concorde and Airbus represent efforts to improve the European position.

As regards military aircraft, the situation is different: in 1975 military aircraft manufactured in the EC area already accounted for 67 per cent of EEC member states' total military fleet. The fragmentation of European industry into several national industries with smaller markets than the United States has been considered one of the main weaknesses in the European aircraft industry. The number of producers in Europe is large compared to the size of markets. There are 19 aircraft manufacturers within the European Community as compared to only eight in the U.S. In 1978 the 19 companies shared a turnover of 7.4 billion units of account in the Community, as against 17.6 billion in the U.S.[16]

The joint European armament programs enlarge European markets because the parties to the programs are also expected to buy the common products. With regard to the intensity the West European armament cooperation can be divided into three main types: joint production, joint development and production as well as joint research, development and production of weapons. In the large aircraft projects (Jaguar, Alpha Jet and Tornado/MRCA) the participating countries have shared the R&D tasks, too, while in some other programs (e.g. Hawk and Sidewinder missiles) the participating countries have only collaborated in the production phase. France, the United Kingdom and the Federal Republic of Germany are the leading participants in transnational R&D collaboration, while minor countries usually participate only in production.

The main aim of the West European industry - to become strong and independent - is reflected in weapons programs. To be able to develop European technology, the companies in different countries pool their resources and seek funding from different national governments for joint programmes. To achieve such collaboration they have to overcome the problem of the national protection of military R&D, which is the usual practice. This collaboration is the only way to become competitive with the U.S. which has its own, enormous funding apparatus for military R&D. Rivalry between the U.S. and Western Europe is also reflected in the fact that there is almost no military R&D collaboration across the Atlantic, but the few joint weapons projects only concern the production phase.

On the other hand the independence of European military technology with regard to the U.S. should not be exaggerated. In the need for new technology the European arms producers often turn to the U.S. firms to get their newest innovations. Thus the Euro-American relationship consists of both signs of independence and dependence, but the overall aim is to get rid of the U.S. technological domination.

A comparison between U.S. and non-U.S. aerospace industries can be made by comparing the number of weapons systems they produce:

Table 11.   Number of Non-U.S. and U.S. Indigenous Weapons Systems in
            Aerospace by Major Categories

	Aircraft	Missiles	Helicopters
France	21	28	11
United Kingdom	20	16	1[a]
Japan	10	6	-
Italy	9	11	2[a]
Sweden	9	5	-
Netherlands	8	-	-
FRG	4	2	3
Switzerland	4	-	-
Norway	-	3	-
West-Europe + Japan	85	71	17
European co-production	6	11	9
Non-U.S. total	91	82	26
USA[b]	58	38	23
Industrialized market economies, total	119	120	49

Source: World Armaments and Disarmament, SIPRI Yearbook 1979,
            London 1979, pp. 72-139.

Notes: [a]Excluding licence production.

            [b]When the different variants of weapons are taken into ac-
            count, the U.S. number of military aircraft rises up to 82 and
            the number of missiles to 58. Cf. the list provided by Aviation
            Week & Space Technology, March 3, 1980, pp. 102-105.

As can be noted, France is the second aerospace producer after the U.S. while
the UK ranks third. No other industrialized Western country has indigenous
aerospace production in all weapons categories. On the other hand Italy,
Japan, the Netherlands and Sweden are notable aircraft producers and Italy,
Japan and Sweden produce several sorts of missiles. Helicopter production is
the weakest part of Western aerospace industry as far as indigenous designs
are concerned. The largest production outside the U.S. takes place in France,
Italy

and the UK, but most Italian models are in fact based on American licences and most British models on French designs.

It is notable that co-production in European armaments industry has not led to international mergers. Only VWF-Fokker was formed in 1970, but the split of the company was announced in January 1980, and the merger movement will now continue within German industry. The co-production projects have been formed for specified weapons systems, and at least so far no permanent transnational companies have emerged on the basis of co-production. On the other hand, co-production in Europe is a young phenomenon and it may very well be that the ad hoc international groupings will later develop into permanent joint ventures if they keep developing new international weapons projects. Some representatives of the European armament industry hope that real transnationals would be created in defence production:[17]

> Enough experience has been gained in managing truly European enterprises, such as Royal Dutch Shell and Unilever, and I trust that what has worked well for oil and soap should work even better for future aerospace efforts.

A representative of British industry has also perceived the emergence of all-European, united companies. After discussing the present status of European co-production he continues:[18]

> Let us now aim, as the next step, for the preservation of these partnerships. Let us now attempt to develop them so that we have one for civil aircraft, one for military aircraft, and one for space - I almost - but not quite - hesitate to suggest - one for aero-engines, where the position at present is sharply divisive, although Turbo-Union is very encouraging bringing together as it does, a powerful consortium consisting of the many engine manufacturers of Britain, Germany and Italy - a very happy augury for the future.

West Europe's aerospace industry is not as big a factor in the total Common Market economy as the U.S. industry is in the U.S. economy. In 1975 the aerospace contribution to the combined GNP of the EC was 0.67 per cent in terms of sales, while the share of the U.S. aerospace sales in the nation's trillion-dollar GNP was 1.75 per cent.[19] Non-economic factors, however, increase the role of aerospace in industrial policy. Military business accounts for 70 per cent of the sales of European industries on average, while its share in the U.S. industry is about 55-60 per cent.[20]

France

The strongest West European aerospace industry is found in France after it overtook the United Kingdom in 1973. In 1978 the turnover of French aerospace industry was Ffr. 24 500 million (approximately $ 6.1 billion), of which 70 per cent went to exports.[21]

Table 12.   Exports of French Aerospace Industry in 1978

Product category	Ffr. Mill.	Per cent
Aircraft	9 892	57.7
Missiles	2 162	12.6
Engines	1 964	11.4
Electronics	1 690	9.9
Helicopters	1 446	8.4
Total	17 154	100.0

Source: Le Monde, March 6, 1979.

Military sales account for 72 per cent of French aerospace exports.[22] The French aerospace exports are dominated by five companies:

Table 13.   The Share of Largest Producers in French Aerospace Exports 1977

Company	Main business	Exports Ffr. Mill.	Per cent
Dassault-Breguet[a]	Mirage	10 000	46.5
Matra	Missiles	4 500	19.6
Aerospatiale (SNIAS)	Helicopters, missiles	3 000	13.0
SNECMA	Engines	1 900	8.2
Thomson-CSF	Aerospace electronics	1 400	6.1
Sum		21 500	93.4
Total aerospace exports in 1977		23 000[b]	100.0

Source: Le Monde, January 21, 1978.

Notes: [a]International production of Alpha Jet with Dornier, FRG, and Jaguar with British Aerospace affect the figure.

[b]The figure was later revised to Ffr. 23 820 million. Le Monde, February 21, 1978.

The profiles of the leading export companies can be summarized as follows:[23]

Avions Marcel Dassault-Breguet Aviation is one of the most export-dependent military producers in the world. Its exports account for about 75 per cent of turnover. The total sales of the company were $ 1.4 billion in 1978. Military orders accounted for 77 per cent of all orders in 1977. The role of military production is particularly strong in exports: 65 per cent of the exports were military aircraft in 1977. By value of export revenue Dassault was the fourth largest export company in France in 1976. Dassault's success in exports also draws other companies into exports. Main beneficiaries are engine manufacturing SNECMA, radar and avionics producing Thomson-CSF and missile and ordnance producing Matra. In 1978 the French government took 21 per cent of the shares of Dassault to be better able to coordinate all French aerospace efforts. The international organization of Dassault is not known, but the company often uses personal agents in marketing.

The state-owned Société Nationale Industrielle Aerospatiale. (SNIAS) produces aircraft, helicopters and missiles. Its total sales were $ 2.5 billion in 1978. In 1977 the share of exports was 45 per cent of the turnover. The lower share of exports results from the fact that SNIAS produces a great deal for the French army. The company exports 77 per cent of its helicopters and 70 per cent of the tactical missiles. Within the last years the company has made losses, due to large civil investments, particularly in Concorde. The company has sold helicopter licences to Westland in the UK as well as Romania, Yugoslavia, India and Egypt. It also cooperates with the German MBB, of which it owns 12 per cent. SNIAS also has foreign subsidiaries or joint ventures, at least in the U.S. and Brazil, but further information is - again - lacking. SNIAS is the second largest helicopter producer in the world after the U.S. Bell. It has joined the loose federation Euroheli for coordination of European helicopter programs (together with MBB, Westland and Agusta). SNIAS itself is also a licence producer of Raytheon's missiles.

MATRA is a diversified company which produces missiles, space systems, automobile equipment, public works, electronics, tele-communication, information systems, optics, semiconductors (to-gether with the U.S. Harris) and services. MATRA is growing very fast: its turnover was $ 609 million in 1978, but according to press information $ 1 billion in 1979 and $ 3.5 billion in 1980. The exact figures are not easy to come by, due to the complicated structure of MATRA as well as various criteria for consolidation. At present about half the business is military, but 75-80 per cent of MATRA's profits were provided by missiles in 1978. The main form of the company growth has been takeovers of smaller companies in high-technology fields, and a wide practice of subcontracting is also used. MATRA cooperates with the Italian Oto Melara and the British Hawker Siddley in missile production (Otomat and Martel). According to company publications MATRA has foreign affiliations and partic-ipations but no further information is disclosed. MATRA produces six types of missiles, bombs, grenades, rockets and cooperates with Thomson-CSF extensively in weapons electronics.

As can be noted, the export dependence of the French companies is very strong - a factor which under fierce international competition encourages transnational cooperation. Another result of the competition is that the companies do not like to disclose their international subsidiaries or affili-ations.

The United Kingdom

The British share in the world arms exports has been slowly decreasing within the last few years, from some 10-11 per cent to some 8 per cent, if calculated on the basis of figures provided by SIPRI. The British aerospace exports, however, have grown continuously within the last few years.

Table 14.   British Aerospace Exports 1972-77, £ Million

1972	1973	1974	1975	1976	1977
418	520	631	801	904	1038

Source: Lawrence Freedman, Arms Production in the United Kingdom. Problems and Prospects. The Royal Institute of International Affairs 1978, p. 33.

The rise of the sales is mainly caused by increased military exports to the Middle East, Persian Gulf area and around the Mediterranean. The total sales of the British aerospace industry were recently estimated as approx. $ 7.3 billion in 1979, of which $ 2.7 billion (37 per cent) were exports.[24] The present composition of exports is not available but in 1977 the composition was as follows:

Table 15.   Composition of British Aerospace Exports in 1977

Product category	Exports 1977 $ million	Per cent
Aircraft and parts	1 061.6	52.4
New engines, repaired engines and parts	843.4	41.7
Missiles	51.9	2.6
Radio, radar, navigation	26.4	1.3
Instruments and equipment	40.7	2.0
Total	2 024.0	100.0

Source: Calculated from figures in Aviation Week & Space Technology, February 13, 1978.

Note: It is a common opinion that the figures on British arms exports are underestimated. Cf. Freedman op.cit., p. 32.

It is typical for the British exports that the share of engines and parts is high. This is explained by the common use of Rolls Royce engines abroad. In 1973 the military element of aerospace exports was 50-60 per cent, depending on the category. The present ratio is not known, but military exports in particular have increased since 1973.[25]

In 1976-77, the main aerospace contractors for the British Ministry of Defence (MOD) were:

Table 16.   British Aerospace Industry with MOD Contracts over £ 5 Million in 1976-77

Company	MOD contracts
British Aircraft Corp.[a]	Over £ 100 million
Hawker Siddley Group[a]	
Rolls Royce	
Westland Aircraft	£ 50-100 million
Short Brothers	£ 10-25

Source: Lawrence Freedman, Arms production in the U.K., Problems and Prospects, op.cit., p. 1.

Note: [a]Now British Aerospace.

The aerospace industry of the UK faced a major reorganization in 1977, when the state-owned British Aerospace was created by a merger of British Aircraft Corporation, Hawker Siddley Aviation, Hawker Siddley Dynamics and Scottish Aviation. The company now employs 1/3 of the aerospace workforce in the UK. In addition to these aircraft producers Britten Norman produces small aircraft suitable for military purposes. Like Cessna in the U.S., this company does not enjoy much MOD funding, but this does not mean that it is excluded from military exports.

The role of the main companies can be summarized as follows:[26]

> British Aerospace had $ 1.7 billion sales in 1978, i.e. it is larger than Dassault and compares with U.S. Northrop in sales. The products include civil aircraft, nine main types of military aircraft (e.g. Harrier, Nimrod, Hawk and Bulldog), seven different types of missiles, space activities and various sorts of military equipment and components (e.g. qyro-instruments, ECM-equipment, testing devices etc.). Its exports account for approximately 55 per cent of the turnover and their geographical distribution is Central and South

39

America 4 per cent, Africa 1 per cent, Middle East 26 per cent, Far East 2 per cent. The company has a very international cooperation and organization. On the European scale it participates in Concorde, Airbus, Tornado, Jaguar and recently also Euromissile. On a larger scale, the company subcontracts for McDonnell Douglas, General Dynamics, Lockheed and Mitsubishi. In missiles production BAe is collaborating with Raytheon (USA) and Matra (France). It has sold missile licences to several countries, including Australia, Iran, and an aircraft manufacturing licence to India (HS 748 transport) and Romania (BAC III). In space programs, the company cooperates particularly with the U.S. Hughes, whose TOW-missiles are also produced in collaboration. One of the most expanding parts of BAe's activities is the so-called defence support program, i.e. the company takes care of some developing country's air defence by sending personnel and equipment and by providing training for local staff. Such programs are going on in at least Oman and Saudi Arabia.

Westland Aircraft produces helicopters, remotely piloted vehicles for surveillance, helicopter TV-systems, weapons equipment, fuel tanks, flotation systems, assault boats, weapons hydraulics, night vision equipment and security alarms, repair and overhaul services etc. Helicopters constitute, however, 72 per cent of the turnover. According to SIPRI only one of the models is indigenously designed, most of them are licensed by Aerospatiale (SNIAS), France and some by Sikorsky, USA. Westland has joined Euroheli for European coordination of policies. In the UK, Westland has a joint venture with the American enginecompany Garrett for overhaul and repair services, as well as marine and aviation related manufacture. Westland has had financial problems within the last few years and internationalization has been seen as one solution. Particularly the contract with the Arab Organization of Industrialization for the purchase of 50 Lynx and for later licence production was welcomed in this respect, but after the project failed the company has expected compensation, or purchases from those who broke it. Westland's turnover was £ 198.2 million in 1979.

Short Brothers is also an active exporter of armaments, although no giant in size. It manufactures transport aircraft, drones, armoured cars and missiles (Blowpipe, Seacat, Tigercat), targets and targeting devices. According to a commercial Seacat is adopted by 16 navies, and it is "the world's most widely used guided weapon system". Although Short Brothers is not very large, its international sales are extensively dispersed in Latin America, Africa and Asia.

The Federal Republic of Germany

When World War II started, Germany was the leading aircraft exporter of the world. The peak year of production was 1944, when the Nazi aircraft industry built 40 593 aircraft. When the industry was demilitarized after the war, many aerospace designers, managers and engineers emigrated and continued their work abroad. Spanish and Latin American aircraft industries in particular received new work forces as a result of German aerospace emigrants. Some of them returned to Germany after 1955 and even had new designs with them when they arrived. Although military production had been forbidden in 1945-55, the knowledge and skills were, however, maintained in some academic institutions. Thus, when the aerospace industry was again started at the end of the 1950s, it did not have to start from zero. The aircraft industry was reborn with the licensed production of the Lockheed F-104.[27]

The aerospace industry of the FRG is the third largest in Western Europe. The aircraft subsector represents 65.5 per cent of the turnover (1976), while engine, equipment and space sectors account for 11.5, 16.0 and 6.9 per cent respectively. Compared to France and the UK, the space subsector is relatively strong while the engine sector is weak. Military sales account for 82 per cent of the aerospace turnover, a ratio which is very high compared to the U.S. 65 per cent and the UK 67 per cent.[28]

Until the late 1960s the main characteristic of the industry has been licensed production for domestic markets. The American dominance was strengthened by the penetration of American companies into German industry with share-holdings: Boeing 8.9 per cent in MBB, United Technologies and Northrop in VFW-Fokker (13.5 and 10 per cent respectively).[29]

At the beginning of the 1970s the position of German industry was reconsidered. From then on, the aim was to develop indigenous production and get a strong industry as part of Europe. Also exports increased after these reconsiderations. Active participation in international military programs was one way to develop the industry; thus the FRG now participates in over 30 European co-production or licensing arrangements. In aerospace, the FRG collaborates with France, the UK, Italy, Spain, USA, Canada, Belgium, Netherlands, Denmark, Norway, Switzerland, Japan. The cooperation concerns all the main subsectors: aircraft, helicopters, engines and space.

As many of the weapons programs are managed from abroad, the result is that some of the West German aerospace exports are not delivered from Germany but from the partner countries, particularly from France. Thus the FRG industry has been able to circumvent restrictions concerning military exports. It is also possible that the extensive sales from foreign countries keep the military exports figures lower than they really are.

In 1977 the German aerospace exports were DM 1877 million, which was a third of the total turnover. The ratio is lower than in the UK and much lower than in France (37 and over 70).[30] The exports have started to rise rapidly since 1974.

The industry is dominated by four companies; aircraft producers Messer-schmitt-Bölkow-Blohm (MBB), VFW-Fokker, Dornier, and engine manufacturing Motoren- und Turbinenunion (MTU).

Table 17.   Largest Aerospace Companies in the FRG

Company	Sales 1977 DM Mill.	Per cent military	Main products
Messerschmitt-Bölkow-Blohm MBB	1 801	60	helicopters, Tornado, tanks missiles
Vereiningte Flug-technische Werke (VFW)-Fokker	1 705	60	transport aircraft, heli-copters, missiles, mine systems
Motoren-und-Turbinen-Union (MTU)	1 063	52	engines for aviation, tanks ships
Dornier	723	51	helicopters, Alpha Jet, liaison aircraft, drones

Source: Arbeitsgruppe Rüstung und Unterentwicklung, Institut für Friedensforschung und Sicherheitspolitik (IFSH) an der Universität Hamburg.

The company profiles - except the MTU which will be covered in Chapter 2.4. can be summarized as follows:[31]

MBB is the largest German aerospace company, where 46.22 per cent of the shares are owned by public institutions, State of Bavaria and City of Hamburg. The French Aerospatiale and the German Siemens own 8.9 per cent of the shares each. The U.S. Boeing sold its shares two years ago. In a commercial MBB describes itself as "a partner in international programs". The characterization is most accurate, since it has been estimated that 60 per cent of the turnover originates in international programs. In civil aviation, MBB is the main German participant in Airbus. In military aircraft, it participates in Tornado with British Aerospace and Aeritalia. It provided technical support for Mc Donnell Douglas aircraft, and has also cooperated with MDD in the development of future high-performance aircraft (TKF) for the 1990's. In helicopter production the company has a joint venture with the Japanese Kawasaki, and it works with Aerospatiale - one of the owners - in the development of new night warfare helicopters. Both companies also own Euromissile in Paris, which facilitates MBB's military exports. In Belgium MBB has a joint venture, European Defence Products EDP with PPB in Brussels, and in space programs MBB cooperates with its European partners. MBB's own indigenous designs include helicopters (BO-105) and the antitank missiles Cobra and Mamba.

The diffuse profile of MBB is further displayed by the fact that it passes 80 per cent of all its tasks to its partners and subcontractors. MBB has foreign co-production in several developing countries, including Iran, India, Indonesia, Philippines, Pakistan, Turkey and Spain.

VFW-Fokker was formed in 1970 as the first - and so far the only - international merger within defence industry. The two parties remained rather independent. The German partner's major shareholders include Friedrich Krupp (36 per cent), United Technologies Corp. (USA 26 per cent) and the state in Hamburg 26 per cent. The Dutch partner has a participation in U.S. Northrop with 20 per cent. Thus, two transnational U.S. defence producers are among the major owners of the company. The company has a 35 per cent share in the German portion of Tornado. It produces military aircraft for surveillance, maritime functions, transport and training. It also overhauls and repairs F-104's, helicopters and transport aircraft. VFW's activities have been particularly successful in European space cooperation. Fokker is the Dutch participant of the F-16 program.

After the split-up VFW is expected to merge with MBB. This merger is also being pushed by the German authorities. It is anticipated that VFW will concentrate on space programs while MBB continues with military aircraft, helicopter programs and missiles. The joint sales of MBB-VFW will total $ 2 billion (according to the present figures) and the new company will be bigger than British Aerospace. The international contacts will be numerous, mainly on the basis of MBB's relationships.

The general profile of Dornier is rather similar to that of MBB: military aircraft, services, armaments, space technology; however it is unusual in Europe for two similar types of aerospace companies to coexist in the same country. Dornier's exports are 85 per cent of its sales and the company has an international organization although details are lacking. Dornier is a partner of Dassault in Alpha jet, and the two companies have an agreement with the U.S. Lockheed for U.S. licence production in case the U.S. decides to choose Alpha jet for its arsenals. Dornier has been particularly successful in Africa with its utility aircraft Skyservant, which is now also being developed for maritime surveillance. Dornier has a marketing agreement with the U.S. Grumman to sell U.S. utility aircraft in Europe, Africa and a number of Middle East countries. In the armament sector, Dornier produces combat area observation systems with French subcontractors and reconnaissance drones with Canadair. It does overhaul work for Fiat, Dassault, Bell, Cessna and Piper. Dornier also produces sophisticated space technology. In the development of future combat aircraft Dornier has cooperated with the U.S. Northrop, and thus competes with the MBB-Mc Donnell Douglas team. The German authorities have told the companies to form a joint task force, since the state cannot afford financing two competitive planning processes.

It is evident in the long run that Dornier is also being pushed toward a merger with MBB-VFW because competition between the industries is very expensive. Without such a merger the companies will compete and seek foreign partners for more technology if their own resources are not sufficient. In this situation exports also play a major role since the life and profitability of the companies may depend on them.

2.2.3.   International Medium-Sized Companies

It would be very misleading to think that arms production and international arms transfers are exclusively carried out by the largest transnational giants. Of course the largest corporations produce and trade the major part of world arms, but smaller or medium-sized companies often play their own role too. Sometimes they operate as independent producers if they have managed to develop a certain weapon or weapons system of their own. Another role of medium-sized arms producers is to act as bridgeheads for the TNCs in their strategies to control global arms production and markets. Certain characteristics of the Italian arms industry in particular and its international operations resemble the role of a bridgehead. The foreign TNCs participate in arms production both as partial owners and as suppliers of design and technology. These South European bases then produce not only for their own army but also for exports, which indicates their role as some sort of regional marketing centres and subcontractors for the TNCs. Not only marketing considerations, but also the availability of skilled and comparatively cheap labour in Italy and Spain has favoured the involvement of Southern Europe in the production schemes of foreign TNCs. Developments within Hellenic Aerospace Industries during the last few years indicate that Greece is also going to assume some role in the international aerospace network, perhaps as a repair and service station for Middle Eastern aircraft fleets. Also in the Greek case the role of TNCs is dominant, a fact which indicates that in general the TNCs are always there when a new aerospace centre is being created.[32]

In the 1950s the Italian arms industry - like that of the FRG - revived with the help of NATO contracts as well as British and American licences. Some exports of simple or outdated weapons also took place. In the 1960s the arms industry entered a new phase, again with the help of foreign licences. The industry started producing jet fighters, helicopters and aeroengines, and also Italian designs appeared. At the end of the 1960s the Italian industry was already able to supply most of the weapons systems ordered by the Italian army. As soon as production grew, exports started to become more important, e.g. licences of MB-326 aircraft were sold to South Africa, Brazil and Australia. Bell Helicopter provided licences to Italian Agusta, and Lockeed to Aermacchi, a company of which Lockheed is also a partial owner (25 per cent since 1959).[33] In the 1970's Italy was capable of producing all major weapon types, and it became one of the leading exporters ranking as number four among Western suppliers in 1978. Its exports increased particularly in 1972-74 and have remained strong since then.[34] While becoming a leading exporter Italy has, however, also remained a leading importer of foreign arms technology. According to SIPRI Italy produced 19 weapons systems with foreign, mainly U.S. licences in 1978, while the number of indigenously produced systems was 36. The role of foreign licences is particularly strong in aerospace industry: 17 of the total 19 licences are provided by this sector.[35]

According to AIA (the Associazione Industrie Aerospaziali), Italian exports of military aircraft have increased as follows:

Table 18.   Italian Exports of Military Aircraft 1967-77, Billion Lire

1967	1972	1973	1974	1975	1976	1977
50	110	135	180	245	300	330[a]

Source: Initiatives taken by the Metal Workers Federation in the Italian Arms Industry, IDOC Bulletin, No. 10-11, October-November 1979, p. 7.

Military production also dominates the turnover of Italian aerospace industry: in 1976 it accounted for 78 per cent of the total turnover.[36] Closely connected to aerospace exports are exports of military electronics, which have increased as follows:

Table 19.   Italian Exports of Military Electronics, 1972-76, Billion Lire

1972	1973	1974	1975	1976
65	93	100	154	243

Source:Initiatives taken by ... ibid., p. 7.

A   summary   of   Italy's   main   aerospace   producers   is   given   below:

Table 20.   Main Military Aerospace Companies in Italy

Company	Per cent military	Main business	Sales in 1976 billion lire
Aeritalia	55	transport, fighter aircraft, space	165
Agusta	85	helicopters	306[a]
Fiat Aviazione	75	engines	n.a.
Siai Marchetti	90	training, COIN, marine patrol aircraft	35
Aermacchi	90	training, attack aircraft, RPVs	40
Piaggio	70	transport, COIN, surveillance	24
Oto Melara	95	missiles, vehicles, naval guns	117[b]
Selenia	75	electronics, missiles	n.a.
Sistel	n.a.	missiles, electronics	n.a.
Breda Meccanica	80	missiles, cannons	n.a.
Breda Nardi	n.a.	helicopters	n.a.

Sources: IDOC Bulletin, No. 10-11, October-November 1979, pp. 13-29,
             Presentazione commento dei dali sulle imprese belliche. Gruppo
             dilavoro sull'industrie bellica italiana della FLM. Roma 1979.

Notes: [a]1978 and [b]1977.

It is characteristic of the Italian industry that it is very dependent on military products, very dependent on exports and quite dependent on foreign technology. Most of the companies are totally owned or controlled by the Italian state. Thus, dependence on military production has been part of the industrial policy. Only Piaggio and Aermacchi are privately owned, the latter partly by Lockheed.[37]

The almost automatic result of the political decision to have a full front of high-technology military production is that the companies seek foreign technology and exports, because it is impossible to raise the necessary amounts of R&D funds for modern industry from local sources.

The Italian companies have been particularly successful in Third World exports. Agusta, e.g.says that its helicopters have been sold to 70 countries. The reason for this may be - besides active marketing - that the Italian weapons systems include smaller-sized aircraft, which may often be more suitable for the Third World conditions and purchasing power.[38] According to a representative of Italian industry, it has also been an advantage "not to be a big power", particularly in those countries which like to diversify their import sources and decrease dependence on the great powers.[39] This sort of political advantage could also explain why Iran has not cancelled the order by the Shah's regime of 50 Agusta helicopters although many other large military orders have been cancelled by the present regime.[40]

Italy's dependence on foreign technology is both intensive and extensive. Aeritalia is a licence producer for Lockheed, and a risk-taking participant in Tornado MRCA program and in the new Boeing civil aircraft. Agusta exports 70-80 per cent of the production. It is a licence producer for Bell, Sikorsky and Boeing, and has co-production with Westland, MBB and Aerospatiale. Siai Marchetti is a licence producer for Boeing and Sikorsky, as a member of the Agusta group of companies. Aermacchi is a licence producer for Lockheed, subcontractor for MRCA, and co-producer with Teledyne, U.S.A. On the other hand it has also sold licences to South Africa, Brazil, Turkey and Australia. The fact that some American aircraft and engines have found their way to the Third World markets via Italian industries has given good reason to speak of "the Italian connection" of American aerospace industries. To complete the picture, the cooperation of Hughes with Breda Nardi, the Swedish Bofors with Sistel and the French Matra with Oto Melara can be added. The Italian aerospace industry uses mostly American and British engines.[41]

There are no analyses available of the real international balances of the Italian armament industry. The sum of licence fees, royalties and other payments for foreign companies must be high, however. In addition, the industry imports many components from foreign producers. It is known that the majority of the components used by the military electronics industry are imported from the U.S. at a cost to the balance of payments of some 50 billion lire annually.[42]

The history of the Spanish aircraft industry also tells of foreign dominance. The Aircraft company CASA (Construcciones Aeronauticas, S.A.) was formed in 1972 by a merger of Hispano Aviacion and Empresa Nacional de Motores de Aviacion, which had cooperated with emigrant German aircraft designers after World War II. The majority of CASA is owned by the Spanish state (65 per cent), and among the private owners the participation of the U.S. Northrop (21 per cent) is notable. CASA is a subcontractor for foreign civil and military aircraft, including Mirage. It has done some licensed manufacturing and assembly of Northrop's export fighter F-5, and it is a licence producer for MBB's BO-105 helicopters. As indigenous designs, CASA produces transport and trainer/ground attack aircraft.[43] CASA's exports have been modest compared to Italian companies, but new efforts have been made to improve export performance. This is clearly indicated by CASA's decision to start a joint venture with the Indonesian Nurtanio for the development and production of aircraft based on CASA's design. Despite exports Spain is one of the largest importers of TNC-built military aircraft.[44]

One peculiar group of aerospace companies consists of small, rather unknown firms which try to make military inventions with limited human and material capacities. Some of them may have been founded by frustrated scientists, engineers or soldiers who try to invent great new weapons. Maybe also some militarist-minded adventurers have started such undertakings. A further reason for the international operations of unknown small enterprises may be the missions given by some governments or major companies or intelligence organizations which try to hide their involvement and rather let unknown, private enterprises take care of their missions. In covert activities in particular small unknown firms may be used.

An example of a mysterious aerospace company in international arms transfers is Orbital Transport und Raketenaktiengesellschaft (known as OTRAG) which is based in the FRG. In 1977 the journal Afrique-Asie published information according to which OTRAG had leased 100 000 km^2 of land in Southern Zaire for rocket launching experiments. The area is almost half the size of the FRG.

According to OTRAG, the purpose of the Zaire operation is commercial and designed to launch inexpensive rockets to carry satellites into orbit for use in telecommunication, meteorology, resource surveys and other forms of earth reconnaissance.

The special arrangements in OTRAG's test area, however, raised suspicions concerning the possible military nature of OTRAG's activities. OTRAG received exclusive and complete rights to use the area for its own purposes, including the exclusive use of airspace. OTRAG controls all access to the territory and has the right to expel local inhabitants. It also has the right to construct whatever it likes in the area, and the staff enjoys diplomatic privileges and immunity although it is officially on a business mission. OTRAG is also responsible for infrastructure and security within the area, and the Zairean government has guaranteed overall security. The area is also freed from customs and taxes.

The strategic location of the area, the top-level expertise among OTRAG's staff, their former experience with Western space administration, as well as the connections with public financial sources in the FRG have, however, caused wide speculations concerning the possible military function of OTRAG's activities. The total secrecy has been one of the main reasons why military operations have been suspected. Some have maintained that the OTRAG area is a vast new military base in the vicinity of Southern Africa, while others have claimed that Western powers, perhaps even the FRG, are carrying out tests with ballistic missiles. In the NATO area it is not easy to find suitable test sites.[45] There is no final answer to such questions. But it is evident that had the Zairean government only wanted a communication or resources satellite, which OTRAG promised to supply, it would have been very simple to turn to those foreign electronic companies which are able to provide these facilities. No vast and protected areas would be needed for such civilian purposes.

OTRAG's operations in Zaire faced, however, increasing difficulties and various rumours of its supposed activities started to spread around.[46] The West German government felt international pressures, some of which were channelled to Zaire, to establish more effective supervision of the activities by OTRAG. The Zairean government was, on the other hand, willing to improve its relations with neighbouring Angola. A combination of these pressures resulted in the decision by Zaire to terminate the contract with OTRAG.[47] The company started immediately to seek alternative launch sites in Latin America and South East Asia, according to some sources of information.[48]

2.3.   Transnational Electronic Industry and Military Electronics

2.3.1.   The Role of Electronics in Modern Armaments

Electronics is a most essential part of modern armaments and defence apparatus. In fact, it is precisely in electronics that the main part of the arms race takes place: electronics can make the arms smaller, more capable and precise. With electronic means you control traffic in the air, ground and sea; by electronic means you try to protect the defendent's arms and jam the weapons of the enemy (electronic warfare, electronic countermeasures ECM). With electronics you navigate, communicate, transmit data and command peacetime as well as battlefield operations. With electronics your enemy tries to hit or jam these activities. With electronics you carry out intelligence, surveillance and reconnaissance. It also helps you in the R&D of new weapons or in testing available ones. In battlefield conditions, targets are identified and guns are fired by electronic means; at night, night vision devices are used, and so on. Military electronics have become a complex and very specialized field of electronics. To be modern in that field requires enormous knowledge, techniques and finances; even to be able to follow the latest developments - not to speak of production - requires capabilities that only few countries possess.

Given the vast economic and qualitative requirements, it is only logical that the major producers of military electronics are the transnational electronic companies, who are able to exploit state funding for their R&D, and thus promote the innovative nature of their industry. There is no doubt that electronics is the most demanding part of defence production. He who controls the latest technology certainly has power over those who do not possess it.

Electronics is also an important way of influencing the military balances in

51

certain areas by technological means. Electronics may cause major changes in security systems; new arms can become old because of the new electronic devices of the enemy, and so on. The problem with electronics is, however, that the public as well as many political or even military decision-makers do not actually know what the latest technology is. The newest electronic devices are the most protected part of armament arsenals; they are kept secret and not transferred to potential enemies. In sum, we can conclude that electronics may bring irrationality to arms transfers. After the Middle East War in 1973 it became clear that the precision guided munitions (PGMs) had changed the nature of warfare. They had increased the vulnerability of fighter aircraft, tanks etc.[49] To avoid this vulnerability of most existing arms arsenals, many efforts were made to find electronic countermeasures (ECMs) for the PGMs. Thus, part of the technological arms race can now be characterized as a chain in which producers develop electronic measures, countermeasures, measures against countermeasures, measures against countermeasures of countermeasures... and so on.

The developing states or other states with more modest technology are outside this process. They cannot be sure whether their weapons are "safe" in the electronic sense or whether a number of electronic countermeasures exist against their technology, which they may have bought as the most modern one. The marketing divisions of armament industries are, of course, always selling the "latest technology".

If it is in this way that the development of military electronics has greatly increased the irrationality of arms transfers, it is possible that a substantial part of the money spent on arms acquisition goes to waste in the military-technological sense - not to mention the social and economic costs.

Electronics may have become one of the strongest elements of international military power. Those who have the latest knowledge of electronic warfare presumably do not transfer this part of their technology abroad because they want to keep the ultimate means for themselves. When one looks at the list of currently available military aircraft one notices for example that for most models there is one version for the national army and another for exports - it is in the electronic capabilities that the difference lies - but we do not know what they really are.[50]

The development of military electronics widens the security and power gap between those who command the new technology and those who do not. This gap has become wider in the 1970's because the developments have been rapid within last years. Thus, much more uncertainty and irrationality is connected with international arms transfers than we can really know. The argument is relevant not only for the developing countries but also for small and medium sized industrialized countries.[51]

Because of the development of electronics the life of a new weapon becomes shorter, according to some estimates 5-7 years. At the same time, the development process of a new weapon requires more time and money whereby the number of new weapon types decreases.[52]

On the other hand the qualitative arms race shortens the life of the weapon systems and thus increases their number. Introduction of new technologies has, consequently, become one of the main causes for the rapid rise in weapons costs - although other causes like raw material prices, inflation etc. naturally are also important. The power of new technology is clearly visible in this process; the performance capacity, i.e. the technical criterion is the point of planning. If the performance of a new weapon exceeds the old one, even the highest costs are paid without complaint. According to a UN expert group, the price of a fighter aircraft has doubled every 4-5 years. At the same t me the maintenance costs of modern weapons have also risen.[53]

Electronic production can be roughly divided into four categories according to who uses it and for what purpose: industrial and business electronics (e.g. data processing, automats, office equipment, tools etc.), consumer electronics (e.g. TV, tape recorders), communication electronics (radio, telephone) and state electronics, of which military electronics is the largest part.

There are some special features which make military electronics very attractive to electronic industries. The first is the availability of state funding for R&D, which goes to the newest technology and innovation. The well-known example is the invention of integrated circuits, which were developed for military needs in the 1950s and 1960s, and established the leadership of the U.S. in this field. The second reason for the popularity of military production is that the state purchases the products and the companies are able to charge high prices because the market is restricted. The market is restricted both because of the classified nature of some products, and because they are often specially designed to fit into certain weapons only. For these reasons the companies compete for state funding although they keep criticizing state planning and procurement policies.[54]

According to a UN study, 20-30 per cent of the workforce in the U.S. electronic industry work in military production.[55] In France the corresponding figure is 20 per cent.[56]

The price of electronics in different weapons categories varies but the general trend is an increase in the electronic components in all categories. The electronic components make up at least 25 per cent of the cost of a warship, over 30 per cent of an airplane, 40 per cent of a battle tank, and 50 per cent of an air defence system.[57]

Because weapons get old rather quickly, armies try to overcome the problem by adding new electronics to modernize old weapons. An illustration of this is the modernization program of the strategic bomber B-52 in the U.S. - the modernization was the policy alternative to a completely new bomber B-1. Electronic specialists say that the electronic components of arms will have to be updated and retrofitted several times during the lifetime of a weapon.[58]

Table 21.   Technological Changes of B-52 Bomber in 1960-90, USA

1960	1970	1980	1990
-Hound Dog Missile (AGM-28)		-ECM Improvements (Phase VII)	
-Quail Missile (ADM-20)		-Tail Warning	
		-Transmitter Update	
-Low-Level Capability Mod (Systems)			
		-Cruise Missile Integration	
-Structural Improvements Wing Body Tail			
		-Offensive Avionics System	
-ECM Improvements (Phase II)			
-High-Density Bombing System (B-52D)			
-Stability Augmentation System			
-SRAM Missile (AGM-69A)			
-Electro-visual Sensors			
-ECM Improvements (Phase VI)			
-Engine Quick Start Capability			
-Structural Modification (B-52D)			
-AFSATCOM			

Source: Electronic Warfare/Defense Electronics, April 1979, p. 45.

In 1974 the professional journal Electronics estimated that the whole electronics market of Western Europe and the USA was about $ 56 billion, of which the market for military electronics was $ 13 billion (23 per cent). At that time the industrial and office electronics was 44 per cent, the consumer electronics 22 per cent and communication electronics 11 per cent.[59]

In 1978 the total electronics market in the U.S., Western Europe and Japan was $ 121 billion; thus the figure had more than doubled in four years. The military sector is now hard to calculate because it is spread over several categories none of them labelled directly as "military". Some approximations can be presented, however.

In the U.S. the total electronics market was $ 67.3 billion in 1978. The defence category in the federal electronics sector was $ 16.5 billion, i.e. 24.5 per cent of the total.

Table 22.   The Spending by U.S. Government on Electronics in 1977-82, Millions of Dollars

	1977	1978	1979[a]	1982[a]
Defence, total	14 963	16 487	18 086	22 258
Procurement, total	7 051	7 932	8 533	10 684
Communications and intelligence	1 205	1 317	1 356	1 697
Aircraft, related ground equipment	1 890	2 212	2 319	2 895
Missiles and space systems	2 310	2 541	2 857	3 478
Mobile and ordnance	436	471	538	683
Ship and conversions	1 210	1 391	1 663	1 831
Research, development, test and engineering	4 945	5 440	6 283	7 732
Operations and maintenance	2 967	3 115	3 270	3 842
NASA, total	810	818	850	972
Transportation, total	405	421	454	582
FAA procurement	240	247	267	343
FAA research and development	100	111	121	165
Highway and transit systems	65	63	66	74
Health, Education and Welfare, total	387	397	428	506
Education systems	107	111	112	125
Health-care electronics	280	286	316	381
Department of Energy, total	73	87	107	142
FEDERAL ELECTRONICS, TOTAL	16 638	18 210	19 920	24 450

Source: Electronics, January 4, 1979, p. 117.

Note: [a] Figures for 1979 and 1982 are forecasts.

As can be noted from above, the federal market for electronics consists almost totally of military equipment. Military devices may not all be calculated under DoD administration, but some equipment of military relevance can exist in NASA category as well.

Taking into account that the communication sector may also contain military electronics (navigation systems, satellite earth stations, radio equipment for aviation and marine activities), the share of military electronics could rise to some 25-30 per cent of the total electronics market, i.e. to some $ 20 billion in 1978 in the U.S. In France the electronics market was $ 10.3 billion in 1978. In the same year the aerospace equipment producers -most of them electronic companies - had a turnover of $ 1.2 billion, thus accounting for 11.7 per cent of the total. If we add to this the sale of telecommunication, radars, navigation aids and military radio equipment, we get $ 1.84 billion more. With this calculation, the French market for military electronics would be $ 3.04 billion in 1978, i.e. 29.5 per cent of the total.[60]

This share of electronic production is by necessity high in countries like the U.S. and France with the most modern and diversified defence production. In countries with modest or small defence production the share of military electronics is naturally lower. Electronics is also a most problematic field for those countries which try to become new, self-reliant producers of weapons. It is evident that for them the only way to acquire military electronics is to try to get complete packages from those who already have the technology. By doing this their self-reliance decreases, however, and they become dependent on critical foreign components.

2.3.2. The U.S. Military Electronic Industry

The Electrical Industries Association (EIA) in the U. S. estimated at the end of 1978 that in the next ten years (1978-1988) they would sell military electronics to the Department of Defense for $ 230 billion dollars.

Table 23.   The Electronic Content of DoD Markets, 1978-88 (constant FY
              1979 dollars)

	$ Billions
Electronics & communication	68.7
Aircraft	41.2
Operations and maintenance	35.2
Missiles	31.8
Space	22.1
Ships	17.8
Ordnance and vehicles	7.3
Management and support, military science	4.0
Total	228.1

Source: Murry Shohat, Military Electronics - a Quarter Trillion Dollar
           Market, Military Electronics/Countermeasures, December 1978,
           p. 30. The figures are adjusted for inflation. If inflation is not
           taken into account, the sum is expected to be $ 351.7 billion.

The EIA expects the annual sales to grow from $ 17.8 billion in 1979 to
$ 21.1 billion in 1983 and to $ 25.9 billion in 1988. This means that during
the ten-year period from 1974 till 1983 the U.S. market for military electronics
will double in real value. The DoD market for military electronics was
$ 10.9 billion in 1974, while the sales of military electronics in Western
Europe were one-fifth of it ($ 2.2 billion).[61]

The EIA has calculated that if U.S. military expenditures grow by 3 per cent
annually, the DoD purchases of electronics will grow by 4 per cent annually. If
now military expenditures grow by 4-5 per cent annually in real value, as has
been proposed, it is likely that DoD procurements of electronics will
correspondingly be higher than expected.

The growth of the military electronics market will, according to EIA, be
strongest in communication, space activities and missiles technology, while
the annual market for aircraft electronics is assumed to stabilize.

Table 24.   DoD as a Market for Military Electronics in 1979, 1983 and
             1988

Category	1979	1983 Billion of dollars	1988
Electronics and communication	5.2	6.2	7.8
Aircraft	3.8	3.8	3.8
Operations and maintenance	2.8	3.2	3.7
Missiles	2.3	2.8	3.8
Space	1.2	1.9	3.0
Ships	1.3	1.6	1.9
Ordnance, vehicles	0.4	0.7	0.9
Management, support	0.3	0.4	0.4

Source: Murry Shohat, Military Electronics - a Quarter Trillion Dollar
           Market, Military Electronics/Countermeasures, December 1978,
           p. 39.

The producers of military electronics can be divided into two main groups. The
first consists of giant transnational electronic companies which maintain
military divisions and receive contracts from the DoD. A comparison between
the list of the 500 largest U.S. companies (according to Fortune) and the list of
the top 100 defence contractors in 1978 looks as follows:

Table 25.   Largest U.S. Electronic/Electric Companies Having Contracts
with the DoD in 1978

Company	Sales in 1978 $ Mill.	Rank in Fortune list of 500	DoD contracts in 1978 $ Mill.	Rank in DoD list of top 100 contractors	DoD contracts as percentage of sales in 1978
IBM	21 076	7	396	27	1.8
General Electric	19 654	8	1 786	5	9.0
ITT[b]	15 261	11	269	37	1.8
Western Electric	9 522	17	131	21	1.4
Eastman Kodak	7 013	25	108	72	1.5
Westinghouse Electric	6 663	29	539	18	8.1
RCA	6 601	30	565	16	8.6
TRW	3 787	70	325	31	8.6
Litton Industries	3 651	72	1 557	6	42.6
Sperry Rand	3 649	73	612	14	16.8
Honeywell	3 548	77	545	17	15.4
Raytheon	3 239	88	1 307	9	40.4
Texas Instruments	2 550	112	434	22	17.0
Singer	2 469	113	282	35	11.4
Burroughs	2 422	118	65	96	2.6
Motorola	2 220	132	123	65	5.5
North American Philips[a]	2 184	136	147	57	6.7
Emerson Electric	2 177	137	112	68	5.1
Control Data	1 846	158	111	71	6.0
Martin Marietta	1 758	165	539	19	30.7
Hewlett-Packard	1 728	167	71	92	4.1
Harris	872	284	105	74	12.0
General Cable	848	289	129	63	15.2

Sources: The Fortune Directory of the 500 Largest U.S. Industrial
Corporations, Fortune, May 7, 1979, p. 270-289 and Defense
Dept. List Top 100 Companies by Military Contract, Aviation
Week & Space Technology, October 22, 1979, p. 75-81.

Notes: [a]Parent company N.V. Philips' Gloeilampenfabrieken in the
Netherlands.

Because Fortune's list concerns manufacturing companies, ITT's finance and insurance subsidiaries, the sale of which were $ 4 138 million, are excluded from the figure.

As can be noted in the table, the military contracts with the DoD account for only a small share of the turnover in IBM, ITT, Western Electric, Eastman Kodak, Burroughs and Hewlett Packard. This does not mean that their defence-related production would be so modest in the absolute sense -it rather means that the civil activities of these companies are extensive.[62]

The role of military production in these companies can be summarized as follows:

IBM is the giant producer of office machines and data processing equipment. Its gross income outside the U.S. was 52.4 per cent of its total sales in 1978. The sales in Europe, Middle East and Africa were 36.9 per cent of the total, while the share of Americas and the Far East was 15.5 per cent. The corporation operates all over the world and favours totally owned subsidiaries. IBM advertises e.g. command, control and communication systems (C^3), navigation equipment, helicopter electronics, electronics for space and satellite use, shipboard sonar, ground tracking and launch control equipment etc. According to the Annual Report, the gross income of "federal electronics" was $ 549 million in 1978.

ITT is a more diversified company. 29 per cent of its $ 19.5 billion sales come from telecommunication and electronics, including defence systems. Other main sectors are engineering, consumer products and services, natural resources, insurance and financing. In 1978 the company reported $ 660 million defence sales, "chiefly for the U.S. Government". Sales to foreign governments, primarily telecommunication equipment, aggregated $ 2.4 billion, i.e. 12.4 per cent of the total sales. Military equipment may be included in this figure. 42 per cent of ITT's sales were in Northern America, 53 per cent in Western Europe which leaves only 5 per cent for the rest of the world. In the mid-1970s the ITT group had about 390 subsidiaries in foreign countries. Among the principal militarily-oriented subsidiaries were Standard Elektrik Lorenz SEL in the FRG and Standard Telephone and Cable STC in the UK. ITT's list of defence products is long and related to military communication: C^3, identification, air traffic control, portable communication, Loran navigation systems, satellite equipment and ground stations, distant early warning systems, ballistic missile warning systems etc.

American Telephone & Telegraph is particularly identified with Bell telephones. It was 21st largest DoD contractor in 1978, the contracts being $ 457 million. The main part of the sum went to its subsidiary Western Electric Company, which manufactures telephone apparatus, cables, switchboards and other communication equipment. In 1975 the military and space work accounted for 7 per cent of the company's sales. Principal defence products are radar control systems for missiles and systems for protection from attack by aircraft or missiles. The profile of the company is mainly national; it does not pursue major export campaigns in international military journals.

Eastman Kodak, Burroughs and Hewlett-Packard do not produce weapons but rather important components of weapons: photographic, micro- and radiographic technology (important for e.g. reconnaissance and surveillance), data processing, computer systems, peripherals and related necessary military elements. Burroughs is very firmly based internationally; it has about 30 plants abroad. In the developing countries its main locations are in Latin America and South East Asia. It has over 900 sales offices throughout the world in 120 countries.

A more militarized group of companies are those whose defence production is large enough to lift the DoD content of sales up to 5-20 per cent of the turnover, despite large civilian divisions. Some of these companies (e.g. General Electric, Westinghouse Electric) have electric power appliances as their main business, but they also have extensive military production. Others, like RCA, Singer and North American Philips are better known as producers of consumer electronics, but are also deeply involved in defence production. Another group are the producers of large-scale computers, components and essential equipment (Sperry Rand, Honeywell, Texas Instruments, Motorola) which have started to design military applications for their products or which prepare important military infrastructures (General Cable).

The profiles of the more militarized electronic companies can be summarized as follows:[63]

General Electric produces jet engines, nuclear power plants for marine propulsion, radars, missile and space systems. It has about 160 plants in 24 countries.

Westinghouse Electric manufactures aviation and marine electronics, motors, radio and TV-equipment, communication equipment, power generators for space, aircraft and ground support systems, nuclear power for outer space, power regulators, transformers, radars, fighting radars, air-to-air and air-to-ground-modes, logistics, electronic countermeasures. It has subsidiaries, holdings and sales representatives in 160 countries.

RCA is involved in space systems communication, C^3, radars, laser technology, ranging and tracking electronics, electronic warfare, test systems, TV-displays, automatic battlefields, power transistors, reconnaissance. It has 76 manufacturing locations in the U.S. - not all for military production of course - and in at least 10 countries.

Sperry Rand specializes in computers for military applications. It manufactures avionics, communication equipment, autopilots, pumps, gyroscopics, radars, sonar and microwave equipment, computers for navigation, guidance, simulators, high-speed data transmission, display systems, deep water technology etc. Defence and space systems are reported as 15.5 per cent of the company's turnover. The geographic distribution of sales: the USA 61.0 %, Europe, Africa and the Middle East 27.8 %, the Americas and the Far East 11.2 %.

Honeywell manufactures space systems, avionics, navigation and guidance equipment, electro-optical, infrared and microwave technology, acoustic sensing, sonar systems, fire controls, displays, trainers, simulators, ocean systems, ship positioning, combat fire controls, munitions, torpedoes, systems analysis. According to company reports, the sales distribution is the USA 70 %, Europe 22 % and other areas 8 % of the total company sales. The company has 370 sales and service offices for Honeywell Control systems and 450 offices for Honeywell Information systems worldwide.

Singer is not a producer of sewing machines only, it produces aerospace and marine systems, equipment for anti-submarine warfare, weapons control systems, tactical computer systems, air defence, displays, simulators, acoustic countermeasures, C^3, visual systems, space systems, inertial navigation for helicopters, missile actuators, intelligence, fire controls, communication security, signal collecting. The company reports its aerospace and marine systems as 21 per cent of the turnover in 1978. According to a company publication, Singer is "a community of some 8000 scientists, engineers, and technicians working in over 100 technical facilities around the world".

Motorola produces semiconductors, power units, space communication, data processing, tracking, navigation, radios, tactical navigation and battlefield communication equipment. The company has offices in Bonn, Kuala Lumpur, London, Paris, Rome, Toronto and Utrecht.

Control Data produces computers, data systems and peripherals. Its sales to the U.S. government were 13 per cent of the total sales in 1978. The sales in the Americas (excluding the USA) and the Far East were 10 per cent of its sales in 1978, otherwise no information of the distribution of sales is available. The company has a large transnational organization, where particularly joint ventures in Iran since 1975 and in Romania since 1973 can be mentioned.

On the basis of available empirical data, it is impossible to identify the extent of military activities within the total production and sales of the companies. It is also difficult to assess the role of military electronics in arms transfers. It is clear that part of military electronic technology in these companies is classified and not traded at all. The nonclassified part may be sold through foreign military sales programs, but it may also be sold using the network of civil electronics. In the last case it is difficult for anyone to track the spread of electronic technology. The companies do not report the marketing of their military products either. So, the conclusion is meagre indeed: the transfer of military electronic technology is a great unknown in military transfers.

It is also worth noting that American TNCs have stopped giving information about their international organization, which again limits research into their international operations.

A third group of electronic transnationals consists of companies like Litton Industries, Raytheon and Martin Marietta which can be considered the most militarized electronic companies if measured on the basis of the DoD content of sales.[64]

> Litton Industries is a diversified company, where the sales are composed of electronics (19 %), advanced electronics (14 %), and marine engineering (13 %), together with business equipment, industrial systems and paper, printing and publishing activities. Defence production can be estimated as about 30 per cent of the sales, consisting of guidance, control, electronic warfare, data transmission for various weapons, C^3, weapons controls, identification, satellite command, inertial navigation and Omega systems. Sales outside the USA are reported as 23.2 per cent in 1978.

> Raytheon and Martin Marietta are electronic companies but their activities are mainly directed to aerospace as they deal with missiles and space systems. They have therefore already been discussed in Chapter 2.2.

The companies mentioned above are by no means the only large producers of military electronics. As this is the most rapidly growing sector of the whole defence economy, the number of companies involved is also large, particularly in the U.S. which is the evident leader of the field. Companies like Emerson Electric, General Cable, Fairchild Camera and Instrument (which was recently sold to French interests), E-Systems, Harris, General Telephone & Electronics, Varian have frequently been among the 100 largest DoD contractors but they are not big enough to qualify for the list of the 500 largest companies which has been used above in Table 25.

One trend in military electronics is that electronic systems have become very complex - the complexity being typical not only of the final electronic systems but also of the components. For arms producers this means that the rapidly declining amount of electronic work is done by the weapons producer, and an increasing amount of work is carried out by the producer of electronic components. In the present situation the weapons producer has two choices concerning electronics: either to reduce the workforce and buy complex electronics from subcontractors or to enlarge the electronic division with the aim to become self-reliant in electronics as far as the company's own weapons are concerned; maybe also to offer electronics to other producers.[65]

The large use of electronic subcontracting usually leads to the formation of industrial groupings where certain weapons producers choose "their" own electronic subcontractors. At the same time more electronic companies are drawn into military industry.[66]

On the other hand weapons producers have also tried to enlarge their electronic divisions. The takeover of Microdata Corp. by McDonnell Douglas, electronic divisions at Fairchild, General Dynamics, Grumman Data Systems, Hughes Electronic Systems, Lockheed Electronics, Northrop's electronic division, Rockwell Electronic as well as Norden Systems within United Technologies are good examples of the growth of electronic production within weapons industries.[67] This means that a division of labour emerges between the electronic divisions and the electronic industries proper. The former is usually producing special electronics for specific use or on a smaller scale while the electronic giants produce large electronic systems like air traffic control, navigation systems, radar networks, etc.

Most of military electronic exports go abroad as subcontracted parts of weapons and weapon systems. Some companies are on the list of top military exporters and also as independent electronic producers. Within the last couple of years the largest five have been:

Table 26.   Five Largest Electronic Companies in U.S. Foreign Military Sales in 1976 and 1978[a]

Company	FMS 1976[b] $ Mill.	Per cent[b] of FMS total	FMS 1978[b] $ Mill.	Per cent[b] of FMS total
Litton Industries	258	5.3	524	9.1
General Electric[c]	248	5.1	177	3.1
Westinghouse Electric	44	0.9	56	1.0
Honeywell	55	1.1	33	0.6
American Telephone & Telegraph	25	0.5	28	0.5
	630	12.9	818	14.3
FMS total	4 860		5 805	

Source: Foreign Military Sales. Department of Defence. Washington Headquarters Services. Directorate for Information Operations and Reports, May 15, 1978 (mimeo).

Notes: [a] The figures published by the DoD are net values of military prime contract awards.

[b] The figures are rounded.

[c] General Electric, although principally an electric company, is on the list mainly because of aircraft engines.

The military sales of transnational electronic companies are most certainly much larger than can be seen in statistics like FMS both in the U.S. and in other countries. The transnational organization, however, keeps such transfers hidden.

2.3.3.   Military Electronic Industries in Western Europe and Japan

It was stated in the previous sections that it was a political priority for Western Europe to become a strong producer of military aircraft, and that the implementation of this aim has required reorganization, rationalization and internationalization. The electronic industry is a comparable field in which Europe has wanted to become strong and independent.

The West European market for electronics was about $ 37 billion in 1978, the largest national market being the FRG ($ 11.3 billion), followed by France ($ 8.1 billion), the United Kingdom ($ 5.7 billion) and Italy $ 3.9 billion. The largest sectors are computers and consumer electronics, each about $ 12 billion. The communication sector was the third largest category $ 7.2 billion, about 19 per cent of the total market. The largest subcategories were radio communication (excluding broadcasts) $ 1.4 billion, radars $ 993 million and navigation aids $ 610 million.[68] The demand for electronics in Europe is big enough to have encouraged the growth of a few transnational electronic companies, which are also the main producers of military electronics. The difference between Europe and the U.S. is, however, that state procurements as well as R&D funding is much more modest in Europe. It is possible that for this reason the European companies are more inclined to resort to foreign markets and commercial operations.

Table 27.   Major   Non-U.S. Electronic Corporations with Military
            Production

Company	Home country	Sales in 1978 $ Mill.	Rank in Fortune top 500
Philips	Netherlands	15 121	5
Siemens	FRG	13 865	6
AEG-Telefunken	FRG	5 998	37
Thomson-Brandt[a]	France	5 076	49
General Electric[b]	UK	4 214	68
IBM Deutschland	FRG (USA)	3 152	90
LM Ericsson	Sweden	2 014	153
Thorn Electrical Industries	UK	1 964	159
EMI	UK	1 595	197
Standard Elektrik Lorenz/ITT	FRG/USA	1 395	223
Plessey	UK	1 099	299
CII Honeywell Bull	France/USA	990	329
Standard Telephones & Cables/ITT	UK/USA	976	333
Canadian General Electric[c]	Canada/USA	970	334
ICL	UK	856	338
AGA	Sweden		376
MATRA	France	609	476
Telefonbau u. Normalzeit	FRG	575	498

Source: The Fortune Directory of the 500 Largest Industrial Corporations
             Outside the U.S., Fortune, August 13, 1979 and TAPRI data
             files.

Notes: [a] Thomson-Brandt is the parent company of France's largest
             producer of military electronics Thomson-CSF, which reported
             its own consolidated sales as 13 089 millions of French
             francs in 1978. With the conversion rate 1 $ = 4.441 Ffr.
             in December 1978, the consolidated sales of Thomson-CSF
             were $ 2 947 millions. See Thomson-CSF Annual report
             1978, p. 4 and for principles of consolidation, p. 51.

             [b] The total name of the corporation is GEC The General
             Electric Company Ltd. It is not to be confused with General
             Electric Company of United States.

             [c] A subsidiary of the U.S. General Electric Company.

The international orientation of European electronic companies varies. AEG, CII-Honeywell Bull, Decca, LM Ericsson, Racal and Siemens are the most export-oriented, whose exports constitute 60-80 per cent of their sales. In Ferranti, GEC and Plessey the share of exports is about 20-30 per cent of total sales.[69] It is a general trend among the European electronic companies that the largest transnationals are also the most dependent on exports. This is naturally connected with the small size of home markets. Thus, the large European companies are more transnational than their American counterparts.

As in the case of American companies, in European companies it is also difficult to separate military activities from the civilian ones. It is also impossible to estimate to what extent the transnational organization is used for transfers of military technology.

The dominance of American electronic industries is clearly visible in the list of the largest non-U.S. military producers. Many largest "European" companies are actually subsidiaries of American companies, while only one European company, Philips, has managed to penetrate the U.S. list of DoD contractors (Table 25). Part of the military electronics in Europe is originally American, and European electronic companies very often seek American partners when they try to improve their technological base. Thus the goal of independent European military electronics is a distant one, although European companies have managed to become strong in many specialized systems.

The nationalist tendencies are also strong in Europe. The Federal Republic of Germany, France and the U.K., for instance, try to favour their own industries in defence procurements. They also try to organize big units which could compete with the Americans.

The U.S. Department of Defence has tried to strengthen the West European subsidiaries of American companies. In 1978 the subsidiaries of IBM and ITT in the Federal Republic received DoD funding as part of the funding of their parent companies.[70]

The military profile of Philips can be summarized as follows:[71]

> Philips' Gloeilampenfabrieken is the fourth largest electronic
> company in the world. Its sales in Europe account for 63.5 per cent,
> in North America 16.9 per cent and in Latin America, Asia and
> Africa 19.6 per cent of the total sales. Philips produces
> telecommunication networks, air traffic controls, radio equipment
> for shipping and aviation, road traffic controls, laser technology,
> space systems, cable and wire, information systems, weapons devices,
> electronic warfare systems, night vision equipment, thermal systems
> etc. but the annual report does not tell much of these functions.
> Philips has about 140 major participations in 66 countries, but many
> military subsidiaries are not mentioned in the list of subsidiaries.
> Military products are manufactured at least in the Netherlands, the
> FRG, the UK, Sweden and the United States. In the UK military
> production is carried out by at least 8 plants and in the FRG Philips
> has five military subsidiaries. In the U.S. list of DoD contractors in
> 1978, 16 different companies were involved - the largest sum was
> awarded to Magnavox, a subsidiary of the U.S. Philips trust. Philips
> operates in at least 43 developing countries. It is unlikely, however,
> that final military systems are produced by these plants; they most
> probably produce components for military systems. In
> telecommunication, Philips has tried to found strong regional
> production centres. They are located in Brazil (two plants) in South
> Africa, in Singapore and Australia.

In the Federal Republic of Germany there is a "leading trio" of military
electronic producers.

The largest, Siemens, has grown as the national electronic company, which has
enjoyed considerable state support. According to one estimate it has received
$ 500 million in investment capital from the government to build a German
national computer industry.[72] The military profiles of the largest German
producers are summarized as follows:[73]

> Siemens is a manufacturer of e.g. radio communication, radars, air
> traffic and airport systems, space activities, C^3 systems, low level
> air defence, power amplifiers for short-wave transmitters, receivers,
> laser technology and on-board power systems. Relevant business for
> the military is also data processing, secure voice and data systems,
> optoelectronics, site protection systems and check-out systems. In
> terms of armament turnover Siemens is the largest military producer
> in the FRG. The share of military sales in its total sales is about 8
> per cent. The company cooperates with e.g. AEG and the French
> Thomson-CSF in the military field. The company is a 12 per cent
> owner in Blohm + Voss and a 8 per cent owner in MBB - both major
> weapons producers. In 24 countries the company has its own manufac-
> turing units, and in 23 countries it has a minority participation in
> manufacturing plants.

AEG is the second largest military producer in the FRG, the share of arms turnover being 10 per cent of its total sales. AEG makes radio and radar equipment, telecommunication and transportation systems for various military purposes. Telecommunication was 17 per cent of its total sales in 1976 but it also makes fast patrol boats and frigates. Aerospace division includes aircraft and missile equipment, ground installations for aviation and space systems, radar equipment, direction finders, missile guidance, avionics, power supply units, de-icing systems, helicopter equipment, radomes. The company is a licence producer for American Texas Instruments (airborne radar) and it participates in the Tornado program. It has several contracts with NATO countries, e.g. the maintenance of the early warning system in West German territory. The company also produces surveillance and space technology and it has been considered a leader in European development and manufacture of solar generators. The company has joint ventures with e.g. General Electric Company, Hughes aircraft, Siemens and Decca. The company has a large international network and it has manufacturing plants in the developing countries.

Standard Elektrik Lorenz AG is a subsidiary of ITT and produces navigation equipment, aircraft electronics, airport projects, and participates in several European arms programs as well as space activities. In 1977 the sales of SEL's navigation division were $ 50 million, of which 85 per cent were exported. Although American by origin, SEL has received funding from the FRG government. It cooperates with the parent ITT and is active in licence- and co-production work with American companies. It also distributes other companies' products, e.g. Singer-Kearfott division has sold its navigation units for anti-tank helicopters with a licence for SEL. The international organization of the parent ITT is available for SEL's marketing.

Also Philips, Honeywell and Litton maintain manufacturing subsidiaries in the FRG which produce military electronics. It is typical of West German military industry that the large electronic companies have formed planning companies together with weapons producers to maximize the technological skills and design capacities. The role of these planning companies is related to efforts at strengthening military production in the FRG after the long low-profile years in the 1940's and 1950's when German industry had to be decomposed and demilitarized.

The existence of a large network of planning units where different international producers pool their resources is unique in Western military industry. As this large-scale planning is of rather recent origin, its total impact on Western arms production may not yet be visible. It would seem that the transnational planning cooperation in West German arms industry has two types of consequences. On the one hand it increases the technological and financial potential of West German arms industry; when planning increases it logically follows that military production is also bound to increase. On the other hand some control of this planning takes place abroad as the participation of foreign TNCs is rather strong.

Table 28. Participation of Transnational Electronic Companies in the Military Planning Companies of the FRG

Company	Business	Participating corporations	Share of the capital, per cent
ESG Elektronik-System-Gesellschaft	Planning, projects, electronic weapons systems for airforce and ground forces. command systems	Siemens AEG-Telefunken SEL Standard Elektrik Lorenz (ITT/USA) Rohde Schwartz	25 25 25 25
FEG Gesellschaft für Logistik	Planning, projects, electronics for aviation	ESG ELTRO (AEG-Telefunken/Hughes Aircraft, USA) Honeywell, USA Litef (Litton Industries, USA) TELDIX GmbH (AEG-Tele-funken/Robert Bosch)	 12.37 12.37 12.37 12.37
GFS Midas Gesellschaft für Führungssysteme	Planning, projects, command systems	Siemens AEG-Telefunken	50 50
Gesellschaft für Raketen-systeme	Planning, armaments, aero-space	AEG-Telefunken Dynamit Nobel (Flick) Honeywell	33.33 33.33 33.33
RTG Raketentechnik	Planning, development and production of rockets and bombs	MBB Diehl GmbH & Co.	
MTG Marinetechnik Plan-ungsgesellschaft mbH	Planning and supervision of warship projects	MEG MSG MUG	

Table 28 continued

Company	Business	Participating corporations	Share of the capital, per cent
MEG Marine-Elektronik-Planungsgesellschaft	Planning, project design, marine electronics	AEG-Telefunken	16.66
		Siemens	16.66
		Krupp-Atlas-Elektronik	16.66
		SEL	16.66
		Hollandse Signallapparaten B.V. (Philips, Netherlands)	16.66
		VFW-Fokker	16.66
MSG Marine-Schiffstechnik Planungsgesellschaft	Planning and management of warship projects	Blohm + Voss (Thyssen/Siemens)	40
		HDW	18
		Bremer Vulcan Schiffbau und Maschinenfabrik (Thyssen-Bornemiza)	18
		Fr. Lürssen-Werft	15
		Orenstein & Koppel	9
MUG Marine-Unterwasser-regelanlagen Planungsge-sellschaft	Planning, project design and management of submarines	AEG-Telefunken	40
		Krupp-Atlas-Elektronik, MaK Maschinebau (Krupp)	40
		Hollandse Signaalapparaten BV/(Philips)	20

Source: Wilfried Klank, Struktur und Entwicklungstendenzen der BRD-Rüstungsindustrie, IPW-Berichte 11.1979, p. 25.

The planning companies are central in armament design and construction for the West German needs, but they are also participating in armament exports by designing special export projects for foreign customers.[74] Thus, the role of the planning companies is one of the factors explaining the rather rapid increase of West German arms exports in the 1970s, from $ 140 million in 1973 to $ 800 million in 1977 in current dollars.[75]

The United Kingdom is a strong defence producer and the third largest arms exporter in the West after the U.S. and France. The role of defence production is traditionally strong in electronic companies - in fact it is considered one of the strongest areas in the British electronic industry. Defence electronics has been backed by the increase of military industry, government funding and purchases as well as growing exports. The industry has also been strengthened by the electronic modernization of older weapons - particularly retooling for electronic warfare capability has been common. The British industry has calculated that an electronic retooling of one naval ship can lead to contracts of £ 1 million or more.[76]

The main electronic companies contracted by the British Ministry of Defence (MOD) were as follows in 1976-77:

Table 29.   British Electronic Companies as Contractors for the Ministry of Defence in 1976-77

Over £ 100 million:	General Electric Co Ltd (GEC)
£ 50 - £ 100 million:	Plessey
£ 25 - £ 50 million:	EMI, Ferranti
£ 10 - £ 25 million:	MEL Equipment (Philips), Racal Electronics
£ 5 - £ 10 million:	Decca,
	Mullard (Philips), The Rank Organization, Standard Telephones and Cables (ITT), Thorn Electrical Industries, Ultra Electronic Holdings (Dowty)

Source: Lawrence Freedman, Arms Production in the United Kingdom Problems and Prospects. The Royal Institute of International Affairs, 1978, p. 1.

British expertise in defence electronics, radar communications and "capital electronics" - a category which includes major military electronic systems - has been considered high as compared to office and consumer electronics. This is also seen in the world sales of the main companies:

Table 30.   Composition of World Sales of Major British Electronic Companies in 1979-80[a)]

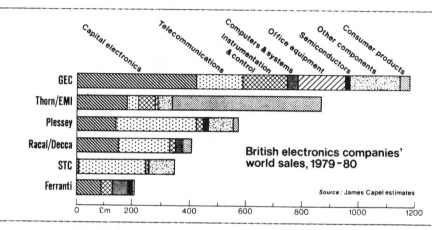

British electronics companies' world sales, 1979-80

Source: James Capel estimates

Source: The Economist, February 23, 1980.

Note: [a)]The military component is strong in capital electronics, telecommunication and instrumentation.

The military production of British electronic companies can be summarized as follows:[77]

> GEC produces aircraft and helicopter electronics, flight controls, navigation equipment, airport equipment, space technology, weapons guidance, anti-missile systems, electronic warfare, RPV's, surveillance, night-vision, sighting devices, marine engineering, radars, naval valves, handling aids, nuclear controls, naval gearboxes, turbines and gearings, underwater communications, ocean survey systems and all sorts of electronic components like laser, thermal devices, gyroscopes, magnetors etc. GEC's Marconi division, which produces avionics, radar systems and space technology, has been described as a company whose "order books are full" because of large undertakings for NATO, British defence industry and the British army. Marconi's R&D capacity has been estimated as one of the greatest outside North America. One of GEC's major owners is the multinational insurance company Prudential Corporation, which has a

subsidiary in South Africa. GEC is a transnational producer: GEC-Marconi Electronic Ltd. alone has subsidiaries in Cape Town, Sydney, Kuala Lumpur, Cyprus, Johannesburg, Caracas, Rio de Janeiro as well as in most NATO countries.

Thorn Electrical Industries produces weapons controls, power supplies, chemical detectors, simulators, anti-submarine trainers, electrical connectors, airfield equipment, test instruments, radio and navigation equipment, data transmission, fire detection and extinguishing systems, measurement devices, avionics. One of Thorn's specialities is magnetic equipment for naval warfare. EMI, which has now merged with Thorn, produces naval warfare equipment, weapons systems, simulators, testing devices, equipment for surveillance, reconnaissance and detection, radios, radars etc. EMI has manufacturing and marketing subsidiaries throughout the world - which may be one of the reasons why Thorn bought it - but the international network has so far been known as a marketer of consumer electronics. The joint sales of Thorn and EMI were $ 3.6 billion in 1978, which brings the alliance into the group of major producers, also in military electronics. Thorn is owned by "family interests and charitable settlements".

Plessey, which had $ 1.1 billion sales in 1978, is the third largest producer of military electronics in the UK. Its main business is telecommunication. Plessey Electronic Systems and Plessey Marine are both considered as the company's most profitable divisions, both produce defence electronics. Plessey has e.g. a £ 100-million contract for a strategic battlefield communication system. In addition, it has a successful ship radar that has been sold abroad to other NATO countries; it has also recently developed a new tactical radar control and display system. Plessey is also known for its aerospace, avionics and marine systems, as well as its R&D capacity. Telecommunication systems require large financing, and Plessey's resources have been considered limited as it has to compete with large transnationals like ITT. That is why Plessey has been seen as a candidate for future mergers. Plessey has an international organization with subsidiaries in e.g. Australia, Netherlands, South Africa and North America. It is also a major owner (24.42 %) of the large British computer company ICL.

Racal Electronics has grown in 30 years from a two-man consultancy to a $ 500-million multinational. It produces battlefield communication (e.g. portable radios), data communication, jamming equipment, antiterrorist weapons, acoustics, antennas, test equipment, instrumentation, communication security, magnetic devices, microwave components, radars, logistics. Radio communication represents 44 per cent of its total sales. 75 per cent of the production are exports from the UK or trade outside the UK. At present the company is growing rapidly and is developing an international organization, emphasizing the private and commercial orientation, i.e. freedom and autonomy in marketing. The international network is not made public, but the principle is to set up cooperative ventures with foreign governments or companies which can assemble Racal's products with indigenous labour. Such ventures are located in Egypt, Spain and Brazil - the latter involving an associate company in which Racal has 49 per cent holding. Prudential Corporation, which was already mentioned as one of GEC's owners, owns 5.35 per cent of Racal's shares. It also owns 7.36 per cent of Decca, which is now being merged with Racal. Decca is a two-direction company, one section producing consumer electronics and the other military products. Decca is specialized in marine radar systems, navigation and electronic warfare. In radars Decca competes with the U.S. companies Sperry and Raytheon. Both Decca's radar systems and growing technology for electronic countermeasures (ECM) were considered reasons for Racal's takeover. Another good reason is Decca's multinational network, which is based on navigation stations built by Decca in e.g. Europe, Canada, Nigeria, Australia, Japan, the Persian Gulf, India and Pakistan. Decca's exports from the UK were 31.9 per cent of its turnover in 1978, but its sales outside the UK were 60 per cent of the total. Kuwait Investment Fund is a 10 per cent owner of Decca, and the holding has stayed in the Racal-Decca merger. Decca has at least 14 subsidiaries abroad.

Among other prominent producers is Ferranti, which is, however, a more home-market-oriented and NATO-oriented company. It has produced radar systems for UK aircraft for 15 years and its naval radars are used by the British, Danish, Dutch and Brazilian navies. Rank Organization produces e.g. night-vision, optical and thermal systems for missiles tracking and guidance, sonar equipment, personal transceivers, microwave products.

France. The production of military electronics in France is characterized by one giant, Thomson-CSF, and many small or medium-sized enterprises. Compared to the UK, which has many medium-sized companies, French production is much more monopolized. The rapid growth of Thomson into one of the strongest producers in Europe is a result of the French policy which favoured strong and large national units of production.[78] The position of Thomson is comparable to Siemens in the FRG or Ericsson in Sweden. The French electronic industry produces a total range of modern military electronics. The main reason for this is the French arms programs particularly in aerospace, which were also created with the emphasis on national self-reliance and autonomy. The French electronic industries avoid cooperation with American TNCs and prefer joint activities with European partners.

Thomson-CSF, a transnational company in private ownership, was established ten years ago by a merger of the electronic activities in Thomson-Houston-Hochkiss-Brandt and CSF (Companie Générale de Télégraphie sans fils). Today more that 7000 employees are engaged in R&D alone, and the central development laboratory employs 500 skilful technicians and engineers. Thomson-CSF's consolidated sales were $ 2.9 billion in 1978, and the share of foreign activities was 41.5 per cent of the total sales. High performance radars have been mentioned as a specialty of the company, which produces an almost complete variety of military electronics: avionics, detection and navigation equipment, underwater systems, weapons systems, simulation, radio communication, microwave and satellite transmission equipment, military data processing, fire controls etc. The company is also a major producer of all sorts of electronic components. The consolidated accounts of the company include 40 companies, 27 of which are French and 13 foreign. According to other estimates the company maintains industrial and commercial operations in 17 countries, and local agents, delegations or representatives in more than 90 countries. During 1978 the company trained 480 foreign trainees who came from 12 foreign countries.

In 1977 50 per cent of the annual turnover was accounted for by defence production. In radio equipment and ground radar installations, 80-90 per cent of the production was exported. One-third of the electronics development at Thomson-CSF is financed by the French government. Thomson sometimes collaborates with other large transnationals. It had a joint venture with LM Ericsson but in 1978 it came under Thomson's control. The two companies also cooperate in Sweden. In the components sector the company cooperates with the U.S. Motorola, the world's second largest producer of semiconductors. In Egypt the company cooperates with Siemens to construct a telephone network. In 1978 the French government gave Thomson and Philips a 600-million-franc credit for the development of the production of integrated circuits.[79]

There is no doubt that Thomson is a major transnational producer of military electronics. As usual, these activities are not reported. The only indication of the possible transnationality is expressed by the Annual report as follows:[80]

> In addition, the company has been in contact with certain foreign governments wishing to create and develop national professional electronics industries capable of covering their own needs.

The exports of French aircraft have spurred the turnover and exports of many French electronic companies, not just the largest one. The equipment group of GIFAS (Groupement des Industries Françaises Aéronautiques et Spatiales) had a turnover of Ffr 5 100 million in 1978 (appr. $ 1 200 million).

Table 31.   Turnover of French Aeronautical Equipment Producers in 1973-
             1978, (million of current francs)

1973	1974	1975	1976	1977	1978
2 490	2 950	3 870	4 700	4 820	5 100

Source: Interavia 6.1979, p. 551.

In 1977 the equipment group had exports of Ffr. 1 043 million, 21.6 per
cent of the turnover. At the same time it had orders for Ffr. 2 180 million, i.e.
twice the sum of its export deliveries. Military electronics forms the largest
part of these equipments. In 1978 the French exports of aerospace electronics
alone were Ffr. 1 690 million (appr. $ 384 million), which was about 10 per
cent of the total aerospace exports (Ffr. 17 154 mill.).[81]

There are also major producers of military electronics in other industrialized
market economies. In Sweden, LM Ericsson, AGA and the Swedish subsidiary of
Philips have emerged as main Scandinavian suppliers, spurred by the defence
production of   Sweden. LM Ericsson is a diversified producer of
telecommunication, data systems, transmission equipment, radio, cables,
electronic components and signalling systems. It has manufacturing and
marketing subsidiaries all over the world. In 1977, its sales outside Sweden
were 83.6 per cent of the turnover. AGA produces navigation aids, measuring
instruments, security systems, thermal devices etc. It also has an extensive
international organization.[82]

The strongest Southern European base for the production of military
electronics is located in Italy:[83]

> The share of the military production of the total turnover is as high
> as 75 per cent in Selenia, 100 per cent in Elettronica and 100 in
> Contraves. The industry has licensing agreements with foreign
> companies - which tells about the dependent nature of the Italian
> military electronics - but the official policy of the industry is "to be
> prepared to operate without foreign support", should the political
> situation change. According to professional estimates Italy is a leader
> in the exports of electronic warfare systems to the Third World.

Italian industry has a wide range of ground, naval and airborne electronics, which serve the growing arms industry, the fifth largest after the USA, France, the UK and the FRG. Although the Italian industries are no transnational giants, they have an active export and licensing policy; their role should therefore not be neglected in the discussion of international military transfers.

The powerful electronic industry of Japan has also made efforts to develop military production as part of the overall aim to strengthen Japanese defence industry. Japanese Defence Agency has contracts with, e.g. Mitsubishi Electric, Nippon Electric and Tokyo Shibaur, which have supplied electronics to the Japanese aerospace industry. Nippon Electric, Mitsubishi and Toshiba are active in the Japanese space program. On the whole Japanese military electronics is a young sector, and the development takes place in cooperation with foreign companies. The Japanese space program is developed by particularly RCA, Ford, MBB and General Electric. Mitsubishi, whose other division produces aircraft, is partly owned by Philips (1/3) and Nippon Electric is 50 per cent owned by Honeywell. Fujitsu cooperates with Siemens and Matsushita with Motorola. Mitsubishi also cooperates with Hughes and IBM in certain projects. The Japanese electronic industries are so far dependent on foreign, mainly American but also European transnational producers.

Although there is a growing military sector, there is not much export yet. This is due to the fact that Japan has not traditionally exported arms or military technology. The Japanese defence industry is growing very strongly, however, and suffering from high development costs. It will therefore not take long until powerful groups start pushing for exports. Voices have already been heard in shipbuilding, which suffers from overcapacity. A similar push for exports may soon be possible in aerospace and electronics. Japan also produces components for transnational producers of military electronics. Some projects like Mitsubishi's construction of satellite-connected telecommunication stations in Malaysia, have not only civilian but also military functions.[84]

2.4.   Transnational Engine Industry

Powerful and efficient engines are a most essential part of modern weapons and weapon systems. Sophisticated aircraft, missiles, helicopters, tanks or ships would not have any military value, unless their power plants provided enough energy, speed and reliability. After the rapid rise of fuel costs fuel consumption has also become a major concern. Particular military requirements, e.g. high speed and quick changes of altitude in an attack aeroplane, make the engine a component on which the functioning of the whole weapon system is based.

To produce such engines is a complex and demanding task, which requires special raw materials, top-class designing talents, specialized tooling etc. Specific testing and research facilities are necessary as well to ensure the high quality and reliability of the engines. Finally, after the engines have been delivered to the customers, there is a need for perfect overhaul and repair services, regular spare part supplies and general logistical know-how both in the home country and abroad.

Because the construction of modern engines is so complex the producers of final weapon systems almost never produce the engines themselves but purchase them from specialized engine manufacturers. For the same reason - i.e. the complexity of production - the number of engine producers is very small. In fact it is justified to state that engine production is the most concentrated part of world armament industry. In aerospace, in which we concentrate in this chapter, there are only a handful of engine producers with independent technology, while there are plenty of airframe producers in different countries. The result of this situation is that many countries which claim to have "indigenous" and "self-reliant" aircraft production are not actually self-reliant but rather dependent because they import the engines. Also, many of the engines manufactured in different countries are based on licences from a few leading companies; thus not all engine companies have technological independence.

Actually it is rather surprising that the security and economic implications of the concentration of engine technology have aroused so little interest among the students of arms production and arms trade. Yet the general situation is that should the few leading companies suddenly stop deliveries of engines or licences, aircraft production would stop immediately in most countries. The engines are so expensive that airframe producers cannot buy them into stocks. Another security aspect is that regulations concerning engine deliveries and transfers of their technology are probably the most efficient immediate way to control arms transfers, because the number of producers is so small.

An economic question that cannot be avoided is whether the limited number of key producers raises the prices of engines, and thus makes purchases of arms very expensive. The question is particularly justified where the companies have managed to agree upon market sharing, cartel or other similar arrangements. Although the present market structure in aeroengine production offers objective conditions for a cartel, available information does not give any justification for such doubts. On the contrary, there are several examples of fierce competition among the leading engine producers.

Engines constitute a notable share of total aerospace sales in the leading producer countries, i.e. the U.S., the UK and France. In 1976 their engine sales were $ 3.5 billion, $ 1 billion and $ 0.8 billion respectively, and accounted for 15 per cent, 30 per cent and 19 per cent of the total sales.[85] Thus, from the relative point of view, the engines were particularly important for the British aerospace industry (cf. Annex A). According to another source, quoted earlier in this study (p. 38) the exports of aeroengines and parts accounted for 40 per cent of the total British aero exports in 1977.

As far as the large engines are concerned, the Western markets are dominated by the so-called "big three", which collectively hold about 76 per cent of the world market in gas-turbine aeroengines. They are Pratt & Whitney (part of United Technologies, USA) with an estimated 42 per cent of the market, General Electric (USA) and Rolls Royce (UK), each with an estimated 17 per cent of the market in 1979. The rest of Western gas-turbine markets are covered by some 50 companies, only a few of whom, however, have indigenous technology, while most of them produce engines with licences from the leading companies, or participate as subcontractors for the leading companies.[86] The leading French companies are state-owned Snecma - the fourth largest in the world - and Turbomeca, the first of which is specialized in aeroplane engines while the latter produces helicopter engines. Both companies have independent technological capability. Other large producers, notably Motoren und Turbinen Union MTU in the FRG, Fiat in Italy, Ishikawajima-Harima, Mitsubishi and Kawasaki in Japan, Volvo Flygmotor in Sweden and KlöcknerHumboldt-Deutz, KHD in the FRG are partly independent in technology, but produce most engines under licences.

As far as engines for lighter aircraft are concerned, there is also a small group of transnational producers. Avco Lycoming, Garrett, Continental and Detroit Diesel Allison Division of General Motors are important suppliers to international aircraft and helicopter industries - all of them from the U.S. Also the Italian Rinaldo Piaggio has extensive international sales, but its engines are based on Rolls Royce's and Avco Lycoming's licences.

If the strength of the companies is measured on the basis of the number of world aircraft models powered by these companies, the positions of the leading companies look as follows:

Table 32.

Table 32.   Number of Civil and Military Aircraft Models Built in Market
             Economies Powered by Leading Engine Manufacturers[a]

Engine producer	No. of models powered	Per cent
Pratt & Whitney	121	29
Avco Lycoming	93	22
Rolls Royce	69	16
General Electric	41	10
Garrett	18	4
Continental	17	4
Allison	14	3
Snecma	10	2
Volvo	10	2
Other	32	8
Total	425	100

Source: Calculated from Aviation Week & Space Technology, March 3,
           1980.

Note: [a]See Annex D for more detailed information.

The engine producers are not, of course, an independent group in world
military production. On the contrary, their production is totally dependent on
the production plans of airframe producers both in the home country and
abroad. The engine producers have four types of markets: 1) engines for new
aircraft produced in the home country, 2) engines for new aircraft produced by
foreign industries, 3) re-engine programs for existing aircraft to lengthen their
time of operation and to improve their performance and 4) supplying of parts,
logistics and overhaul services for old engines both at home and abroad.

The first market is the production and exports of new aircraft in the home
countries. If there is a political decision to have strong aircraft production and
exports - like in the U.S., France and the UK - the engine producers
automatically benefit from such a decision. Thus, Snecma benefits from
Dassault's sales, General Electric from Northrop's sales and Rolls Royce from
British Aerospace's sales, and all of them become major military exporters not

so much on their own initiative but because of the expansion of the others.

Thus, the interests of the engine producers are very closely connected with the activities of the aircraft producers. Some engine producers supply engines mainly for one aircraft producer - which makes them an intimate pair - but a more common practice is that aircraft producers have diversified their engine supplies. This is partly a normal division of labour: for different sizes of aircraft you need larger or smaller engines which are often produced by different producers because of specialization. But it is also evident that the aircraft producers have tried to avoid dependence on one engine supplier only, probably to maintain price competition among suppliers and to secure engine supplies in case one supplier has problems. In the table below we have studied the links between the leading aircraft and engine producers in the U.S. military aircraft industry:

Table 33.   Connections between Leading U.S. Military Aircraft and Helicopter Producers and Leading Engine Manufacturers

Aircraft/helicopter producer	P&W[b]	GE	ALL	CONT	LYC	GARR	Other
General Dynamics	x	x					
Textron/Bell	x	x	x		x		
Lockheed	x	x	x				
McDonnell Douglas	x	x					
Northrop		x					
Hughes		x	x		x		
Grumman	x		x		x		
Sikorsky[b]	x	x	x				
Boeing	x	x					
Rockwell	x	x			x	x	x
Vought			x				
Cessna		x		x			
Fairchild	x	x					
Beech	x			x	x		

Engine producer[a]

Source: Aviation Week & Space Technology, March 3, 1980.

Notes: [a]Abbreviations: P&W = Pratt & Whitney, GE = General Electric, ALL = Allison, CONT = Continental, LYC = Avco Lycoming, GARR = Garrett.

[b]Both Pratt & Whitney and Sikorsky belong to United Technologies Corporation.

In the above table we can observe that the leading competitors in large engines, i.e. Pratt & Whitney and General Electric usually supply engines for the same aircraft companies and have not divided their customers to make any cliques. Allison, Continental and Lycoming also compete for the same customers.

The second important market for engine industries is the participation in foreign aircraft industries. As was mentioned in the beginning, the engine technology is controlled by a small group of producers, who extensively supply engines for industries at home and abroad. Some engine producers are very home-industry oriented (like Snecma in France and Volvo in Sweden), while some other companies have very modest sales at home but extensive operations abroad. Among the U.S. producers, particularly Avco Lycoming and Garrett have modest national but extensive international profiles. This can be noted by comparing information in Annex D and Table 34 below:

Table 34.   U.S., British and French Engine Producers as Suppliers to Foreign Aircraft and Helicopter Industries

Aircraft producer and country	Engine producer[a]								
	P&W	GE	ALL	CONT	LYC	GARR	R-R	SNEC	TUR
Aeroboero, Argentina					x				
FMA, Argentina									x
GAF, Australia			x						
Neiva, Brazil				x	x				
Embraer, Brazil	x			x	x	x			
Canadair, Canada	x	x			x				
Omnipol, Czechoslovakia	x				x				
Dornier, FRG	x				x	x			
MBB, FRG			x		x				
Valmet, Finland					x				
SNIAS, France	x		x		x			x	x
Dassault, France	x	x				x	x	x	
Reims Aviation, France				x	x		x		
HAL, India					x		x		x
IAI, Israel	x	x				x			x
Macchi, Italy							x		
Aeritalia, Italy		x					x		
Piaggio, Italy					x		x		
SIAI Marchetti, Italy			x		x				

Table 34 continued

Aircraft producer and country	Engine producer[a]								
	P&W	GE	ALL	CONT	LYC	GARR	R-R	SNEC	TUR
Breda Nardi, Italy			x		x				
Agusta, Italy	x	x	x		x				
Fuji, Japan					x				
Kawasaki, Japan	x	x	x		x				
Mitsubishi, Japan	x	x				x	x		
Shin Meiva, Japan		x							
Fokker-VFW, Netherlands							x		
Atlas Aircraft, South Africa					x		x		
CASA, Spain		x			x	x	x		
Pilatus, Switzerland	x								
AIDC, Taiwan					x				
BAe, UK					x	x	_x_		
Norman, UK					x				
Short Bros., UK	x					x			
Westland, UK							_x_		x
Soko, Yugoslavia					x		_x_		
Utva, Yugoslavia					x				

Source: <u>Aviation Week & Space Technology</u>, March 3, 1980 and TAPRI data files.

Notes: [a]Abbreviations: P&W = Pratt & Whitney, GE = General Electric, ALL = Detroit Diesel Allison div. of General Motors, CONT = Continental, LYC = Avco Lycoming, GARR = Garrett, R-R = Rolls Royce, SNEC = Snecma, TUR = Turbomeca.

x = Primary supplier.

As can be observed in the above table, the leading engine producers are in general very important for foreign aircraft industries. In fact very few aircraft models in the world - excluding the Soviet Union - are powered by companies not mentioned in the table. The dependence of aircraft producers on these engine supplies can thus be considered one of the most critical points in the industry. If the dependence on foreign aeroengines is typical of industrialized countries, it is not too surprising that the dependence is even pronounced more in the case of developing producers.

On the basis of Table 34 above we could say that the Western aircraft industry is dependent on seven transnatioal engine producers. It is interesting to note that Western engine technology is also used by the Czechoslovakian industry together with its own designs and Soviet imports, as well as by Yugoslav industry, all of whose models are powered by Western engines.

Some countries which have tried to achieve self-reliance in aircraft production have worked hard to be able to construct their own engines. In the developing countries particularly Israel and India have such programs. So far they have, however, not succeeded in these efforts. They produce engines for their models with foreign licences and their indigenous models have been in the stage of development for many years. The aircraft industries of other developing countries have not even tried to develop their own models. The role of the leading engine producers in developing aircraft industries has been studied in Table 35 below:[87]

Table 35. Developing Aircraft Industries as Markets for Leading Engine Manufacturers[a]

Country	Number of models powered by						
	LYC	CONT	P&W	R-R	GARR	GE	TUR
Argentina	1						1
Brazil	10	2	9	1			
Taiwan	3						
India	2			5			
Israel			2		1	3	
South Africa	2			1			
Yugoslavia	4			4			

Source: *Aviation Week & Space Technology*, March 3, 1980, World Armaments and Disarmament, SIPRI Yearbook 1979, London 1979, Jane's All the World's Aircraft 1973-74 and ibid. 1976-77.

Notes: [a] The table does not distinguish between indigenous/licensed or civil/military models.

The above information shows that on the basis of the number of aircraft models Avco Lycoming is the dominant supplier for developing aircraft industries, followed by Rolls Royce and Pratt & Whitney. This measure is not the best one because it does not estimate the amount of production and sales but it can be considered a sufficient approximation of the role played by the dominant engine suppliers.

Western helicopter production is also dependent on the leading engine producers. The same companies which dominate aeroplane engine markets also dominate markets for helicopter engines, only in a different order. Judged again by the number of models powered by each producer, the situation looks as follows:

Table 36. Helicopter Production of Major Producing Countries as a Market for Leading Engine Manufacturers

Producer country	Number of models powered by							
	LYC	GE	TUR	ALL	P&W	R-R	Other	Total
United States	27	21		7	10			65
France	1		16	1				18
Italy	4	4		5	2		1	16
Japan	3	4		2				9
United Kingdom			2			6		8
India			3					3
FR of Germany	1			1				2
Brazil			2					2
Total	36	29	23	16	12	6	1	123

Source: Aviation Week & Space Technology, March 3, 1980, Flight International, February 25, 1978.

Avco Lycoming is a clear leader in helicopter engines, followed by General Electric, Turbomeca, Allison and Pratt & Whitney.

One could expect that because the world aircraft and helicopter engine production is dominated by only a handful of companies, they would be powerful, rich and capable of continuous new development programs. This, however, is not quite the case. The development of new engines is so expensive that the companies are not expected to invent totally new, revolutionary types. Instead, they develop new variants from their existing engine models, which has resulted in the emergence of "engine families".[88] Even though the development is based on the existing types, it becomes very expensive. When Rolls Royce decided to develop a new engine to replace its old Spey, the cost of the program was estimated as $ 700 million, and the company turned to rich Japanese firms to share the burden.[89] When Pratt & Whitney decided to start co-development with the German MTU and the Italian Fiat, the cost of the program was estimated as $ 500 million.[90]

Because of the high development and production costs, the engine companies have joined their forces and formed international groupings. Besides sharing the costs, the companies naturally also compete by forming these groups, trying to ensure wider markets with international cooperation. At present, the main groupings are as follows:

Table 37.   International Groupings between Leading Manufacturers of Gas Turbines

Companies		Models powered
General Electric, USA Snecma, France	CFM	Boeing KC-135 MDD DC-8 Boeing 707
Rolls Royce, UK Turbomeca, France		Jaguar Hawk New development
Rolls Royce, UK Allison, USA		Vougt A-7D Vougt A-7E
Rolls Royce, UK Snecma, France		Concorde
Rolls Royce, UK Fiat, Italy MTU, FRG	Turbounion	Panavia Tornado
KHD + MTU, FRG Snecma + Turbomeca, France		Alpha Jet
Garrett, USA Volvo, Sweden		New development
Rolls Royce, UK Mitsubishi, Kawasaki IHI, Japan		New development
Pratt & Whitney, USA[a] MTU, FRG Fiat, Italy		New development

Source: Aviation Week & Space Technology, March 3, 1980, p. 133 and The Economist, August 18, 1979, p. 66, Aviation Week & Space Technology, June 6, 1977.

Notes: [a]Rolls Royce originally participated in this group but it withdrew in 1977.

As can be noted, in the composition of each group there is one leading company which is bigger and technologically superior, and then one or two smaller, more dependent partners which are, however, technologically and financially capable of participating in the program. The withdrawal of Rolls Royce from the company of Pratt & Whitney shows that there is no room for two leaders or competitors in the groups.[91]

The experience of international engine cooperation shows that notable strategic and political problems exist. In particular the newest military engines are considered as strategic technology the transfer of which is not permitted even to political allies. When General Electric started engine development with Snecma, it first wanted to use technology developed for the engine in B-1, the new bomber. The transfer of such technology was not permitted by the U.S. authorities, and GE had to revise the plans before the cooperation with Snecma could be continued.[92] A comparable situation has arisen in the co-production program of F-16. Fifteen per cent of Pratt & Whitney engines are considered strategic secrets, and these parts cannot be produced by NATO's West European members. Instead, the critical parts are produced in the U.S. and then assembled in Europe under close supervision.[93]

The participation of engine industries in foreign aircraft production does not lead to transfers of strategic technology for several reasons. The first is that most engines are sold to foreign aircraft producers and afterwards the engine producer is also responsible for services. The second reason is that licences are usually granted to models which do not represent the latest technology. This is connected to the fact that foreign producers usually produce smaller aircraft and do not threaten the air superiority of the main producers. Consequently, the foreign-made engines do not threaten the technological dominance of the leading powers either. In licence production the supplier of technology usually reserves the most complicated parts for its own production, while the licenser makes more simple parts and assembly. The fact that many developing producers lag very much behind the leading producers in technology also has caused a situation in which licences of older models are sold to them. In this way the production time of old engine models is made longer by selling licences for production abroad while the supplier is already occupied with the development and production of new models. Thus, Rolls Royce lengthens the time of Spey engines by letting Rumania and China produce them with licences while the British headquarters plan a new model to replace it.

The aircraft producers have sometimes found that dependence on foreign engines may cause restrictions on their exports. In particular the United States has vetoed military aircraft sales on the basis that the plane has American engines. Sweden's Saab was not able to export Viggen-fighters to India because of the U.S. veto. Aeritalia could not export its G-222 military transport aircraft to Libya because it had General Electric's engines and the U.S. vetoed the sale - worth $ 382 million to Aeritalia.[94] The solution found by Aeritalia was to turn to Rolls Royce for engines to avoid such restrictions. This was not pleasant for Alfa Romeo and Fiat which produce General Electric's engines with licences. Rolls Royce's engines will have to be imported to Italy.[95] The effort by Israel to sell Kfir-fighters to Ecuador and Central America was also vetoed by the U.S. on the basis of U.S. engines in 1978.

The examples of using engine supplies to restrict arms transfers are not very numerous, however. On the whole the political authorities have let the arms trade grow, although engine control would offer perhaps the most efficient immediate way to restrict sales and foreign production, if the political will to do it exists.

2.5.   Summary

Western conventional arms production is a) concentrated in a few countries, b) concentrated in a few companies which are c) large and transnational by their character. Such "triple concentration" results mainly from two factors: complexity of technology and high development and production costs. The tendency is towards weapon systems which consist of several technologically complex parts, each being produced by a specialized producer. For a modern aircraft special raw materials, airframe, engine, electronics and other special components are needed, and the final system is so complex that few producers possess independent development and production capacities.

The cost crisis is also limiting the number of producers. Technological specialty, large R&D needs, long development periods, consumption of scarce, top-grade materials, high labour costs, expensive machinery and related factors make the production very expensive. Another aspect is that military production is not a pure free market sector guided by economic efficiency. On the contrary, state authorities often maintain companies which would go bankrupt without state support, as shown by examples like AEG-Telefunken, Chrysler, Lockheed and Rolls Royce. The Western military production is hence a combination of strong state intervention and free-market behaviour, the purpose of which is to decrease the unit costs of weapons. Rationalization, mergers, market expansion and intensified internationalization are strategies to overcome the cost crisis of production.

The armament leader is the U.S., followed by France and the UK. Only these three countries can be considered autonomous as far as technological capacity is concerned - but they are in turn dependent on raw material supplies and arms exports. The FRG is making efforts to enter the company of France and the UK, and it has strong technology in some areas, while being dependent in some others. In addition, it is to a certain extent penetrated by foreign capital. A candidate for an independent military technology is also Japan, but so far it has produced weapons for internal needs. Italy is a strong producer, too, but technologically dependent on foreign TNCs. The technological capacity of other Western industrial countries is more partial and limited to less sophisticated weapons.

The largest and most powerful companies are located in the U.S. which supports them with remarkable R&D funds and large procurements. The companies enjoy the benefit of a large home market, and the DoD seems to distribute the procurements so that all leading companies "get their share". The U.S. firms are also most capable of development and production of new technologies.

In Europe there is a tendency toward one company per country, as shown by the developments in France and the U.K. In most weapons categories the French and British companies are already competitive vis-à-vis the U.S. firms, but this situation has only been possible with heavy investments, rationalization and market expansion. The European firms are in general more dependent on military exports than the U.S. ones, as far as export ratios are concerned. In absolute terms the U.S. military exports are bigger.

It is important to know the TNC-model of arms production, because Western arms technology has become a model for the socialist countries and increasingly also for the developing countries. The faith in the superiority of this technology in guaranteeing the military security is thus spreading, and its impact is becoming global. Very few countries are brave enough to seek for new, alternative conceptions of security and military technology.

The military TNCs have become a giant social institution, but they are largely unknown due to the military and commercial secrecy covering their operations. Since the access to information is troublesome and often blocked, we have in Chapter 2 presented three sectors in somewhat more detail. Our hope is that the information facilitates future research of military production and gives empirical background for its political evaluations.

3 Military industries of the socialist countries

The military industries of the socialist countries are problematic for any serious research effort: almost no empirical information is published by the countries concerned, due to very strict secrecy rules in matters related to security.[1] Due to lack of direct, primary sources research of defence apparatuses of the socialist countries is often very general, indirect and imprecise, compared to studies on Western defence apparatuses. Furthermore, studies are written by Western scholars and political motives are sometimes connected, or have even replaced pure intellectual interest.

3.1.   The Soviet Union

The development of military production is related to the general industrial development of the Soviet Union. The foundations for armament industries were laid in the 1920s and 1930s when heavy industry was being created as one of the priorities in the new socialist planning. In World War II, enormous efforts were required by the newly created industries to supply the country with all necessary war material.

After the war the Cold War policies, emerging arms race with the West and the technological leadership of the U.S. in many crucial areas forced the Soviet defence industries into new, large programs. Programs for nuclear weapons, strategic and tactical missiles, naval warfare etc. had to be started, and the Soviet Union followed the U.S. with the time lag of 1-5 years in each field of the arms race.[2] In the 1960s strategic parity between the U.S. and the Soviet Union was achieved, but the arms race continued in space, in aviation, in ballistic weapons and in the qualitative development of missiles as well as anti-missile programs.

In the 1970s the arms race continued: new weapons were included to already enormous arsenals, and qualitative advances were added to old platforms; e.g. precision guidance, range and accuracy increased. There is no doubt that the main role of Soviet defence production has been to react to the technological leadership and the new weapons of the West.[3]

David Holloway, a British scholar, has differentiated three levels in the Soviet weapons program. The first level is the armed forces, which order the military equipment and use it after procurement. The chief institutions are the General Staff and the Ministry of Defence, which supervises the fulfilment of armament programs, plans new production and carries out technological research.

The chief mechanism of coordination is the Military-Industrial Commission attached to the USSR Council of Ministers. The Commission supervises the management of defence industries at branch and subbranch level. It implements the main directions of military-technical policy, determines appropriate specialization of production and sets up interbranch and intrabranch links.

The third level consists of different Ministries which are responsible for R&D establishments as well as the production processes. Each Ministry has a technical administration which guides, plans and supervises the Ministry's R&D institutes. Each Ministry as well as each branch of the armed forces has a Scientific and Technical Council which deals with technical policy and technological innovation. Outside scientists and engineers can also serve in these councils as advisors or consultants, thus providing links with other scientific institutions, e.g. to the Academy of Sciences.[4]

The military industries are subordinated to their respective Ministries and their responsibilities are divided as follows:

Table 38.   The Responsibilities within the Soviet Defence Industry

Industry	Responsibility
Defence Industry	Armaments, e.g. tanks, artillery, ammunition
Aviation Industry	Aircraft, aircraft parts
Shipbuilding Industry	Warships
Electronics Industry	Electronic components and parts
Radio Industry	Radio and communication systems and equipment, radars, computers
General Machine Building	Strategic missiles
Medium Machine Building	Nuclear devices and warheads
Machine Building	Ammunition

Source: Andrew Sheren, Structure and Organization of Defence-related Industries, in Economic Performance and the Military Burden in the Soviet Union, A compendium of papers submitted to the Subcommittee on Foreign Economic Policy of the Joint Economic Committee, Congress of the United States, Washington D.C. 1970, p. 127 and David Holloway, Technology and Political Decision in Soviet Armaments Policy, Journal of Peace Research, Vol. XI, No. 4, 1974, p. 261.

In the West the large military industries are often pressing for new weapons programs and technological innovations. Apparently, the Soviet armament industry does not have a similar role. Innovation and expansion are rather imposed upon the armament industry as a result of political decisions which also accord the industry favoured treatment by providing it with the best materials and labour force.[5]

According to Checinski, the Soviet industry is divided into four categories:

1. Enterprises which are entirely engaged in producing armaments and military equipment;

2. Enterprises which cooperate with armament industry but at the same time produce for the civilian market;

100

3. Enterprises which mainly produce for the civilian market but which also supply elements to the armament industry;

4. Enterprises which do not assist armament industry.

The rank of an enterprise in one of these categories corresponds to its priority on the list of factors of production as distributed through the central planning system. Enterprises in groups 1 and 2 are given priority when high quality raw materials, machine tools and skilled specialists are distributed across the economy. The priority status of space and defence industries also guarantees good quality and sufficient financing.[6]

The scientific research and educational systems, especially in technical fields, are also affected by the priority status of defence production, as well as its secrecy rules. All military scientific and technical knowledge is secret. Research and educational systems are divided into secret and non-secret areas, e.g. scientific information which has significance for armament industry is not available in a non-secret library.[7]

The development of weapons is carried out by defence design bureaux, which often carry the name of some famous designer like Tupolev or Iljushin. Some of the design bureaux have their own experimental factories which are under the control of the chief designer; thus they are able to produce their own prototypes of new weapons. The status of the leading design bureaux is believed to be rather strong. The design bureaux and plants must compete for new weapons contracts.[8]

The strength of the leading design institutions may be a common feature in Western and Eastern armament industries: power tends to concentrate in those who command the new, complex armament technologies. Without the technological skills and good understanding of the rapidly changing requirements of military technology, the whole defence production would soon become senseless. The technological imperative, thus, tends to strengthen the position of scientific, designing and engineering personnel, compared to the military and administration.

A Soviet scholar confirms this view:[9]

> "for a long time science and military affairs were related to each other in this way: from military affairs to science and back to military affairs. In military practice a definite requirement arises. At a certain stage this is realised by military specialists and formulated by them as a concrete request which is presented to the competent scientific establishments and finds there its solution. With the development of science and growing complexity of the tasks of strengthening the country's defence another type of relationship begins to become widespread - from science to military affairs, since contemporary science is able to find ways of raising the combat capabilities of the army and navy which are new in principle and do not flow directly from the traditional forms of their existence."

The same tendency appears very clearly in a statement by Marshal Crechko.[10]

> Scientific and technical progress is one of the chief factors in improving the country's defence potential and in advancing the art of war and military work generally. The fruits of scientific and technological progress allow new types of weapons and military hardware to be developed more quickly and efficiently and this in turn augments the fire power, striking power and manouverability of the Armed Forces and gives rise to new methods of military operations.

Crechko furthermore considers that changes in the military technology are the main factor in shaping the tactics, strategy and the organization of the armed forces. The improvement of the technical performance of the weaponry appears to be a universal feature in the arms race. For this purpose the development of conventional weapons aims, inter alia, at

> a longer range, increased fire power, higher accuracy, increased mobility, higher rates of fire, greater survivability and reliability, more stable functioning in the face of enemy electronic countermeasures, and greater ease of handling and operation. The main areas in which R&D are concentrated are the development of indigenous designs and systems, the use of new materials and explosives, and the development of improved sighting and guidance systems with increased accuracy.[11]

This quotation indicates that the development of military electronics has a rather high position on the agenda of Soviet military programs.

The major Soviet military industries and their responsibilities are presented in the following table:

102

Table 39.   Major Soviet Military Industries and Their Responsibilities

Manufacturer/designer	Responsibility
Antonov	transport aircraft
Beriev	transport aircraft
Iljushin	transport aircraft
	marine patrol aircraft
Kamov	helicopters
Mikojan	fighters
Mil	helicopters
Sukhoi	fighters
Tupolev	bombers
Yakovlev	transport aircraft,
	fighters
Soviet State Arsenal	armoured personnel carriers
	tanks, self-propelled guns and
	hovitzers,
	missiles
Leningrad	aircraft carriers,
	destroyers, corvettes
	patrol boats, submarines
Nikolayev	cruisers, aircraft carriers
	frigates, minesweepers
Kaliningrad	destroyers
Zhdanov	cruisers
Gorky	submarines, torpedoboats
Severodvinsk	submarines
Sudomekh	submarines

Sources: SIPRI Yearbook 1979 and The Military Balance 1979-1980.

Because information on production, turnover and employment of these enterprises is not available, quantitative comparisons with Western armament
enterprises are not possible. Instead, attention is often paid to similarities or
dissimilarities of the general social position and to the role of armament
industries in different societies.

The first observation in this respect is that socialist armament industries are
not comparable to transnational or international armament industries in the
West. They are totally under political control and cannot have independent
operations, while the Western industries sometimes carry out operations
outside government control. In a socialist society, the profit motive for arms
production is lacking; on the other hand, the economic risks of production are

also lacking as all the financing comes from the public budget. The public ownership of the socialist enterprises also prevents penetration of private interests into defence policies and armament production. As the profit motive is lacking and the production is shared among different plants according to authoritative production planning, there cannot be any pressures for economic expansion and continuous occupation of new armament markets. For the same reasons, foreign arms deliveries are not motivated by economic competition between different producers or a "sell or die" philosophy as is often the case in capitalist armament enterprises.[12] In sum, socialist armament production and international transfers are carried out on the basis of security, political and military considerations, not because of economic expansion.

There are also indications that the Soviet military production and arms exports show some regularities which are connected with the dynamics of budgeting and planning. According to Hutchings, the totals of Soviet arms exports to the Third World display a cyclical pattern which is influenced by the timetable of the Soviet long-term economic plans. Exports to the Third World surge upwards in the second year of each five-year plan, and this may have some connections with the overall foreign trade policy. On the other hand the allocation of resources to military purposes tends to be highest in the mid-point of the five-year plan. This may be a consequence of the fact that the civilian expenditures appear to be more concentrated at the beginning and the end of the plan.[13]

However, armament production, modern R&D activities and the permanent pressures for inventing new, better technologies are expensive both in the East and in the West, although the pricing policies of the participating units differ in both societies. The unit costs of weapons are rising with technological sophistication and rising raw material prices, and public authorities will have to be concerned with the means to decrease unit prices of weapons. The economic realities will have to be considered by the political authorities also in socialist societies. It is not out of the question that decisions concerning the number of produced weapons or the deliveries of some weapons abroad may be affected by economic factors, too, although the primary considerations are always related to security, international commitments and political goals.[14]

3.2.   Other European Socialist States

The armament industries of the member countries of the Warsaw Treaty Organization (WTO) are based on common planning and coordination. A special WTO committee, composed of the directors of the military departments of Planning Committees, determines which kind of arms or components are to be produced in each country and which armies of the WTO will be supplied with them and at what time.[15]

The role of the Soviet defence industry is dominant within WTO, and the arms production of the other member countries can be considered as complementary to the Soviet production.[16] While the Soviet Union maintains large-scale production in all armament areas, the production of the other member countries is more limited and specialized. The technological leadership of the Soviet Union is indicated e.g. by the fact that the other member countries often produce arms or components of arms with Soviet licences and designs.

According to the Sofia Agreement of 1948 the CMEA countries are entitled to adopt the technique or technology of member countries without paying licence fees.[17] This is in line with the overall practice of inventor's certificates in the socialist countries instead of monopolistic patents.

The question of specialization and decisions over the location of specialized plants within the WTO are solved on the basis of technological level and the best skills in each country - i.e. a kind of comparative-advantage principle works within the WTO defence production.

According to Checinski the size of defence production is fixed according to the assumed level of demand in the event of war. In this case the WTO would meet the armament needs from both national arsenals and from the stocks in the member countries. Quotas concerning domestic production are set for each armament plant and reserve production forces. Raw materials reserves are planned accordingly.

The armament plants produce a) quantities needed at home, b) those needed for the other WTO countries and c) quantities needed for international aid and political cooperation. The remaining productive capacities are either frozen or used for buffer production of e.g. civilian goods.[18] During the political crisis of Afghanistan towards the end of 1979, it could be noted that the socialist countries maintained enough armament stocks to be able to act at short notice if considered necessary from the security point of view. Also during the 1973 Middle East War the Soviet Union was able to supply large quantities of arms to the battlefield. The need for large supplies emerged because new armament technologies proved to cause large material damage.[19]

Outside the Soviet Union, the most developed armament industry is in Czechoslovakia. The largest enterprise is aircraft producing Aero, which produces trainers, fighters, transport and acrobatic aircraft. One of the newest models of this factory, L-39 Albatross, has been selected as a standard trainer for WTO. According to company representatives, the demand for L-39 has been so great that the original production forecast of 1 000 has been revised to over 3 000 jet trainers. According to SIPRI, the fighter/ground attack version of L-39 has been exported to Afghanistan and Iraq. The company itself has declared its aim for Western and Third World markets with this model.[20] This means that a new category has appeared in WTO arms production: arms for commercial exports.

The USSR is the largest customer as well as the largest supplier of the Czech aerospace industry. Since 1975, an intergovernmental agreement between the Czech and the Soviet aircraft industries provides for scientific and technical information. The L-39, which is considered a second-generation jet trainer in WTO, was designed by a Czech team working with USSR designers.[21] Czechoslovakia is also capable of producing sophisticated aircraft parts and equipment. The Motorlet aircraft engine factory produces engines, some of which are based on Soviet models or licences.[22] Rudy Letov National Corp. produces mobile control and test units for aircraft systems, equipment and instruments. It has also developed advanced simulators.[23]

Czech State Arsenal produces armed personnel carriers (OT-64) which are also produced in Poland and Hungary with a licence. Soviet designed tanks (T-62) are also produced in Czechoslovakia with a licence.[24]

Defence industries in Poland include an aircraft factory <u>PZL - Polskie Zaklady Lotnicze</u> - which produces multipurpose and trainer aircraft in the Warsaw plant and Iskra trainers in the Mielec factory. In Swidnik PZL manufactures four models of helicopters, one of which is based on a Soviet licence while the others have Polish design. Poland also produces aircraft engines. Shipbuilding is traditionally strong in Poland. The Gdansk Yard produces tank landing ships and fast patrol boats. In addition, Poland produces armed personnel carriers (OT-64) and tanks (T-62) with Soviet licence.[25] According to a Western estimate, 10-12 per cent of Poland's mechanical and electric industries work in military production.[26]

The military production in the German Democratic Republic has not tradition- ally been comparable to Czechoslovakian or Polish production, although the GDR is a developed, industrialized society. According to Western estimates, the defence production has grown within the last few years, however. Today, production includes naval vessels (at least torpedo boats, minesweepers and tank landing ships), armoured vehicles, engineering equipment, sophisti- cated optical instruments, chemical products, munitions, artillery and various infantry weapons.[27]

The Romanian aircraft factory <u>CIAR</u> and the Yugoslav <u>Soko</u> produce together Orao fighter/ground attack aircraft, which is powered with British engines and made its first flight in 1977. Another Romanian aircraft company, CAB, produces transport aircraft with licences from <u>British Aerospace</u> since 1978 and <u>Pilatus Britten Norman</u> since 1968. <u>ICA-Brasov</u> produces helicopters with a French licence from <u>Aerospatiale</u> granted in 1971. In 1971 Romania also signed a licence agreement with the People's Republic of China for producing fast patrol boats. The Romanian State factory produces armoured personnel carriers, which are developed locally on the basis of a Soviet model.[28]

Yugoslavia has two aircraft factories. The larger one, <u>Soko Metal Industries</u> in Mostar, produces indigenously designed aircraft for training, strike/reconnais- sance, tactical reconnaissance, attack and close support purposes. All Soko's models are powered by British engines and the company exports some of its models. Soko also produces helicopters with a licence from the French <u>Aerospatiale</u> since 1971. Another enterprise, <u>Utva Aircraft Factory</u> in

Pancevo, produces utility and training aircraft. The Yugoslav shipyards Uljanik, Brodotehnika and Tito Yard construct submarines, tank landing ships, minesweepers and fast patrol boats. In their efforts to diversify dependence on foreign technology sources, they import essential parts from the Soviet Union, Sweden, the United Kingdom and Switzerland.[29]

3.3.   The Electronic Industry of the Socialist Countries

One of the least known fields within the Soviet unknown defence industries is the production of electronics in general and military electronics in particular. An advanced space program or modern armaments arsenal cannot exist without advanced electronics. Participation in the arms race would also be senseless without modern military electronics, since it is precisely in this field that the qualitative arms race takes place.

The Western defence community usually thinks that the West is superior in military electronics. It also tries to maintain this presumed superiority with embargoes on new electronic equipment. COCOM - the Western coordinating commission consisting of the NATO countries and Japan - has been particularly reluctant to make electronic exports to the socialist countries.

According to Checinski two separate ministries are concerned with electronics in the Soviet Union: 1) Ministerstvo Priborostroyenija, and 2) Ministerstvo Radioelektroniki, each with its own enterprises and research institutes. All scientific and productive activities of the 'Priborostroyenija' Ministry follow the requirements of the Ministry of Defence, and are listed in the first and second priority categories within the industry. The branches of the 'Radioelektroniki' Ministry are listed in the third and fourth categories, unless they make discoveries or have projects which have special relevance for the Army; in that case the project is lifted to the first or the second category. Correspondingly, a project under 'Priborostroyenija' can be transferred to lower categories if it has no military significance.[30]

The ministry of electronic industry (also known as M.E.P.) does not publish information about its production and the activities of the research institutes are kept secret. The ministry produces: electronic components (tubes, integrated circuits, optoelectronics etc.), equipment for production and control of production, lasers and laser equipment, auxiliary equipment like transformers, advanced finished products (e.g. pocket calculators).

Within the last few years, the M.E.P. has encouraged the creation of large production units which are specialized in certain types of electronic products. Scientific-technical councils coordinate the activities of scientific research institutes, education, experimental production and mass production. The general aim is to encourage electronic production and rapid solutions to electronic problems. Large centres for electronic research and production have been founded in Leningrad, Kiev, Minsk, Voronej, Moscow, Vitebsk and other places.[31]

In the 1950s and 1960s the Soviet Union lagged behind the U.S. in many fields of electronics. The USA introduced the first transistors in 1948 while the first Soviet ones appeared in 1952-53, and the industrial production was started in Svetlana plant, Leningrad in 1956. Texas Instruments and Westinghouse presented the first integrated circuits in 1958 while the first Soviet circuits appeared in 1962.[32] This indicates that the Soviet Union is lagging behind in military electronics by the same interval as in military technology in general. In connection with the major reorganization of the Soviet industrial production around 1965 major efforts were also made in organization, education and information to improve the level of electronic industry.

It was a common opinion that the Soviet Union lagged behind the West in military electronics in the general sense but, at the same time, it had made advances in certain fields. The radar equipment of Soviet arms was, for example, found "near parity, sometimes surpassing U.S. technology" by Western military experts in 1971. The Aviation Week & Space Technology wrote at that time:[33]

> Soviet Union is making substantial progress in developing and deploying military radar as an essential corollary of its emergence as a world-wide military power.
>
> The Russians apparently have embraced the new maxim that he who controls the electromagnetic spectrum controls the outcome of any conflict in modern war or global politics. They understand and appreciate the essential role radar plays in fulfilling this dictum.

At the end of the 1970s the Western experts paid increasing attention to electronic improvements in Soviet weapons. A NATO report noted in 1978 that new Soviet developments include e.g. electro-optically guided missiles, laser-guided bombs, sophisticated reconnaissance aircraft, new target data equipment, improved sensors and improved versions of remotely piloted vehicles.[34] When it comes to electronic countermeasures (ECM) - a fastly improving part of military electronics - such capabilities have been observed in several new-generation military aircraft.[35]

In 1975 the Soviet Union imported electronic and radiocommunication equipment for 68.5 million rubles. Imports from the German Democratic Republic were 18 million rubles. Electronic production in the GDR has strong traditions based on Carl Zeiss factories. The company produces instrumentation for the manufacture of integrated circuits. The second largest import partner was Japan, which benefited from the vetoes of the U.S. government against electronic exports to the Soviet Union. The USSR also imported equipment from Canada, the FRG and Switzerland, and it was suspected that some firms in these countries acted as middlemen for American companies whose direct export from America met political obstacles.[36]

In certain fields of electronics the socialist countries have been very willing to increase trade with the Western countries and with the large transnational electronic companies. The transnationals have also been willing to sell both finished products and production technology because the markets of the socialist countries are very large. The major export offensive by the TNCs took place around the mid-1970s.

Already in the 1960s Sescosem, a subsidiary of France's largest electronic company Thomson-CSF, built a semiconductor microcircuit factory in Poland on the condition that the company could sell semiconductor devices to Poland. In 1973 the U.S. company Westinghouse received approval from the U.S. government to construct a $ 10 million facility near Warsaw for the production of semiconductor rectifiers to be used in welders, motor controllers and other industrial applications. This technology was not considered to have military significance. In 1974 Teledyne Microelectronics Co. received an export licence to build a hybrid microcircuit assembly facility for Cajavec, a Yugoslav electronic company. This facility assembles and interconnects microcircuit chips purchased from abroad.[37] Other Western electronic industries having licensing arrangements with socialist partners are the U.S. Control Data, ICL in Great Britain, Siemens in the FRG, CII-Honeywell Bull in France and Fujitsu in Japan. Much of the technology thus released has been considered obsolete by Western standards. Control Data is participating in a joint venture in Romania for the production of peripheral equipment.[38]

Most of COCOM's vetoes in electronics have dealt with high capacity computers, their possible components and know-how because of their potential military use. In case such exceptional sales have been accepted for civil purposes, the COCOM has created safeguards, e.g. Western expert visits to the socialist installations at regular intervals in order to determine that computers are not used for military purposes.[39]

Large-scale air traffic controls are one field of both military and civilian electronics which the socialist countries have preferred to buy from Western transnational companies on a turnkey basis. The French Thomson-CSF has sold such equipment to Bucharest and ITT's German subsidiary SEL has sold navigation aids to Poland, Romania and Bulgaria.[40]

3.4.   The People's Republic of China

For many years China's defence policy has had to balance between two extremes: nuclear deterrence and the tradition of People's War. During the 1950s the defence of the People's Republic of China was mainly based on weapons captured in the Civil War and Soviet military aid. The tradition of the people's liberation struggle as well as China's vast manpower resources emphasized the role of infantry in defence.

However, China started the construction of major weapons in the 1950s, due to the very unstable political situation in Eastern Asia at that time. This production was problematic for a country with poor material resources, and there was a continuous dialogue over military vs. civilian needs in the building process of new industry.[41]

China's indigenous armament industry was largely based on technology and plants furnished by the Soviet Union before the break in Sino-Soviet relations. China started the production of destroyers, aircraft, a range of various army equipment and also electronics later on. According to U.S. General George Brown, China has since the mid-1960s been engaged in broad-based efforts to expand and modify military R&D as well as production facilities. Despite the shortage of skilled personnel there has been a growth of defence production, particularly in army material and aerospace.[42]

Since the adoption of the principle of self-reliance in China's political profile, indigenous production and design capability have been emphasized. On the other hand a change in this respect can be noted at the end of the 1970s, when a growing interest in Western military technology was expressed by the Chinese authorities. This interest is connected to the "four modernizations", of which the modernization of the army is one.

China produces transport aircraft, helicopters, fighters and bombers in the Shenyang factory. Some of these designs are Chinese versions of original Soviet models, which indicates that China was forced to base its designing activities on such equipment as it already had. The volume of the production of these aircraft is presumably not very large by international standards, due to the low level of mechanization in Chinese industry and various technological bottlenecks. The transport aircraft will presumably be powered with Canadian engines. The F-12 fighter is based on Mig-23, which China has recently bought from Egypt. The engines for this aircraft will come from Rolls Royce, UK; according to an agreement, valued at $ 195 million, China will import 50 Spey engines from Rolls Royce. In addition, an unknown number has also been manufactured by the Chinese with a licence. F-12 is planned to start the flight tests in 1980.[43]

China has also been interested to buy Hawker Siddley's Harrier VSTOL-fighters from the United Kingdom. This aircraft can use very small airfields. According to newspapers the purchase would be 80 aircraft. The final destiny of this deal is not solved at the time of this writing, however. The deal lies on the table of the Western coordination committee COCOM.[44] According to SIPRI's informa-tion, China has also received a production licence for Harriers in 1979,[45] but this production has not started either because of the political obstacles. Some doubts have been expressed concerning China's capacity to maintain modern, complex aircraft. At least in the civil aviation field China has been able to maintain only older piston-engine aircraft and turboprop aircraft in China, while jet-powered aircraft have been sent abroad for service. Most of this work has been done by Hong Kong Aircraft Engineering Co. (HAECO) which services China's Boeing civil aircraft.[46]

China has also been very willing to acquire Western helicopters as well as technology for helicopter production. Officially, the aim is to increase the manufacturing capability of commercial transport helicopters, but in reality this is dual technology which can also be used for military purposes. Obviously transport helicopters are needed to increase the mobility of the Chinese troops as well as to increase their material support capacity.

The Chinese helicopter program has proceeded in stages. In the first stage, smaller quantities of several helicopter models were bought. The U.S. Bell, MBB in the FRG and Aerospatiale in France sold a few units each.[47]

In the second stage China entered into negotiations over the co-production of Western helicopters. Bell Helicopter (Textron), together with its engine manufacturer Pratt & Whitney Canada (United Technologies Corporation), has negotiated the assembly and production of 50 advanced helicopters (model 412) at People's Republic Aircraft Factory at Harbin. Bell's preliminary agreement - the final destiny of which is not clear - also covers training of engineering, management and other technicians in the USA, furnishing some tooling and sending of Bell's specialized personnel to Harbin. China would supply Bell with some components, not more than 30 per cent of the value of the contract.[48] It has also been announced in the U.S. recently that Lockheed and Boeing Vertol are discussing potential sales of C-130 and CH-47 transport helicopters to China. All U.S. helicopters, which are being discussed, can be used for both civil and military purposes, but according to the Pentagon and the U.S. State Department potential transfers to China will not include weapons.[49] According to the policy of the Carter administration the U.S. transfers can include dual purpose technology and military support equipment but not direct weapons.[50]

The Euro-American competition over the Chinese military markets is fierce, however, as China is supposed to buy military equipment for about $ one billion over the next few years. In particular France and the FRG are actively involved in the competition over the Chinese markets. In July 1980 Aérospatiale in France announced that the company will sell 50 Dauphin-2 helicopters to China; the agreement also contains licences for Chinese production. The sale was estimated by industry sources at around $ 75 million. It is not known yet whether the French sales will jeopardize the above-mentioned negotiations of Bell Helicopter.[51]

The question of weapons may have been one reason why China preferred French helicopters. Although China produces various indigenous types of missiles, it has been very anxious to acquire Western missile technology. In 1978 the French government announced a $ 700 million order for Milan and HOT anti-tank missiles, produced jointly by Aérospatiale and MBB, and Crotale anti-aircraft missiles, which are produced by Thomson and Matra. According to some sources, at least Aerospatiale and MBB (partners of Euromissile) would also provide the Chinese with production equipment to make their own version of the HOT-missile system. A recent Western delegation to China did not observe evidence of any deliveries of these missiles, but now that Aerospatiale has sold a large number of Dauphin helicopters the delivery of HOT is most probable, too, since the HOT system can be fitted to the military versions of Dauphin helicopters.[52]

China produces several types of indigenous missiles for airborne, naval and ground functions. Many models are copies of Soviet models. It is also notable that China is developing intercontinental ballistic missiles which are inertially guided. A successful test was reported in the summer of 1980. China is working on a ballistic early warning program and a modern radar network, but the level of military electronics is far from sufficient according to Western standards.[53] This is the field where the U.S. has actively promoted sales of military equipment. Current Sino-American discussions include potential sales of tactical air defence radar sets, pressure transducers used to test jet engines, an antenna for an early warning radar set, tropospheric communications equipment and passive devices for electronic countermeasures. During a visit to the U.S. in May 1980 the Chinese military experts visited U.S. military bases and a number of industrial plants: IBM, Westinghouse, General Motors, American Motors, Honeywell.[54] The list indicates that China is only interested in sophisticated technology provided by the largest transnationals.

China's space activities have both civil and military functions, and again participation of Western technology can be noted together with China's indigenous programs. RCA in the U.S. has participated in China's weather satellite program together with the Japanese Hitachi which has provided computers.[55]

China has a program for communication satellites, too, but so far no information is available about Western participation. China has recently joined international space programs, such as Comsat and Landsat, and the U.S. NASA has given approval for China to acquire a ground station for Landsat data.[56] China has shown interest in remote sensing techniques and maintains its own satellite control facilities for military purposes.[57]

China's electronic industries have been evaluated as being about 15 years behind Western technology; such an opinion has been expressed by a representative of a large American electronic company. According to the same estimate, China would stay even more behind if it tries to rely on indigenous technology only.[58] Some foreign electronic companies have already penetrated into China's markets; in addition to those already mentioned, at least Hewlett Packard has made sales of electronic equipment since 1973. Despite negotiations between China and some other Western companies, no major sales have so far been reported. China has also shown its own, indigenous computers and other equipment to foreign visitors.[59]

An indication of China's problems in the field of electronics is its interest in Western telecommunication equipment. Both Western Germany and the U.S. have preliminary agreements with China for the development and launching of communication and direct broadcast TV-satellites.[60] Some transnationals have already been successful in this area: three ITT's subsidiaries (one in the U.S., two in Europe) have sold marine radio equipment to the PRC.[61]

China's shipyards produce patrol boats, torpedoboats, frigates, destroyers, submarines and gun boats, which are both powered and armed by Chinese equipment. Many of the models are locally developed from Soviet models.[62]

There is a disagreement about China's role in international arms transfers. According to ACDA, China's arms exports in the 1970s surpassed its imports until 1976, and there has been a continuous decrease of arms exports since. According to the same source, China's arms imports were bigger than exports in 1976, and in 1977 both figures were equal, $ 85 million at constant 1976 prices.[63] If, however, all those arms imports of which China has made enquiries in the United Kingdom, France, FRG and Italy come true, which is not very likely, China is on the way to change into a major importer.[64] China's import of MIG-23 aircraft, T-62 tanks and surface-to-air and anti-tank weapons from Egypt can also be noted in this connection.[65]

According to SIPRI, China exported arms for $ 214 million in 1978, i.e. the exports more than doubled since 1977. Aircraft, armoured vehicles, missiles and warships are being exported by China, but they are nearly always refurbished or second-hand. China has exported major weapons to Pakistan, Bangladesh, Zaire, Kampuchea, Albania, North Korea, North Vietnam, Cameroon, Guinea, Tunisia and Zambia. One of the largest ones is the sale of 50 F-6 fighters to Bangladesh, whereby China also trained the pilots in China.[66] China has not actively sold arms technology abroad. It has, however, sold a licence for building fast patrol boats in Romania in 1971.[67]

In civil aviation, China has also sought Western technology. In 1979 Chinese authorities reached a preliminary understanding with McDonnell Douglas Corp., USA, for the assembly of the DC-9 Super 80 jets in China. China would buy an unspecified number of the $ 14 million Super 80s for use in domestic flights. Some of the planes would be bought outright, but Chinese technicians would assemble others or portions of them in Shanghai using U.S.-made parts. China would then pay for the deal with other manufactured goods rather than cash.[68]

For future purchases of Western technology China has recently approved a law concerning joint ventures with foreign companies. The law specifies that foreign participation must constitute at least 25 per cent of the venture. The foreign participation may, according to informal information, be also more than 50 per cent and a foreigner can serve as the chief operating officer of the company. The rule makes the participation of foreign producers possible in cases of complex technology.[69]

4 Forms of internationalization within military industry

After the description of large armament industries <u>as an institution</u> in the leading capitalist and socialist states we now turn to analyze the forms of their internationalization and expansion. We shall focus on their expansion in the Third World, because that process most often means exporting not only arms but also arms races into new areas. When this expansion takes place on a large scale - as has happened in the 1970s - it obviously affects the conditions of development in the Third World.

The post-war internationalization of armament industries started in the 1950s when the Cold War policies led to a revival of arms production in major Western countries. The U.S. industries with their superior capacity and technology started to expand into the arms production of the Western military allies, mainly in Western Europe and Japan. Internationalization also extended to Southern Europe, notably Italy and Spain, where the lower price level together with existing industrial plants offered comparative economic advantages. Also obvious political reasons favoured armament cooperation with Southern European industries. Arms exports to the allies were followed by licence agreements and minority holdings in European armament industries, whereby the American companies could secure their footholds in this growing sector.

Toward the end of the 1960s the European industries had become competitive vis-a-vis the American companies, and a major export drive took place. The Euro-American competition in the arms market was not only felt in Europe, but also became visible in the Third World. While the American arms industries had a large home market, particularly because of the Vietnam War, the European companies were able to penetrate into markets which had traditionally been dominated by the American companies.

In the 1970s it finally became evident that mere exports were not enough for the companies if they wanted to secure their share of the market or occupy new ones. More intensive measures were needed, and thus various forms of offset deals, licence agreements and other forms of production cooperation contracts were concluded in connection with arms sales. On the one hand this was part of a conscious company strategy, a sign of the fierce competition. On the other hand such arrangements were increasingly often demanded by the purchasers of weapons, including in the Third World. In this chapter we shall focus on internationalization strategies from the point of view of the companies, while Chapters 5 and 6 are devoted to Third World considerations.

The international expansion of the armament industries takes many forms. The most important one continues to be the export of finished weapons. In this form of trade the fierce competition between the companies has led to a buyers' market, where arms producers intensively compete for customers using not only conventional sales promotion methods but sometimes also most unconventional or even questionable measures. The traditional arms exports can be seen as the first stage of the internationalization process.

Arms sales often lead to the second stage of internationalization, whereby arms technology - or rather a part of it - is sold to foreign customers together with arms . Various licence and co-production agreements represent this type of marketing, which has nowadays not only become a common practice in arms sales to the industrial countries but also to the developing customers. Licence trade and exports of finished products by no means exclude each other. On the contrary, very often part of a deal consists of finished exports while another part concerns licence production. What is more, the licence agreements are usually concluded for a certain part of the weapon or weapon system while the original producer reserves for itself the production of the most important and complex parts.

Licence and co-production agreements may lead to a third stage, i.e. a more intensified cooperation between the supplier and the recipient company. The licensee may become a subcontractor for the company supplying the technology. In such a relationship the licensee produces parts or components for exports to the main producer. The transnational arms company usually moves into international subcontracting after economic calculations which show cheaper labour costs, raw material prices and other economic advantages in foreign subcontracting. The high production costs in the home countries of the

TNCs often lead to international subcontracting as one means to decrease the prices of the final products. In electronic production this subcontracting has been a common practice for some 10-15 years, and the producers of military electronics make use of it. To some extent it also works in other fields of the armament industry.

It should be noted that there are two main types of international subcontractor relationships between technologically less developed and more developed military industries. In the first type the subcontractor is a developing or a newly industrialized producer whose cheaper labour costs or rich natural resources are being exploited for the benefit of transnational military production. In the second type of relationships the subcontractor is the technologically superior company which supplies complex military electronics, engines or armour to the weapon systems manufactured by the developing producers. Both of these subcontracting types are common in modern military production - in fact, they greatly strengthen the transnational character of that production.

A stronger control of foreign arms production and markets can be achieved by direct investments in foreign companies. However, military production is not very easily obtained by foreign capital, because national ownership is preferred for security reasons. Consequently, totally owned foreign production plants are very rare in the armament industry. Joint ventures and minority holdings are more common because countries with poor capital resources often invite foreign capital to share the large investment burdens and to secure the availability of modern technology from the participating foreign companies. Although totally owned foreign production plants are rare the military TNCs own numerous sales offices and service plants abroad. As the weapons have become technologically complex overhaul and services have become increasingly important, which favours the establishment of an international network.

4.1. Arms Exports

The justification for arms exports has been presented in many ways and at various levels of analysis. The transfer of arms always has strategic and political effects in the recipient societies - whether intended or not - and the arguments related to this aspect are presented by military and foreign policy authorities.

The economic justification has, however, become increasingly common in the 1970s. With the growing structural crisis of arms production and the heavy burden it constitutes for the taxpayers, it has become common to justify arms exports with arguments related to the national economy. The main idea is to show the benefits of arms exports for the national economy. Arms sales, according to this line of thinking, ameliorate the balance-of-payments deficits, spur increased commercial transactions between the arms supplier and the recipient, contribute to the viability of defence industries, reduce unemployment and lower the costs per unit of production of weapons. After the oil crisis of 1973 a new economic argument was added: arms are sold to obtain oil and to recycle petrodollars.

In this type of economic arguments arms production is seen as an essential sector, whose contribution to the national economy is substantial. Let us have a closer look at the role of arms exports for the national economies of the leading exporting countries:

Table 40. Arms Exports, Total Exports and GNP in Some Exporting Countries in 1976 according to ACDA (constant prices, $ million and per cent)

	GNP	Arms exports	Total exports	Arms exports/ total exports %	Arms exports/GNP %
USA	1 611 439	4 960	109 557	4.5	0.3
France	353 452	800	54 493	1.5	0.2
UK	231 100	608	44 109	1.4	0.3
USSR	960 000	3 570	35 308	10.1	0.4
Italy	174 956	263	34 963	0.8	0.2
China	307 515	108	6 592	1.6	0.04
FRG	447 452	625	97 172	0.6	0.1

Source: World Military Expenditures and Arms Transfers 1967-1976, U.S. Arms Control and Disarmament Agency, Washington 1978, Tables II and VI. For statistical notes, definitions and sources, see ibid., p. 20-26.

It is a common argument that arms sales are particularly important to the defence production and economies of the United Kingdom and France.[1] The figures from the above table show, however, that the contribution of military exports to the total exports is much greater for the Soviet Union and the United States than for the other exporters.

The share of arms exports of the GNP is about the same in all arms exporting countries. Thus their national economies are just as much - or rather just as modestly - dependent on armament exports. In the light of the percentages of arms export/GNP it is actually possible to question the common arguments of national economies being by necessity pushed towards armament exports. As arms exports constitute less than 0.5 per cent of the GNP in all main exporting countries, the national economic argument is rather a myth. The GNP of these countries does not substantially rise or fall with arms transfers. The fact that this argument is often used, however, tells more of the need to find legitimation for arms transfers in the eyes of taxpayers than of the willingness to present empirical facts.

The balance-of-payment argument of arms exports is somewhat different. After the industrialized countries ran into balance-of-payments troubles in the mid-seventies, they were desperately looking for any commodities to improve their international balances. Arms were suitable for this purpose because the leading producers had superior technology, and beccause their strategy also aimed at strengthening the military power of the oil-producing states.

Thus the short-term impact of arms sales looked positive in the post-1973 situation. We can assume, however, that increasing military sales to countries whose import needs of all capital goods are large reduced their ability to import necessary civilian goods.[2] Arms exports thus took place at the cost of non-military capital goods exports, as very few developing customers can afford much of everything.

In the longer term the balance-of-payment impact of arms transfers on the exporting countries is fairly unknown, due to a lack of empirical analyses. In the case of the U.S. it has been suggested that rising arms sales (or any exports) bring about an appreciation of the exchange rate. The strengthening U.S. dollar would eventually cause exports of non-military goods to decline, a condition which might cause lower employment in non-defence industries. Assuming a fully recovered economy, total U.S. employment would be approximately the same with or without arms sales, but the relative positions of specific firms and of the military and civilian industries would be different.[3]

Actually the balance-of-payments argument of arms sales is not too convincing for several reasons. First, arms constitute only a minor component of the major suppliers' exports. Second, balance-of-payments provide open-ended rationales since they can be used to justify any arms sales. Third, sales of any domestic products help the balance-of-payments; civilian goods produce the same balance-of-trade benefits as military exports.[4] The employment argument for arms exports is in the same way unconvincing: any exports promote employment and there is no reason to assume that employment in military production would somehow be more beneficial than employment in non-military production.

The conclusion regarding the most common national-economic arguments for arms exports is that they are generally unconvincing. Arms exports are not important for the GNP; they are with some exceptions of minor importance for total exports; they can as such improve the balance-of-payments but other exports have the same impact, and finally they reduce the recipient's ability to buy non-military goods which may limit the marketing of civilian goods. The fact that the national-economic justification is often presented tells of the need to find arguments for increased arms transfers which would legitimize them. At the same time, not as much energy is used to find arguments against arms transfers and their long-run negative impact for both the arms supplying countries and receiving countries.

While none of the arms supplying nations is substantially dependent on arms exports, individual industries and companies within each country often are. For the United States as a whole, foreign military sales are only about 15 per cent of the U.S. procurement. Individual firms, however, depend much more on exports. In 1978 the most export-oriented military contractors were Textron/Bell and Northrop which exported about half of their military contracts. General Dynamics and Litton Industries exported a third of their military contracts, and Raytheon 20 per cent.[5]

The dependency of companies on arms exports is much more pronounced in Europe. Dassault-Bréguet, the French producer of Mirage fighters, exported 75 per cent of its production in 1978 - and 65 per cent of its exports were of a military character. When British Aircraft and Hawker Siddley merged in 1977, 70 per cent of all orders on hand at that time were for export. French Aerospatiale (SNIAS) exports 77 per cent of its helicopters and 70 per cent of its missiles.[6]

The British shipbuilding industry is also increasingly dependent on military exports, which rose from 10 per cent of production in 1971 to 38 per cent in 1974. As for the United States and France, the shipbuilding industry has not been highly dependent on exports. The share of exports for the United States shipbuilding industry fluctuated between 3 and 11 per cent from 1971 to 1974, while the French percentages varied between 3 and 14 per cent for the same years.[7]

In Europe military exports are often regarded as vital for the continued viability of the industry. An executive at Thomson-CSF, the French exporter of military electronics, describes the situation of the industry as follows:

> Exports are not an economic necessity for the Americans ... because the U.S. military machine absorbs such enormous quantities of equipment. But the day we stop exporting, that's it. We close up shop.

Other European industries, such as West Germany's $ 1.2 billion tank-builder Krauss-Maffei or Italy's $ 213 million munitions company Oto Melara also export roughly 45 per cent of their production.[8]

The large European arms companies are clearly more dependent on military exports than their American counterparts, if measured by the relative share of military exports. On the other hand there are a number of American companies which are bigger than the biggest European ones, i.e. their production capacity is much stronger. In aerospace, which is the dominant part of arms industry both in the U.S. and Europe, the combined sales of American industry were three times bigger than those of European companies in 1976.[9] When we add to this that the U.S. companies are financially and technologically strong, and the U.S. is the number one arms exporter in the world, we can conclude that the economic pressures for increased arms exports, as constituted by the companies, are just as strong in the U.S. as in Europe.

In Table 41 below we have listed the 20 largest arms exporters in the West in 1979, according to Business Week. The figures are not comparable between the U.S. and non-U.S. companies because the U.S. figures are preliminary DoD estimates on 1979 foreign military sales orders, while the figures for non-U.S. firms are export sales either in 1978 or 1979 as reported by the companies.

Table 41.   Twenty Biggest Arms Exporters in the West in 1979

Top-ten U.S. exporters	FMS orders 1979 $ million	Top-ten non-U.S. exporters	Sales 1979 $ million
Lockheed	1 400	Dassault-Bréguet, (France)	1 170
McDonnell Douglas	638		
General Dynamics	518	MBB, (FRG)	756
Northrop	456	British Aerospace, (UK)	730+
Sperry	249	Aérospatiale, (France)	650
Raytheon	132		
Vinnell	110	Royal Ordnance Factories, (UK)	639+
Textron/Bell	109		
General Electric	101	Thomson-CSF, (France)	625
Westinghouse Electric	85	Krauss-Maffei, (FRG)	540
		Israel Aircraft Industries	326
		Rolls Royce, (UK)	236+
		MATRA, (France)	210

Source: Business Week, March 24, 1980, p. 69. Data for the U.S. firms are DoD preliminary estimates, while figures for other firms are based on company and government reports, or estimated by Business Week.

Note: + = 1978 export sales.

The leading U.S. exporters supply either military aircraft, missiles, electronics or engines for their foreign customers. Vinnell Corp. is an exception; it exports military construction training and repair services.

The group of non-U.S. leading arms exporters is also dominated by aircraft, helicopter and missile producers, but one producer of tanks (Krauss-Maffei) as well as ordnance and ammunition is also included.

Some producers (e.g. McDonnell Douglas) base their exports on a number of aircraft and missile models, while others depend on one or two leading export items. It can be noted, however, that due to the high production costs even the largest companies cannot simultaneously maintain very many production lines.

The tendency is therefore towards a longer series of fewer models. The selection is then composed of different variations of a few basic models rather than many totally different weapon systems.

It is the pressure on economic efficiency at company level that limits the possibilities of one company to maintain many production lines of weapons simultaneously. On the other hand the continuous development of new weapons and the shorter life of existing weapon systems - a result of technological innovations - are causing opposite pressures at national and international level: the total number of produced weapon types may still be high. Thus the arms production authorities in the main producer countries are faced with a dilemma: company considerations call for a limited number of arms production lines while the arms race and technological development push the number of produced weapon systems upwards.

An example of a company whose export sales were mainly based on one item is the U.S. Northrop. Its large sales to the Third World were for many years based on F-5E jet fighters. Now that the plane is getting old and the rank of the company among the leading exporters has started to decline (cf. Annex J), the company has launched a plan for a new FX fighter which is designed exclusively for export. This example shows that companies which are used to a strong export orientation tend to maintain this profile. The FX-plan is on the face of it contradictory to the arms restraint policy of the Carter administration, which was declared in May 1977 and stated that "development or significant modification of advanced weapons systems solely for exports will not be permitted". After permitting the FX-project the State Department solved the contradiction between the FX-plan and arms restraint as follows: the FX aircraft

> will contribute to arms transfer restraint objectives by discouraging purchases of more sophisticated first line aircraft from the U.S. and other suppliers.[10]

Arms manufacturers often claim to have a passive role in foreign arms sales. They claim to act only in response to demand from abroad, and in conjunction with state authorities. According to this claim, corporations just implement foreign policy and do not have any active role.[11]

127

These claims are not, however, supported by the fact that arms manufacturers use very active, sometimes even aggressive, sales promotion techniques abroad. More conventional techniques include the use of sales agents, sales offices, military exhibitions, military visits, publications, advertisements, compensation deals, professional conferences and related techniques. Unconventional techniques include bribes and other questionable or illegal practices, the wide use of which confirms the fierce competition and almost desperate export pressures.

The role of efficient sales agents has always been crucial in arms sales. Thus the export manager of the French Dassault - one of the most export-dependent military producers - has said in an interview, that when sales efforts are started in country X, the first thing to do is to acquire a good, influential and well-informed agent who promotes the sales, knows the right persons and informs the company about the needs.[12] It has sometimes been suggested that one of the explanations for the rapid growth of the French arms exports is the intermediary between the seller and the buyer, who gets a commission of up to 15 per cent which is usually included in the price. Other countries selling weapons have blamed the French for having increased the standard agent commission of between 3-5 per cent to three times this amount.[13] With regard to the bribery cases the role of intermediaries, such as Khassoggi in Saudi Arabia, has also been notable.

The general sales promotion efforts have become very vigorous in all leading arms exporting countries. In addition to traditional happenings like the Paris Air Show or the Farnborough International Air show, there are nowadays tens of exhibitions every year. Earlier they used to take place in the industrialized countries, but after sales promotion efforts were intensified in the Third World, special regional arms exhibitions have been designed. As an example, see the following advertisement:

Source: <u>Defence</u>, September 1979, p. 721.

The role of training programs, seminars and professional conferences is perhaps most intensive in conventional sales promotion. At such occasions not only weapons are introduced but a general way of thinking which prepares the ground for future purchases.

The role of the <u>military journals and advertising</u> is also crucial in arms marketing. The amount of journals has rapidly risen in the 1970s, and their general outlook is very commercial. These journals are often printed on expensive paper, and they are full of large commercials by the arms manufacturers. The arms advertisements have developed a special style of language which cannot be analyzed here but which calls for future research.

Every weapon system has a striking name. Some manufacturers prefer negative connotations which can be connected with efficient killing: e.g. Brazilian armoured vehicles are named after very poisonous snakes. Others prefer friendly types of names, which disconnect the weapons from their real destructive functions. The U.S. foreign military sales names for the most active aircraft sales projects are Peace Eagle (F-15 to Japan), Peace Fox (F-15 to Israel), Peace Sun (F-15 to Saudi Arabia), Peace Farrow (F-4 to Egypt) and Peace Marble (F-16 to Israel).[14] In the Western industrialized countries the killing and destruction aspect of the weapons is almost totally ignored, and the language thus aims at <u>alienating</u> the public from these functions. Instead, the most common theme is the admiration of technology, <u>the Machine</u>, as an ultimate achievement of Man also in military functions.[15]

The arms sales are in principle under <u>foreign policy guidance</u>. Actually the foreign embassies of the main arms producing states often have special personnel for the promotion and supervision of arms sales, and they are supposed to be impartial advisors and contact staff, free of commercial motives or commitments. Whether these persons can resist the advantages offered by the arms manufacturers is another question. When the U.S. Senate was investigating corruption by the Iranian military in connection with large military contracts, the Shah complained:

> It is hard for me to believe that your MAAG officers (the military advisory group at the U.S. embassy) haven't already been hired by American companies and aren't under their influence. Are they giving me the real advice or just promoting companies?

In fact it emerged later that the doubts of the Shah were fully justified. The military advisers in Iran, indeed, had very close links with the arms manufacturers.[16]

Although all the leading arms producing countries have official defence sales organizations, which aim at sales promotion, this is not always sufficient from the point of view of the companies. A Pentagon memo in Iran in 1973 told that "the Shah was unhappy about the independent agents running around his country on commission even though the aircraft being purchased go through the U.S. government".[17]

One of the reasons why independent agents have been "running around" is the practice of bribes and other questionable payments which cannot be arranged with official contacts. As far as the U.S. corporations are concerned, the cases of bribery are well publicized. Arms sales practices have been studied by the Securities and Exchange Commission SEC, the Justice Department, the Department of Defence and the Department of State, the Federal Trade Commission, the subcommittee on multinational corporations of Senate Foreign Relations Committee, Senate Banking Committee and International Revenue Service. Based on press data, we have compiled a list of the best known cases but it is of course not complete:

Table 42. Examples of Questionable Payments by U.S. Arms Producers: a Tentative List

Company	Country of operations	Year	Source
Boeing	Egypt and other Arab countries	1972-74	WSJ Dec. 1, 1977
			WSJ June 28, 1978
	Japan	1972	WSJ Feb. 16, 1977
	Canada	1970-71	WSJ March 16, 1977
	United Kingdom		WSJ Dec. 28, 1976
	Pakistan, Kuwait, Nepal,	1960s	WSJ June 15, 1976
	Greece, Honduras, South	1970s	
	Korea, Lebanon,		
	Spain		BW Feb. 11, 1980
Grumman	Japan	1972	HS Feb. 2, 1979
	Iran		IA 11, 1976
	Peru	1970s	Fortune, Feb. 1976
Hughes	Indonesia	1973	NYT, Jan. 25, 1977
GTE	Philippines		"
Lockheed	Europe		Atlas, May 1976
	Japan	1972-74	BW, May 30, 1977
			DoJ, June 1, 1979
	Taiwan, Malaysia, Mexico,		WSJ
	Morocco, Kuwait, Argentina,		
	Colombia, Peru, Venezuela,		
	Spain, Saudi Arabia,		
	Indonesia		Progr., Dec. 1975
	Libya	1973	IHT, Nov. 5, 1979
Martin Marietta	United States	1960-	WSJ, Feb. 26, 1972
McDonnell Douglas	Several countries	1969	AWST, Dec. 18, 1978
	Pakistan, South Korea,		IHT, Nov. 10-
11, 1979			
	Philippines, Venezuela,		
	Zaire,		
	Japan		NYT, April 15, 1979
	Canada	1972	WSJ, Dec. 1, 1975

Table 42 continued

Company	Country of operations	Year	Source
Northrop	Iran, Indonesia Malaysia, Thailand Saudi Arabia Brazil		AWST, April 28, 1975 FEER, Jan. 16, 1976 NYT, June 10, 1975 NYT, Jan. 7, 1975
Raytheon	Jordan Saudi Arabia		NYT, June 27, 1975 WSJ, May 23, 1978
Textron/Bell	--- Ghana Nigeria, Iran, Morocco, Sri Lanka, Mexico, Indonesia, United Arab Emirates, Colombia, Dominican Republic, Jamaica, Ceylon, Philippines		BW, Oct. 8, 1979 AWST, May 15, 1978 IHT, Febr. 9-10, 1980 WSJ, Oct. 24, 1979

Abbreviations: FEER = Far Eastern Economic Review, NYT = New York Times, IHT = International Herald Tribune, WSJ = The Wall Street Journal, AWST = Aviation Week & Space Technology, BW = Business Week, DoJ = U.S. Department of Justice, IA = Interavia, HS = Helsingin Sanomat.

The methods of payments have been varied. Often the payments are made to foreign "consultants" who are top-level officials or even members of the purchasing government or the ruling family. The payments are often channelled through a third country on foreign bank accounts in e.g. Switzerland or Liechtenstein. Cover organizations are often involved, like the Widows and Orphans' Fund (based in Singapore) in the Lockheed case or Economic Development Corporation EDC (based in Switzerland) in the Northrop case.

It is unfortunate that the possible questionable practices of non-U.S. arms producers have not been paid as much public attention. In 1974 Dassault was found guilty in a bribery case in the Netherlands but information on other non-U.S. cases is not available. It is also not known how the socialist countries promote their arms deliveries in the Third World. The U.S.-bias in corporate practices reflects a certain openness by the U.S. society, although not all details of the bribery cases are disclosed.

It is useful to realize that the U.S. administration has a very concrete interest in finding out about illegal financial transfers; when they are a common practice in the huge companies they damage the balance-of-payments and the companies may escape taxes and other duties. The interests of the shareholders and financing bodies are damaged because of inaccurate accounts and, finally, the international reputation of the TNCs is damaged because of corrupt practices. These are some of the reasons why the U.S. authorities have introduced several measures to increase the control of foreign payments by the U.S.-based TNCs. The U.S. has also agreed bilaterally with some countries on the exchange of relevant information. Finally, it has advocated collective international action to establish international rules against corrupt practices by the TNCs.[18]

In a class of their own are the totally illegal arms transfers, some of which occasionally have been documented. A few examples may suffice to indicate how these transfers are being arranged. In February 1980 the Sunday Times reported that French Crotale missiles and armoured vehicles had been sold by French manufacturers to South Africa, using Egypt as a route. The weapons were declared as being made in Egypt. In 1979 a private air-freight company was hired to fly Italian-made missile parts to South Africa via the Federal Republic of Germany.[19]

Modern transport technology, like the use of containers, makes certain illegal transfers easier than before. Arms can be sent in pieces with falsified cargo declarations as, for example, "machine parts". The contents of the containers are not usually checked, but the transportation is based on papers. The Canadian-based Space Research Corporation used this method when it smuggled arms to South Africa. It also used stops at Antigua, the Canary Islands and Barcelona to cover the final destination of the shipments. Furthermore, the ships concerned were registered in West Germany, the United States and the Netherlands to mask the operations. A comparable case is the shipment of Colt and Winchester rifles, shotguns and ammunition to South Africa via phoney firms in the Canary Islands, Austria, Greece, West Germany and Mozambique.[20]

The information given by the military producers about their operations is not always reliable. A West German company Meravo Luftreederei, a subsidiary of Motoflug of Baden Baden, claimed to train Libyan police and civil pilots in the use of Bell helicopters at a school in southern Germany. Later on, the foreign office was, however, investigating the training program which was thought to concern soldiers.[21]

It should finally be noted that the civilian production of transnational arms producers may offer one legitimate-looking method for the promotion of military sales. Sperry has sold agricultural machinery in China, Litton Industries has sold "economic development studies" in Turkey in the 1960s, United Technologies has sold industrial turbines in Saudi Arabia, Textron/Bell has sold steel mills in Poland and Raytheon sells telephone networks in Egypt.[22] The possibility of military activities in connection with these civilian operations cannot be ruled out, given the predominantly military character of the corporations concerned. On the other hand the military activities in connection with civilian sales cannot be documented, either.

The dual function of many technologies also makes the identification of civilian and military operations difficult. A helicopter can be used for rescue as well as for counterinsurgency, and a computer can be used towards a good health-service as well as for the implementation of, for example, apartheid-policy. Thus the dual function of many technologies as well as the diversified profiles of many arms producers make detailed studies of military marketing very difficult.

4.2. Licence Production and Co-production of Arms

Besides exports, various co-production and licence production arrangements have become very common in international arms transfers, both among developed and between developed and developing countries. Competition among arms suppliers has fostered these arrangements, because arms buyers often prefer licence puchases to mere imports of finished products. Those arms producers which offer the most advantageous terms for a partial transfer of technology are often the winners of the competition.

The licence arrangements usually involve licensed production by foreign firms or joint enterprises which agree to produce separate components of a common weapon system. The F-16 project between Belgium, Denmark, Holland, Norway and the United States is a well-known example of this type of multilateral co-production.

Another form of licence production is <u>bilateral</u> collaboration, whereby the licensee buys patented foreign technology and combines it with its indigenous knowledge for the manufacture of the weapon system. The more sophisticated the weapon system is, the higher usually the share of foreign parts and know-how. Multilateral and bilateral co-production forms are arranged either <u>vertically</u> or <u>horizontally</u>, as will be discussed on pages 138-139.

A preliminary conception of the extent of U.S. co-production and licence projects abroad can be obtained from the following table, which gives the number of these projects by leading arms manufacturers as well as their distribution between developed and developing countries:

Table 43. U.S. Military Co-production Projects Abroad

	Developed countries	Developing countries	Total
General Electric	12	-	12
Bell	8	2	10
Northrop	3	2	5
Sikorsky	5	-	5
Cessna	-	4	4
Hughes	3	1	4
Pratt & Whitney	4	-	4
Boeing	4	-	4
Lycoming	3	1	4
Raytheon	3	-	3
General Dynamics	2	-	2
Lockheed	2	-	2
Pazmany	-	2	2
McDonnell Douglas	2	-	2
All Others	7	8	15
Total	58	20	78

Source: Calculated from data in Michael T. Klare, Arms, Technology and Dependency: U.S. Military Co-production Abroad. NACLA Latin America and Empire Report 1.1979, pp. 25-32. The total value of these ventures amounted to $ 8.5 billion in 1975 dollars.

A number of conclusions can easily be drawn from the above table. First, practically all the corporations on the list are aircraft manufacturers which seem to be most internationalized both in terms of exports, direct investments and co-production patterns. There are more joint projects with governments and manufacturers from developed rather than developing countries. Japan and Italy are very central partners; U.S. aircraft manufacturers have concluded altogether 40 joint projects with them. Of individual firms the two most dominant ones are General Electric and Bell, while United Technologies has in fact third ranking because both Sikorsky and Pratt & Whitney are its subsidiaries.

In the Third World the United States has concluded co-production agreements with eight countries. More than one contract has been concluded with Taiwan (5), Pakistan (4), South Korea (3), Argentina (3) and Iran (2). The five most important destinations of U.S. arms exports in 1965-74 were, in descending order, the following countries: South Vietnam, Iran, Israel, South Korea and Taiwan.[23] Three countries, viz. Taiwan, South Korea and Iran, are on both lists, which indicates that co-production and exports are not alternative but rather complementary means of obtaining weapons and military technology. The overlap between major arms importers and major partners in co-production enterprises casts some doubt on the validity of the product cycle model, which would suggest a temporal order between exports and the transfer of production abroad.

One may postulate that co-production creates more influence over the recipient than the mere transfer of arms. The influence gained through co-production is more material, more permanent and hence more difficult to compensate, at least in the short run. The United States with its military industry has concluded a total of 78 co-production agreements with 22 countries. This naturally creates a transnational production network which facilitates further integration of production on an international scale and tends to increase U.S. political and economic leverage.

As pointed out above this transnational production and influence network is most intense across the Pacific and across the Atlantic. It may be worth pointing out here that crosslicensing and co-production between Western Europe and the United States have been proposed in NATO circles as a potential strategy for solving the economic and military problem of destandardized weapon systems. Co-production schemes within Western Europe are, however, more frequent than deals made across the Atlantic.

The West European arms manufacturers are not concluding co-production projects only within their own subregion, but they are also extending their activities to the developing countries. Although reliable comparative data do not exist, there are indications that in particular French and West German

137

firms are almost equally active in this field as the U.S. arms manufacturers, while British and Italian companies have opted for a somewhat lower level of internationalization in terms of licence production. As an example we may again refer to MBB which has sold licence rights for the production of missiles in Brazil, Iran, Pakistan and Turkey. West German warships are, in turn, produced in Argentina, Brazil, Columbia, Greece, Spain and Turkey.[24]

These examples may suffice to indicate that the process of internationalization is taking place partly through joint ventures. It would appear that the aircraft industry is most rapidly internationalizing, and also centralizing. Direct investments in the ammunition and small-arms sector are also worth mentioning, as are joint projects in the production of missiles. The proneness of the aircraft industry to this development may be due to the prevailing intense competition, which necessitates seeking partners in other countries to guarantee the expansion of production and marketing.

It is worth observing that almost all the leading U.S. manufacturers of military aircraft have expanded to Europe. This means a gradual modification of the fact that the French and British producers of military aircraft have traditionally relied on exports in their efforts to maintain production on acceptable economic terms, while the U.S. firms have oriented more to domestic markets. Now the situation is also changing in the United States, which is beginning to feel a similar pressure.[25] One source has estimated that over 20 per cent of U.S. military aerospace production in 1976 was devoted to foreign military sales.[26] It is also interesting to note that in 1964 the corresponding share was only 4 per cent; in other words there has been a considerable increase in this share from 1964 to 1976.[27]

For major arms manufacturers one of the main rationales of licence production in a developing country is the attempt to cut down production costs. The licence production of Northrop's F-5 fighter in Spain is a case in point. Rough estimates indicate that the production costs of a unit amounted to 590 000 dollars in the United States, and even to 770 000 dollars when it was produced in the Netherlands by Fokker. In Spain the production costs were around 500 000 dollars, so that some savings could be achieved. A more detailed analysis of the licence production of F-5 in Spain shows that all the components which could be produced cost-effectively in the United States were imported and only technologically less complicated, labour-intensive parts were produced in Spain. In other words Northrop organized such an international division of labour that F-5 was produced in the cost-optimal manner as seen from the standpoint of the corporation.[28]

Relatively speaking licence production seems to be favoured more by firms from medium-size countries than from big powers. Many of these projects are probably motivated by the reduction in production costs, but this can hardly be the sole reason for the proliferation of licence-production contracts. The economic benefits and spin-offs of a co-production project are largely determined by its organization. In this respect it is possible to make a distinction between two types of arrangements; vertical and horizontal co-production.

Vertical co-production means that the industry of the purchasing country not only produces components for the particular weapon system bought by the country, but also produces those components for all the systems which are constructed abroad. These components can be totally or partially indigenous.

Horizontal co-production, in turn, contains only the production of components for those weapons acquired by the country herself. It is almost self-evident that vertical co-production is more profitable to the producer of the components than horizontal because in the vertical arrangement the factors reducing unit costs are more visible. Also from the standpoint of the seller the vertical version would be more useful because the cost reduction is also beneficial to him. The economic factor may be the main explanation of the fact that vertical co-production projects have been recently on the increase.[29]

The vertical arrangement may contain, however, some marketing aspects which may become problematic; the producer of components may start in the longer run competing with its 'master'. TNCs usually adopt a positive view towards licence production and co-production because in this way they are capable of enhancing their influence in the local market and reducing the market shares of their rivals. The threat of competition from a subproducer is eliminated by the condition that the grant of a production licence is usually accompanied by a ban on exports to third countries or parties. This means that a licence producer cannot normally start competing with the company which has granted the licence.[30]

4.3.   Subcontracting

Subcontracting is often used for the same purpose as co-production projects, i.e. to exploit a cheap labour force. Subcontracting is probably most common in electronics, where components are assembled in a low-wage country and exported back to the centre.[31] Electronics in general is strongly geared to military markets. According to one calculation, close to one-fourth of all electronics was used in 1974 for military purposes in the United States and Western Europe. In the United States alone the proportion was 30 per cent.[32]

We have no precise data available as to the extent of foreign production of components for various weapon systems. This phenomenon must be, however, fairly widespread because concern has been expressed by the Department of Defense that the United States is too dependent on the foreign production of critical components, in particular in a situation in which there may be only one U.S. supplier in the field concerned. The increasing use of foreign parts is also seen as a consequence of the greater involvement in co-production and offset agreements for major weapon systems.[33]

Foreign operations of the electronics industry having military relevance can be explored to some extent by noting the appearance of electronic firms with offshore operations in the list of 100 leading DoD contractors. This admittedly very tentative investigation resulted in the following overall picture:

Table 44.   The Extent of Offshore Operations by U.S. Producers of Military Electronics in 1974

Rank in DoD contracts	Firm	Number of employees in offshore factories	Location of operations
1.	General Electric	1 000	Singapore
22.	RCA Corporation	3 000	Singapore, Malaysia, Taiwan
25.	Teledyne	3 300	Singapore, Hong Kong, Malaysia
36.	Fairchild	13 300	Hong Kong, South Korea, Singapore, Mexico, Indonesia
41.	Texas Instruments	11 300	Singapore, Malaysia, El Salvador, Taiwan
63.	Motorola	7 800	South Korea, Mexico, Malaysia, Hong Kong
97.	Hewlett Packard	2 600	Singapore, Malaysia
–	Eight other firms with information on offshore operations	21 250	Singapore, Malaysia, Thailand, Indonesia, Hong Kong, Mauritius, South Korea, Mexico
	Total	63 550	

Source: International Subcontracting Arrangements in Electronics between Developed Market-Economy Countries and Developing Countries. UNCTAD, TD/B/C.2/144. Supp. 1, New York 1975, p. 16-17, and United States Armament Industry: The 100 Largest Defence Contractors in FY 1976. Government Business Worldwide Reports, August 1977, p. 6.

We can calculate from the table that those electronic firms which were among 100 major prime military contractors in the United States had in 1974 on an average 6 043 workers in their offshore plants, while the corresponding average for corporations outside this category was 2 656. This would represent evidence to the effect that the main producers of military electronics have fairly extensive international operations. On the other hand one should notice that the difference between averages is due to the fact that the size of a firm explains both its importance as a military producer and its extent of offshore operations.

141

One should also pay attention to the fact that offshore operations are strongly concentrated in certain countries in Asia, in particular South Korea, Taiwan, Singapore and Hong Kong, and to a lesser extent in Mexico. Electronic components are normally produced or assembled in free-production zones, which are established to attract international business to a developing country.[34] Thus the foreign production of military electronics is closely related to the overall international economic division of labour.

4.4.   Foreign Investments in Arms Production

The armament industry has not been very prone to invest in foreign production plants. This may have been caused by at least two factors. For reasons of security policy there has been a preference to keep arms manufacturers in domestic hands, or at least in majority control. On the other hand research-intensive corporations, especially in the aircraft industry, have not had any particular motive to make direct investments, as long as there was no competition. This state of affairs is, however, gradually breaking down as the following examples indicate.

Since 1964 Boeing has controlled about 10 per cent of Messerschmitt-Bölkow-Blohm (MBB) in West Germany, while United Aircraft owned 26.7 per cent and Northrop 20.0 per cent of the shares of the West-German joint venture VFW-Fokker, which has recently split into its national components.[35]

To continue examples, Lockheed has since 1959 controlled one-fifth of Aeronautica Macchi SpA and Raytheon 24 per cent of Selenia in Italy. Pratt & Whitney has a 10 per cent share in the French Snecma, Northrop controls 24 per cent of CASA in Spain and Cessna Aircraft owns 49 per cent of Reims Aviation in France.[36] EMBRAER, the biggest aircraft producer in Brazil, is 49 per cent in private hands, Volkswagen do Brazil being the biggest private shareholder. Imperial Chemical Industries (ICI) together with the Anglo American Corp., control ARMSCOR, a notable South African producer of ammunition and explosives.[37] The Belgian arms producer Fabrique Nationale, which belongs to the giant Société Générale de Belgique group, is bidding for Browning, a U.S. distributor of guns.[38]

Rockwell International, a relatively important TNC in the military sector, is operating 120 subsidiaries in 30 countries, including Brazil, Hong Kong, Singapore, South Africa and Taiwan. Sales by Rockwell's foreign subsidiaries have rapidly increased during the 1970s: in 1972 foreign sales accounted for only 5 per cent of North American Rockwell's total, but two years later, in 1974, the corresponding share was already 13 per cent, amounting in absolute terms to $ 562 million. In that year foreign profits contributed to 21 per cent of Rockwell International's total profits.[39] Rockwell is also planning to expand its international activities:

> The company is actively exploring opportunities in such countries as Iran, Egypt, Saudi Arabia, Kuwait, Nigeria and Zaire ... Efforts are also being made to tap markets in the People's Republic of China as well as to locate sources of products and material needed by Rockwell.[40]

Naturally not all these foreign operations by Rockwell involve a military component, but it seems self-evident that its activities in the electronic and communications industry have considerable relevance also from the military point of view.

A considerable number of additional examples could be mentioned, especially in the production of small arms. To take examples from the Federal Republic of Germany we may point out that Fritz Werner AG has military production plants at least in Israel, Indonesia, Guinea, Nigeria and Iran. Other West German munition firms have established production facilities, for instance, in Thailand, Burma and Sudan.[41]

5 Transnational military industries and arms production of the developing countries: five cases

In this chapter we shall study the activities of transnational armament industries in the military sectors of five countries: Brazil, South Africa, Egypt, Iran and India.[1] All these countries have tried to become independent and self-reliant armament producers, although for different political reasons and in different international and national circumstances.

Military self-reliance is a common aim of those five countries and they are cooperating with foreign TNCs to fulfil this aim. Their cooperation with the military TNCs has not been similar, however. Brazil and South Africa have been selected for closer analysis because both of them can be considered, in a way, successes for the military TNCs. Brazil used to be very liberal towards the foreign capital and this policy was also visible in the development of the military sector. South Africa has done its best to attract foreign military companies in the fear of an armament embargo. For the TNCs South Africa is a special case because the companies participating in its military build-up risk their international reputation by operating in an embargoed country. For this reason many military companies try to hide their participation in South African arms programs.

Egypt and Iran have been selected because in certain aspects they represent failures for the military TNCs. In Egypt the failure of the Arab Organization of Industries (AOI) in 1979 was a big disappointment and financial loss for certain West European industries, which had planned large sales and investments in that undertaking. On the other hand the failure of West European countries as well as their military industries in Egypt was replaced by the increase of U.S. political and economic influence in that country.

As a result of the active U.S. foreign policy the U.S. military industries increased their sales to Egypt and thus profited from the failure of their West European counterparts. The West Europeans are not the only ones who have failed in Egypt - at the beginning of the 1970s the Soviet Union had also become disappointed in Egypt when Egypt unilaterally broke the military cooperation between the two countries.

Another failure for the military TNCs as well as for their home countries is Iran, where the collapse of the Shah's regime cancelled or interrupted large investments, and where large military orders have been cancelled. Many TNCs are now wondering how to compensate the financial losses suffered in Egypt and Iran and where to put the weapons produced or planned for delivery in those two countries.

India, then, is again a different case. It is cooperating with the TNCs but at the same time it is very firm in efforts to achieve self-reliance in military technology. The TNCs operating in India cannot expect to have a freedom of manoeuvre, and they can expect firm demands concerning the transfer of production technology for the Indian industry. Thus the TNCs cannot - in principle - expect that they can go to India to stay forever but only for a temporary period until India's self-reliance is achieved.

It is common for all these countries that they have turned to transnational armament industries to get new and sophisticated technology. On the other hand the transnational arms industries have also turned to them in their efforts to conquer new markets, maintain the existing ones or to exercise control over new, emerging industries.

Thus, the activities of the transnational armament industries in the weapons production of developing countries can be approached from two different angles: from the control and marketing point of view, which concerns the transnationals, and from the standpoint of self-reliance, which is the general aim of the developing countries starting to produce their own weapons.

Basically, the idea of the military self-reliance of the developing or semi-industrialized countries can be seen in a historical context, as discussed in the introductory Chapter 1. First, the developing countries wanted political independence, then economic independence and now they - at least some of them - want military independence, too. For some developing countries it has been enough to choose the political road in the non-aligned movement and to emphasize their independence mainly in political and economic terms. But some developing countries - particularly those who want to become influential in their regions and who have some industrial base - have chosen to arm themselves and to create their own military industries.

5.1. Brazil

Latin America has traditionally not been a leading Third World market for major weapons. Between 1960-70 its imports of major weapons even decreased in value, and its share in the Third World imports was declining.

Table 45.   Latin American Imports of Major Weapons, 1960-76, $ Million and Per Cent of Third World Total Imports

Region	1960	1962	1964	1966	1968	1970	1972	1974	1976
South America	146	124	96	127	156	209	296	490	732
Central America	120	139	93	19	12	21	46	75	118
Latin America total	266	263	189	146	168	230	342	565	850
Third World imports, total	1 516	1 409	1 574	1 989	2 582	3 118	3 762	5 156	8 158
The share of Latin America from above total	17.5	18.7	12.0	7.3	6.5	7.4	9.1	11.0	10.4

Source: World Armaments and Disarmament.SIPRI Yearbook 1979, London 1979, pp. 170-171. The figures are five-year moving averages at constant (1975) prices.

The modest armament profile until 1970 can be explained by two main reasons. The first one was the dominant position of the United States in the region, which has, until about 1970, minimized the arms supplier competition in the area. On the basis of 'Western Hemisphere' policies there has been a regional security system and the Latin American countries - with the exception of Cuba after the revolution - have received U.S. military assistance under MAP. This relationship made the U.S. the dominant arms supplier, but it also offered a tool for the U.S. to regulate the armament processes of its Southern neighbours. In 1950-78 the Latin American countries received U.S. military assistance worth about $ 0.7 billion under the MAP - a figure which is also low indeed compared to the $ 28.6 billion received by South East Asia and the Pacific region, and the $ 18.6 billion received by Western Europe.[2]

The U.S. Congress did not favour exports of sophisticated arms by the end of the 1960s. In fact various legislations in 1967 and 1968 provided backing for the U.S. to withhold economic assistance to countries which purchase sophisticated weapons. Thus, the U.S. arms exports to Latin America remained on a low level.[3] On the other hand the U.S. arms industries became occupied with production for the Vietnam War and were perhaps not so interested in the Latin American markets at that time.

The Latin American countries were not satisfied with the U.S. restrictions at the end of the 1960s. When some of them wanted supersonic fighters, and the U.S. refused to sell them, they turned to Western Europe and bought, for example, Mirage-fighters from France. At the end of the 1960s, the Latin American arms imports indicated the existence of a regional arms race, since one country after another wanted to buy major arms from the international markets. It was mainly European arms industries which benefited from that arms race. In four years from 1968, European countries sold arms to Latin America worth over $ 135 millions. It was not until 1973 when President Nixon reversed the U.S. restrictions concerning sales of major arms that the U.S. companies started making big sales again in Latin America.

The second reason for modest Latin American arms imports has been the absence of international armed conflicts. As there were no clear international hostilities, there was no great need for imports of major weapons, either. The armament needs were of a different kind; guerilla warfare and severe internal tensions led to the need for appropriate weapons like armed trainers, patrol boats, helicopters and hovercraft. These are called counterinsurgency (COIN) weapons, and because the category includes many small weapons which are less expensive, the international transfers do not raise the figures in statistics as the major weapons do.[4]

Brazil managed to achieve a rapid economic growth in the first half of the 1970s. It was based on industrialization with the help of foreign capital and strong export promotion. The 'Brazilian miracle' became a slogan, although it could be shown that large parts of the population did not enjoy the benefits of that growth, but their position was marginalized.[5]

The expansion of the Brazilian economy was accompanied by strong military build-up. In the 1950s the country had mainly relied on arms imports and it was the largest receiver of U.S. military assistance on the continent.[6] Around 1970 Brazil started to emphasize military self-reliance and made several major efforts to build a strong indigenous defence production. Today it produces fighter and light aircraft, helicopters, missiles, warships, armed vehicles, small weapons and military electronics either as indigenous designs or with licences from foreign TNCs. At the same time it is the largest importer of major weapons on the continent.

Such a strong emphasis on armaments is surprising for the reason that there are no major international conflict formations or threat of international military conflicts in Brazil's neighbourhood. Thus, it seems that for Brazil the armament build-up is more a prestige question than a result of prevailing international tensions. Having a powerful weaponry is also related to Brazil's position as a regional big power, as well as to the military rule since 1964 which favours such a policy.[7]

In 1973-77 Brazil's arms import pattern looked as follows:

Table 46.   Brazilian Imports of Major Weapons by Major Suppliers in 1973-
               1977, Million Current Dollars and Per Cent

Supplier	Imports 1973-1977	Per cent
United Kingdom	180	31.5
United States	172	30.1
France	130	22.7
Italy	60	10.5
Federal Republic of Germany	30	5.2
Total	572	100.0

Source: World Military Expenditures and Arms Transfers 1968-1977,
             U.S. Arms Control and Disarmament Agency, Washington D.C.
             1979, p. 158.

In 1978 Brazil and Argentina were the two largest arms importers in South
America. They imported arms worth $ 371 million and $ 265 million respectively,
which amounted to 35 and 25 per cent of the total South American arms
imports. Together these two countries, which have a traditional rivalry as far
as armaments are concerned, accounted for 60 per cent of South American
imports of major weapons.[8]

Since 1970 Brazil has systematically diversified its arms import sources, and
as Table 46 shows, the policy has succeeded. A major step in this respect was
the purchase of Dassault's Mirage fighters from France in 1972-73 and
Northrop's F-5 fighters from the US in 1974. Similar diversification is
observable in all armament categories: transport and training aircraft were
bought from Italy, the UK and the US. Missiles were purchased mostly from
Europe (SNIAS, Matra, BAe, Short Brothers, MBB) and to a lesser extent from
the U.S. (Hughes, Raytheon). Warships were bought from the UK and the FRG,
and helicopters from the UK (Westland) and the US (mostly Bell),[9] Thus, there
was a clear-cut policy to buy in at least two countries for each weapon
category. In this way Brazil wanted to take advantage of the buyers' market in
international armament economy. Perhaps it was able to bargain and receive
better terms in arms deals as the suppliers were competing for customers.
Although the diversification of supply sources decreased dependence on one

supplier, it did not, of course, decrease the total dependence on transnational armament industries as far as high-technology weapons are concerned.

The aim to become independent and self-reliant was also the main motive for the reorganization of the Brazilian armament industry and for the increase of its production capacity. Ten years ago Brazil was not yet any notable arms producer - now it has become one of the main armament centres in the Third World. The development process of armament industry has been rapid, indeed, and it must be connected with Brazil's aim at becoming a regional power centre since no major international threats call for such a rapid growth in armament production. The idea of independence and freedom from foreign dominance is also clear in armament build-up. Thus, the Brazilian Air Force Minister Campos told a Chilean audience in December 1977: "The time has come to free ourselves from the United States and the countries of Europe. It is a condition of security that each nation manufacture its own arms".[10]

As a proof for these words Brazil unilaterally cancelled the 25-year old bilateral military assistance agreement with the U.S. in March 1977. This was the result of the submission of the first 1977 human rights report by the U.S. State Department to the Congress. [11]

Brazil had experience in the production of light aircraft for more than twenty years. Yet it was the founding of Empresa Brasilieira Aeronautica (EMBRAER) in 1969 that changed the country into a major aircraft producer. EMBRAER is 51 per cent owned by the Brazilian government; among the private owners the second largest is Volkswagen do Brazil, a subsidiary of the FRG-based transnational company.[12]

EMBRAER makes 11 different types of aircraft in all, in 50 separate models which in the military field include transport planes, maritime patrol aircraft, fighters, trainers and other military aircraft. Many of these models are of indigenous design, but often the avionics and engines are imported from North America (in the case of the engines the exporters are Lycoming, Pratt & Whitney, Continental and Rolls Royce). EMBRAER has more extensive trans-national collaboration with Northrop, Piper, Aeronautica Macchi and the list used to include Fokker in the 1950s. Thus the U.S. Lockheed has a foothold in

EMBRAER through its Italian partnership (cf. p. 45). EMBRAER employed 4 500 workers in 1978, which is 4.5 times more than it employed in 1970.[13]

The most important foreign partner for EMBRAER is U.S. company Piper, which beat its competitors Cessna and Beech in 1974 as it was more responsive to Brazilian demands. The agreement with EMBRAER and Piper concerns mainly business aircraft, but some of the models are also suitable for military purposes. Because the agreement is one of the very few where the content is known, we will below summarize the agreement as an example of an extensive licensing agreement between a developing producer and a foreign TNC:[14]

> The agreement between EMBRAER and Piper was signed in 1974 for five years. Under the terms of the agreement EMBRAER may select any Piper model for local production - EMBRAER selected five. Piper is responsible for providing the necessary assembly and parts, manufacturing know-how as well as for assisting in such areas as quality control, materials handling and manufacturing. Piper has an option to use its international distribution system for aircraft that may be exported from Brazil. The U.S. firm's compensation is primarily a percentage return on the components it ships to EMBRAER. As the licensee progressively substitutes local content for these imports, the returns will diminish. However, even at 100 per cent production in Brazil, Piper will still be paid a fee for service in support of those aircraft. The agreement specifically permits EMBRAER to fabricate Piper aircraft for sale in the domestic markets and, on occasion, to produce jointly with the U.S. company for foreign market sales.
>
> Production capability of the Piper models is being transferred to EMBRAER in three stages. During phase I, completed structures such as fuselage, empennage, and wings are shipped to EMBRAER for final assembly and installation of all systems and components. During phase II, EMBRAER receives structured subassemblies for mating in jigs, in addition to the functions achieved in phase I. By phase III, Piper will be shipping all component parts for assembly by EMBRAER and in three subphases will 1) begin replacement of Piper-supplies by Brazilian-made equivalents, including interiors and 50 per cent of both fiberglass and acrylics; 2) complete replacement of all remaining fiberglass and acrylics and produce all harnesses; and 3) produce the aircraft completely with Brazilian-manufactured parts and components, with the exception of those that cannot be economically produced in Brazil. By the end of phase III-3, EMBRAER estimates the Brazilian content to be 66-70 per cent. Subcontracting is a general feature of EMBRAER-Piper production program and was one of the reasons why EMBRAER was able to start the project rather quickly. Its subcontracting network is extensive in Brazil, since over fifty Brazilian firms participate as subcontractors for Brazilian aerospace industry.

As can be noted, Piper uses EMBRAER to enter Brazil and export markets in third countries, and EMBRAER is extensively subcontracting for Piper. On the other hand the program successively increases the domestic content of EMBRAER's products and hence makes the Brazilian aircraft industry more self-sufficient.

On the military side an example of a subcontractor position is the production of parts for Northrop's F-5 fighters (vertical tail assemblies and pylons) to be exported to the U.S. This contract was an offset agreement in connection with the Brazilian purchases of 42 Northrop fighters.[15]

EMBRAER is located at Sao José dos Campos, in the vicinity of Sao Paolo. This manufacturing centre of some 250 000 inhabitants is the real centre of the Brazilian arms production. Engesa (= Engenheiros Especialisados) is located in the same centre and is now one of the main suppliers of combat vehicles - including Urutu, Cascavel, Jararaca and Sucuri armoured personnel carriers - to the Brazilian Army and Marines. The carriers are of indigenous design, but for most of them the engines are produced by Mercedes Benz do Brazil. Avibras is a private company which manufacturers solid-propellant artillery rockets and it also produces Carcara air-to-surface missiles. In general the missile industry is firmly under the influence of foreign military technology. Commission Central de Misseis is producing Roland and Cobra missiles with the aid of the French and West German licences (MBB, Aerospatiale). Various air defence systems are manufactured in cooperation with the French Thomson-CSF.[16]

After the break-up of the military assistance of the U.S., Brazil increasingly turned to European arms producers to acquire new technology. As a result a new Brazilian company Helibras was founded, 45 per cent of which is owned by Aerospatiale, 45 per cent by the state of Minas Gerais and ten per cent by Aerophoto Cruzeiro do Sul. Two hundred Ecureuil and 30 Lama helicopters will be built in a new factory at Itajuba, near Sao Paulo, over the next decade. The new plant cost $ 4 million in April 1978, but the final costs are much higher because of the rapid rate of inflation in Brazil. Aerospatiale has agreed to supply all parts and components for the systems and progressively transfer technology so that in the second year of production (1980) the Brazilian-made content will increase to 27 per cent, reaching 65 per cent by 1983. Aerospatiale has also planned to export 25 per cent of the output. The Italian Oto Melara also started a joint venture for the production of howitzers and heavy arms with two Brazilian partners.[17]

With the establishment of a modern, high-technology army and large military industry Brazil has become a big market for military electronics. According to some estimates, the Brazilian government intends to spend $ 2 billion on military electronics in 1978-83.[18] During the "Brazilian miracle" period, when transnational corporations were welcomed in Brazil, most transnational producers of military electronics started business there. Many of them, like LM Ericsson, Philips, General Electric, Siemens, Texas Instruments, ITT had already been in Brazil for a long time for the civilian markets. The large size of Brazil and its industrial centres were a big market for telecommunication, cable producers, electrical companies etc. Because of the liberal policies, the TNCs were largely free to import raw materials and components, and the government offered export incentives. Brazilian electrical and electronic sectors are known as examples of very strong TNC-domination.[19]

When the demand for military electronics grew, many companies active in civil projects offered their services to the army: among them at least AEG-Telefunken do Brasil, Philips do Brasil and Ericsson do Brasil.[20] But also new companies were invited in connection with new Brazilian projects, e.g. Thomson-CSF, which is specialized in military electronics, signed a $ 70 million contract with the Brazilian Ministry of Aeronautics for the construction of an air traffic control and defence system over Brasilia-Rio-Sao Paulo region. The system will include radars, flight controls and a team of specialized operators. According to some estimates the main purpose is to control an area which includes the Angra dos Reis nuclear power plants, Brazil's largest industrial concentration and a number of hydroelectric power plants and dams in the River Plate region.[21]

After 1975, the Brazilian government has become more restrictive toward foreign electronic companies in Brazil. The reason for this change of policy is the growing balance-of-payments problem. Imports of components and raw materials are discouraged, and the companies are encouraged to find Brazilian partners to supply necessary equipment. Government finance and contracts are promised to companies which follow the line suggested by the government.[22]

This policy is also visible in the efforts to promote Brazilian military electronics production and to decrease the power of the TNCs in this field. The largest electronic firm in Brazil, government owned Digibras, has formed a joint venture with the British Ferranti for the development of military electronics. On the whole the Brazilian state has very strongly intervened in electronic production to decrease the power of TNCs and to develop a national electronic industry. The state computer commission CAPRE, the federal government data processing service SERPO and the state telecommunication company TELEBRAS are examples of these efforts. The state favours projects whose decision centre, capital control, administration and technology are located in the country. The state-controlled firms try to produce both software and hardware for the armed forces. In addition, CTA (Aeronautics Technical Centre) is developing and manufacturing electronic components for the armed forces with the participation of local suppliers.[23]

The conclusion is that in principle the time is over when the TNCs had a freedom of manoeuvre in Brazilian electronic markets and in military electronics. It will, however, totally depend on the technological capabilities of the Brazilian companies whether the Brazilianization of this sector will succeed. So far the technological requirements in many Brazilian military or military-related projects have been so sophisticated that cooperation with foreign TNCs has been necessary. One example is the Brazilian satellite communication system, which serves both education communication and military functions.

In 1971 the Brazilian government signed a contract with General Electric (USA) and Hughes Aircraft (USA) for exploration concerning the installation of a national communication satellite system. The plan included three satellites to be launched from 1976 on, covering 86 per cent of the country's large territory, each satellite carrying three TV-channels and twenty radio chains, as well as necessary ground installations. The system, which General Electric was authorized to design, has many educational functions but it will also be used for military and police control purposes. According to General Electric's reports, the functions include "collection, transmission, switching, reception, recording and display of information" and can be used for "law enforcement, business, medical, safety, security, control and navigation" purposes. The Brazilian Ministry of Interior is among the main users of satellite information, which also indicates the police functions of the satellite station network.[24]

As was mentioned at the beginning of this chapter, security problems in Brazil are more often related to internal than international problems. Therefore electronics are extensively used to maintain internal order and repress the political opposition, but Brazilian technology in this field is not sufficient. The Brazilian police have purchased a Printak 250 computerized fingerprint system manufactured by Rockwell International in California - the system will form the nucleus of a nation-wide identification network.[25] During 1969-72 Brazil was a major participant in the Public Safety Programs, designed for police operations by the Office for Public Safety in connection with the U.S. Agency for International Development. The official U.S. participation in such police programs ended, however, in 1975, when Section 660 of the Foreign Assistance Act took effect. It became illegal to use aid funds "to provide training or advice, or provide any financial support, for police, prisons, or other law enforcement forces for any foreign government".[26] What the law did not prevent, however, was the flow of privately produced technologies for such purposes, technology which Rockwell itself calls - "skunk work".

The general aim of Brazil is evidently to become a self-reliant producer of military technology, and policies are carefully coordinated to fulfil that goal. The main organ for this is the War Material Industry of Brazil IMBEL (= Industria de Material Belico do Brasil), which was created in 1975 as a government holding company to coordinate and modernize Brazilian armament production. While IMBEL aims at technological self-reliance it also recognizes the need for foreign technology. Foreign producers are required, however, to bring technology with them and possibly share it with Brazilian partners in joint ventures. The Brazilian partners are often state-owned or state-controlled companies. To be able to afford production of complex weapons, IMBEL has launched plans for extensive exports, particularly in the Third World countries. The policies are very liberal; according to IMBEL's director, Gen. Arbaldo Carderari, "we will sell to the left, to the right, to the centre, up above and down below. If the government authorizes it, we'll do it".[27]

Brazil started to export arms in 1975, and it has been estimated that it would be marketing military hardware worth $ 500 million annually in the 1980s. The most successful export items so far have been Engesa's Urutu, Cascavel, Jararaca and Sucuri armoured personnel carriers - all named after very poisonous Brazilian snakes. An unknown number of these vehicles have been sold to "undisclosed customers in Latin America", and over 600 have been sold to the Middle East. Libya alone has bought 400 vehicles for $ 400 million from the Engesa factory. Brazilian-built aircraft are rather small and suitable for military transport, patrol, COIN and reconnaissance purposes; the main customers have been in Latin America, where at least Bolivia, Chile, El Salvador, Panama, Paraguay and Uruguay have bought Brazilian aircraft. Brazil has also launched a major export campaign in Africa for both civilian and military products. Libya, Sudan, Togo and Nigeria for example have bought Brazilian weapons systems.[28]

The conclusion regarding Brazilian armament build-up is that despite efforts at military self-reliance this goal has not been achieved. The reason is that every time new technology is sought, it has been bought from foreign, transnational armament industries. The Brazilian achievements have so far consisted of better terms in the deals with the TNCs, increased control of TNC activities, and increasing Brazilian share in armament projects.

It is impossible to estimate the overall role of armament production in the Brazilian economy, because transfers of arms and technology cannot be easily isolated from other international transfers. Toward the end of the 1970s it became evident, however, that the Brazilian miracle was over and Brazil had run into serious economic troubles. This means that the overall economic strategies, which were also practised in the armament sector, cannot be followed any more. Brazilian foreign debt totalled $ 52 billion at the end of 1979, and the annual rate of inflation was 77 per cent.[29] In such circumstances the armament policy which requires imports of arms, parts or payments for technology and services will only contribute to increasing economic burdens. As long as Brazil wants to maintain its high level of arms production, it can be said that it is forced to strong export promotion to balance the foreign import bills of the military sector.

The armament industry is no exception among Brazilian industries. One of the main consequences of the 'export-led' growth model has been the steady increase, most often through the network of TNCs operating in the country, of the import of capital goods and advanced technology to prop up the export industries. The demand for imported inputs has been so conspicuous that the exports have not been sufficient to cover the import bill, which has led to balance-of-payment difficulties and foreign indebtedness.

5.2.   South Africa

The history of South Africa is the history of the White minority strengthening its presence in the area and expanding over surrounding regions. This has resulted in the gradual subjugation of the overwhelming Black majority under the White dominance. The expansion of the minority rule within South Africa has led to a special form of internal colonialism known as apartheid which is the most visible manifestation of the doctrines of separate development betwen races. The constant strengthening of the political and economic position of the White minority has been the primary target of the apartheid policy.

The expansion outside the South African borders, with the exception of the illegal occupation of Namibia, has been only a secondary target of the White regime. In fact its policy vis-à-vis Black Africa has hovered between the emphasis on dialogue and intensified contacts and the relative isolation of the country, i.e. the laager option, in which the interests of the White could be supposedly better defended. The scope of direct expansion to the North has become, after the developments in the former Portuguese territories and Zimbabwe, even more difficult and in fact South Africa's options have considerably narrowed. It has tried to respond to these challenges by planning a subregional constellation of states, dominated by Pretoria, but the success of this strategy, in its original meaning, is increasingly doubted.

South Africa is on the defensive. That is why it has tried to increase the autarchy of the economy, especially in such critical sectors as energy, military production, electronics and certain manufacturing sectors. The aim of this policy is to transform the South African economy so that it is better able to tolerate the possible economic sanctions against it. An important instrument in this policy has been the establishment of several state-controlled corporations or para-statals, in the key sectors of the economy.[30] The public sector is in this respect the backbone of the South African politico-economic system.

On the other hand the economy is by no means autonomous. It is strongly dependent on the capital and perhaps even more on the technology acquired abroad; often from a handful of transnational corporations. The external dependence thus restricts considerably the opportunities of the White minority to achieve any true autonomy and autarchy. They are, in other words, forced to find out ways and means by which a compromise between these two tendencies can be made. The intermediate position of South Africa in the international division of labour[31] can be illustrated by its main contradiction. On one hand it is a major exporter of strategic minerals, especially gold, to the industrialized countries of the West, but on the other hand its resources are drained by the continued technological dependence. This is an important factor in the severe and chronic balance-of-payments crises which South Africa has temporarily faced. The domestic system of South Africa is one of polarized accumulation, which is in an international perspective connected with its semi-peripheral position.[32]

It is most apparent that these features of the South African society and its external relations are manifested also in the military sphere. One could assume that the White minority has been building up a strong military apparatus by which both the internal Black opposition and the external challenges can be deterred and, if needed, defeated. On the other hand South Africa's technological dependence necessitates the imports of arms and military technology and, in general, reliance on the skills, capital and technology of transnational corporations. The autarchic strategy means, however, that constant efforts are made to indigenize the foreign technology and to develop national capacity, partly by the aid of TNCs, in this field.

The conventional military capacity of South Africa can be summarized by the following pieces of information:[33]

Table 47.   Military Expenditures and Arms Imports of South Africa in
             1968-77 at Constant 1975 Millions of Dollars

	Military spending	Share of GNP, per cent	Arms imports	Share of total imports
1969	670	2.8	31	1
1971	692	2.6	42	1
1973	860	3.0	101	2
1975	1 353	4.3	137	2
1977	1 764	5.5	123	2

The real value of South African military spending almost trebled from 1969 to
1977, and after that the growth has been at least equally fast. The rapid
growth of the military budget started in fact in 1973 when the Defence White
Paper strongly propounded the idea that all the country's resources must be
mobilized to increase military preparedness. One consequence of this new
'awareness' was the division of the army into a counterinsurgency, for use in
'small wars' against the liberation movements, and a conventional force. The
search for full military preparedness was documented in a five-year defence
expansion program approved in 1974.[34] Since then the growth of the South
African military budget has been rapid and continuous.

The arms imports have remained, according to Table 47, rather constant
throughout the 1970s and not at a very high level. This can be partly explained
by the relative self-sufficiency of the South African military industry, a
position has attained through a gradual shift from imports through licence
production to the domestic manufacture of arms. A relevant factor, though
not yet visible in the table, is that in November 1977 the UN Security Council
placed South Africa in a mandatory arms embargo which in principle forbids
any transfers of arms to the country. The embargo has been circumvented,
however, by a variety of means.[35] This is well indicated by the announcement
that in 1978 South Africa imported arms by some $ 350 million.[36] If this figure
is correct serious doubts can be raised about the reliability of the import
figures presented in Table 47.

159

The only problem is not, however, the conventional military capability. Claims that the South African minority regime possesses a number of <u>nuclear explosives</u> are increasingly common. The bombs could have been developed either by relying on the enriched uranium, imported or domestically enriched, or on the plutonium which could have been reprocessed from the output of the Safari research reactors. Technically speaking South Africa could without any major doubt possess a fission bomb, although the final proof of this is lacking. There are, however, doubts that South Africa exploded - either alone or in cooperation with Israel - a nuclear device in the Southern Atlantic towards the end of September 1979.

South Africa would not have been able to develop its nuclear capability in that relatively short time without the contribution of foreign governments and transnational corporations. The main projects in the South African nuclear industry are at present the commercial uranium enrichment plant, which is located at Valindaba, and the construction of the nuclear power plant at Koeberg. During the 1950s South Africa's nuclear industry and research community was mainly supported by the United States. Thereafter the West Germans were instrumental in assisting South Africa in the development of the uranium enrichment capability, while a French consortium has been delivering reactors and other nuclear technology to the Koeberg plant.[37]

Armaments and military equipment needed by the South African army are acquired by the <u>Armaments Board,</u> which controls military research projects and development of armaments. This state-controlled body was preceded by the <u>Munitions Production Board</u> which was created in 1964 as a response to the decision of the Labour government in Britain to introduce an arms embargo against South Africa. The responsibility for the production of arms belongs to the <u>Armaments Development Production Corporation</u> (ARMSCOR) and private industry. ARMSCOR was established in 1968 with a capital of $ 144 million. In 1978 its turnover was reported to be $ 1.1 billion and the employment factor in the vicinity of 100.000 people.[38] In August 1976 the Armaments Board and the ARMSCOR merged to form a single organization, which is a major instrument in the hands of the South African government in integrating the military industry and coordinating its activities with the needs of the South African armed forces.

The establishment of the ARMSCOR coincided with the shift of South Africa from the arms-import strategy to the licence production of various weapons systems, which took place in the middle of the 1960s. As the local production gradually started to grow stronger, the state assumed a more dominant role in guiding the development and production of arms. Besides ARMSCOR this tendency is illustrated by the takeover of <u>Atlas Aircraft Corporation</u>, original-ly established by the assistance of <u>Sud-Aviation</u>, by the South African government in 1969. These examples refer to the second stage in the development of the South African military industry; imports are replaced by the licence production of weapons, normally in the state-controlled enter-prises. In the second stage the local content of the production programs is, almost by definition, rather low and hence they rely to a considerable extent on foreign technology and parts.

The licence production of various weapons systems has been fairly widespread in the South African military economy, and it has been in fact the dominant way of successfully achieving higher degrees of self-sufficiency. This strategy has been implemented partly by various legal and economic measures by which the activities of TNC subsidiaries have been 'internalized' and so they have been made more integral parts of the South African economy. At the same time the domestic production capacity has also been strengthened. The prevailing situation can be characterized as the third stage of the South African military industry. It is more autonomous than the previous phases, but still in some crucial sectors dependent on foreign technology and capital. The increase in the self-sufficiency of the military industry coincides with the decrease in South African security options, which is reflected in its resort to the 'fortress Southern Africa' or to the <u>laager</u>.[39]

The shift of the arms industry through different phases to indigenous production does not remove the problems, but rather replaces old problems with new ones. As stated repeatedly above, the continuation of technological dependence is probably the most serious problem. This is also officially acknowledged by the South African authorities:[40]

> Confronted by an irrevocable arms embargo, a new dimension was added to self-sufficiency, and the achievement of a greater degree of local content can no longer be regarded as the final and only criterion. The South African industries and Armscor, through its

subsidiary companies, must also become technologically self-sufficient in order that, in the case of a more extensive boycott of
components and raw materials, available alternatives and substitutes
can be utilized, and that new generations of advanced systems based
on local components and raw materials can be developed.

A natural conclusion of this analysis is the emphasis on the need to develop
technologically sophisticated sectors of the economy in general and to gear
them simultaneously to serve military purposes. In other words the
strengthening of the arms production of a country cannot be separated from
the general technology policy. They are mutually reinforcing activities,
although the overall technological base has apparently a determining role in
this relationship.

The autonomy of the South African military industry has increased step by
step. In the beginning it was able to turn out explosives, ammunition and small
weapons. Later on artillery, armoured cars, missiles and aircraft were added
to the production list. Nowadays this agenda is gradually extended to the
production of naval vessels, tanks, helicopters and military electronics.[41] This
development has led to a shift from a traditional war-fighting capacity to the
greatly enhanced ability to carry out counterinsurgency operations as well as
to the capacity to wage a 'modern' conventional war by missiles, tanks and
aircraft. In fact South Africa is intensively developing capacity to deter and,
by implication, to launch heavy conventional attacks. At the same time it is
again increasing the geographical reach of its armed forces as the extensive
operations in the Southern Angola in May-June 1980 show.

Aircraft and engines. According to one source of information South Africa had
acquired 127 weapons-production licences from foreign sources by 1965. Most
of them were for the production of various small arms.[42] One of the first
major arms programs based on the licence production was the assembly of the
Italian ground attack aircraft - MB 326 - powered by Rolls Royce engines. This
is indicative of the reason that most of the aircraft produced under licence in
South Africa have originated either in France or Italy. The only exception
appears to be the T-6G Texan trainer and counterinsurgency plane, 150 of
which have been produced under North American licence. It is to be noted that
also MB 326 or Impala I, as it is called in South Africa, and its successor

Impala II are particularly well suited to counterinsurgency activities. In total 400 of these two versions of Impala have been produced in South Africa.

The production of Impalas and their engines in South Africa tell an interesting story of the existing corporate linkages. The production of the aircraft was licensed by Aermacchi. The Italian government participated in the negotiation of the deal. The Rolls Royce turbojet engines, which are powering both Impalas are produced in Italy, under British licence by Piaggio which is, in turn, controlled by Fiat. The necessary production lines in South Africa have been established largely with the aid of British and Italian engineers. The production of Impala was started by using Italian components, but the declared local content of 70 per cent was reached before the middle of the 1970s. So far in total 300 Impala I and about 100 Impala II planes have been produced (but there are also lower estimates).[43]

The Italian connection can be also discovered in the licence production of C4M Kudu. It is a derivative of the Lockheed AL-60, which is a single engine cabin monoplane produced by Aermacchi, which since 1959 has partly been controlled by Lockheed Aircraft International, which, in turn, is a wholly owned subsidiary of Lockheed Corp. The AL-60 aircraft is powered by the engines of Avco Lycoming, which is also directly active in South Africa.[44]

Since 1976 South Africa has been producing C4M Kudu under licence. It also contains some indigenous design, but inherits on the other hand some technology from the Lockheed/Aermacchi AM.3C, which is produced in South Africa as Bosbok. It is a three-seat cabin monoplane which is used as a trainer, but can also be armed with rockets, bombs, machine guns and napalm tanks (napalm can be, by the way, produced indigenously in South Africa). The story of Kudu and Bosbok, which have been both produced by the Atlas Aircraft, has been similar also to the extent that several of them were first transferred from Italy and only thereafter the domestic production was started.

In 1965 Atlas Aircraft received a licence to produce Italian Partenavia P-64B Oscar-180 light aircraft which has a dual civilian/military capability. Two years later the licence production of RSA-200 Falcon, as it is called in South Africa, was started in new facilities at Bloemfontain by the AFIC Company, which was established to manage this project. By 1974 some 40 planes, powered by engines of Italian origin, were produced for likely use for the South African Commando Air Force, but since then the production has most probably been halted.

In addition to Italy, France has been an important supplier of arms and military technology to the apartheid regime. In the aircraft sector the question is, first of all, of the licence production of Mirage F-1. In June 1971 it was announced that a licence agreement was concluded between ARMSCOR and Dassault/Breguet to produce Mirage F-1 for the South African Air Force. The agreement covered the supply of 48 planes, 16 of which were delivered directly from France before the initiation of the licence production. The remaining 32 Mirages were assembled by Atlas Aircraft, the engine being imported from France. The total costs of the agreement have been estimated at $ 300 million, which also contained the training of South African staff by Dassault/Bréguet in France. There has been widely different information on the total number of Mirage F-1s actually produced for the use of the South African Air Force. By now a relatively well established fact appears to be that 48 of various versions of Mirage F-1s in total have been supplied to the SAAF.

There are also some references to the licence production of aircraft systems in South Africa which are somewhat difficult to verify. It has been stated that in 1969 British Westland and French SNIAS licensed to South Africa the assembly and production of 20 SA-330 Puma helicopters at the cost of some $ 28 million. There are now 19 Puma helicopters in operation in South Africa. Apparently there has also been discussion about the construction of an indigenous military transport plane which would have been modelled on the Israel Aircraft Industries' Arava.[45]

The construction of military aircraft in South Africa has progressed through a number of stages. During the 1960s most of the aircraft was imported, while the early phases of the licence production simply meant the local assembly of the components, imported either from Italy or France. The share of domestic components gradually increased largely as a consequence of the deliberate efforts of the Atlas Aircraft Corp. in this direction. The autarchy of the South African aircraft industry was hence enhanced. Although it is by no means self-sufficient - engines are still imported - the progress can be substantiated by the fact that Impala Mk.II, which is an improved version of Impala II, is now fully made in South Africa. It is the first plane in this category.[46]

The increase in the self-sufficiency of the South African aircraft industry is partly due to the intensive R&D effort carried out in the sector. Most of the aeronautical R&D is undertaken by the Aeronautics Research Unit of the Council for Scientific and Industrial Research (CSIR). The military interest in the work of this unit is revealed by the composition of its advisory body which consists of the representatives of the Armaments Board, SAAF, the Atlas Aircraft Corp., South African Airways and the Department of Transportation. The research done within the unit has focused on low-speed aerodynamics, atmospheric turbulence, high-speed aerodynamics, aircraft structures and propulsion. The unit has been given for the research purposes rather advanced equipment and technical systems. Aeronautical R&D is also done to a certain extent at the universities of Stellenbosch and Witwaterstrand.[47]

Missiles. The development of the South African missile capacity was initiated by the West German and French support. In 1964 the Rocket Research Institute as well as an ionospheric station were established, under the aegis of the University of Pretoria, by the Max-Planck Institute for Aeronomy (FRG) and by the Institute for Stratospheric Physics at Lindau/Harz (FRG). The ionospheric station is located at Tsumeb on a stretch of land in Namibia which is owned by the OTAVI-Minengesellschaft (FRG). According to some sources of information the West German Ministry of Defence has been directly financing the Institute for Stratospheric Physics. In the middle of the 1960s at least two West German companies were involved in the missile operation in South Africa, viz. Herman Oberth-Gesellschaft from Bremen and Waffen- und Luftrüstung AG, which was an umbrella organization of some 30 West German firms involved in the rocket industry.

The activities of Bölkow AG have also included missile research and testing in South Africa where it has been closely connected with the local projects to construct missiles and relevant launching sites. The company also constructed in 1968 a rocket test station at St. Lucia, north of Durban in Northeastern Natal. In 1973 the South African government and Deutsche Forschungs-und

Versuchsanstalt für Luft- und Raumfahrt, financed partly by the Federal government, concluded a ten-year agreement, called project 'Blue Grotto', to develop missiles at a site near Kimberley. Several West German companies which have established themselves in South Africa produce components for rockets. These firms include BMW (S.A.), Diesel Electric (Pty.) Ltd., which is a subsidiary of Robert Bosch Gmbh, Liebherr-Africa (Pty.) Ltd. and Siemens Ltd.[48]

An interesting story is related to the construction of the Cactus ground-to-air missile, which took place in France on the basis of South African specifications and with the participation of South African scientists. The technological responsibility was, however, mainly on French shoulders, while South Africans were predominant in financing the project. In France Matra was responsible for the development and manufacture of the missile, while Thomson-CSF built the ground equipment, which was initially designed to be fitted into C-130 Hercules or Transall C-160 transport planes, both of which were delivered to South Africa. Hotchkiss-Brandt also participatged in this project. The Cactus project, known as Crotale in France, was originally kept secret and was not revealed until 1969 when Defence Minister Botha visited France. Initial deliveries of operational missile systems to South Africa were started in 1971 and by 1973 three batteries were deployed in the vicinity of the Mozambique border.[49]

These foreign contributions have also strengthened the domestic missile industry of South Africa. Over the last 15 years South Africans have developed several missile systems in which the domestic content has apparently been pretty strong. As early as in 1968 the first short-range missiles were successfully tested, and a year later a locally developed air-to-air missile was launched at the St. Lucia range. In 1971 the South African Defence Department announced that an indigenous missile was fired from a Mirage fighter and had successfully hit a supersonic target drone. This air-to-air missile was jointly developed by the National Institute for Defence Research, South African Air Force and ARMSCOR. The development of this missile, Whiplash, took approximately five years. It is produced by the Atlas Aircraft.[50]

It was recently announced that South Africa has procured another air-to-air missile which has been developed by Kentron, the newest branch of ARMSCOR. In this connection it has been stated that this missile was entirely developed and produced in South Africa, and that it has good fighting capabilities. If this is the case the South African missile industry has achieved a relatively high degree of self-sufficiency. Doubts have been raised, however, on the origins of the new missiles and it has been claimed that the missiles fitted in the Mirage F-fighter are in fact Matra R.550 Magic missiles. Provided that this is true the most probable explanation of the apparent controversy is that the Matra missiles are produced under a licence in South Africa and the announcement of the indigenous missile is only a cover-up for the production, needed because of the mandatory arms embargo declared by the UN Security Council.[51]

Electronics. The transnational corporations active in the military sector of South Africa are almost solely of French and West German origin. These two countries have been the most prepared to serve the military needs of the apartheid regime. The situation is, however, quite different in areas where various kinds of dual-purpose technologies are in question. Electronics is one such field and its products can be used almost equally in both the civilian and the military sectors. In these grey-area industries the strong overall position of British and U.S. companies is better manifested than in the "pure" military sector.[52]

The accelerated industrialization of the military sector of South Africa has led to previously unexpected demand for the electronics. The problem is, however, that South Africa has not been able to progress very far in its own electronics industry, and it has had to rely on foreign technology. In fact one has to conclude that even though the South African military industry has become more indigenous during the last years the electronics industry has been an exception to this rule; actually it has become a bottleneck. The circumstances are, however, about to change and the local content of military electronics has increased, even though the reliance on TNCs has persisted.

This can be illustrated, for example, by the active role of the British electronic companies in South Africa. Plessey owns in South Africa a subsidiary which further controls two other companies. One of them has been responsible for the development of a tellurometer needed in the missile production. Plessey has also participated in a new factory manufacturing integrated circuits for electronic weapons. The establishment of the factory, opened in August 1976, was financed by the Council for Scientific and Industrial Research, while the necessary technology for the licence production came from Plessey. In the opening ceremony Defence Minister Botha pointed out that

> integrated circuits form part of all sophisticated weapons using electronic systems. A local manufacturer of integrated circuits will be invaluable from the point of view of defence strategy.

It is claimed that Botha continued his statement by saying that the South African electronics industry could not have undertaken the manufacture alone because of the technical complexity involved. Integrated circuits are necessary elements in, for example, the homing devices of missiles.[53]

Plessey, together with other electronics companies, has had to face the policy by ARMSCOR which aims at increasing the local ownership in the industry. This aim has been pursued by suggesting to TNCs involved that unless they give the majority ownership to the local companies they may lose some advantageous contracts with the South African military authorities. The response of the transnationals has been varied: some of them have sold their local subsidiaries or taken in local partners, while some others - including Plessey in the integrated-circuit factory - have rejected the demands and considered that the South African military industry is too dependent on them to be able to cut down the business relationships.

This is no doubt true, but at the same time the local authorities are busy enhancing the self-sufficiency of the electronics industry, for which the local companies now account for some 20 per cent of the demand. The South African government apparently tries to establish a domestic stronghold around Allied Technologies which took over STC, a subsidiary of ITT, in 1978, and Barlow Rand which has, in turn, swallowed GEC-Marconi, a subsidiary of the British company. Barlow seems to be moving amongst domestic companies towards dominance in military electronics.[54]

The British General Electric Company (GEC) is the biggest electrical concern in South Africa. At the beginning of the 1970s it employed some 4 000 people and had a turnover of £ 25 million a year. In addition, Marconi South Africa, which assembled close-circuit television to the South African army and used to be a subsidiary of GEC-Marconi, is now acquired by South African interests. In 1968 Marconi South Africa opened a new factory which has produced, among other things, the ADF-370 radio compass for the Impala jet trainers. In 1970 Marconi confirmed a new contract amounting to some $ 70-80 million for military radar and other electronic communication equipment used as part of the radar defence network known as the Northern Air Defence System. In general Marconi appears to have been willing to utilize the loopholes in the arms embargo legislation by exporting and partly locally producing such systems as data link equipment for the South African air defence network and Marconi Troposcatter Communications System, exported for use, for instance, in Namibia.[55]

While Plessey rejected the pressure from the South African authorities to strengthen cooperation with the local firms, Racal Electronics, another British company, found a different solution and merged with the Grinaker Co. Racal is said to control outside the United States 75 per cent of the world market in military mobile communications equipment and systems. The activities of the company, which was founded in 1951, are highly international: its electronic equipment is sold in 100 countries, and at least 70 per cent of the total production is exported. Racal is a leading supplier of radio manpacks, tank radios, monitoring and surveillance equipment as well as fixed and mobile radio stations specifically designed for military use. In South Africa well over one half of Racal's local production goes directly to the armed services.[56]

Other British electronic firms have also supplied radar equipment to South Africa. Thus Decca, which has a subsidiary in South Africa, provided the local army with a radar screen, which was erected around the coastline of the Cape sea route to give a protective cover, for 200 miles or more, out to the sea.[57] It may be also worth mentioning that in 1969 the British EMI Electronics and Racal Electronics established, together with the Dutch company Philips Telecommunications, the International Aeradio Southern Africa Ltd., which has obvious military implications. The Philips subsidiaries in South Africa have also been in intense contact with the local military establishment.

They have supplied, for instance, mobile telephones and other telecommunication equipment, including ground-to-air radios, to the South African military and police forces. Furthermore, Philips and its subsidiaries, of which the Transvaal-based Philips Telecommunications Ltd. represents Telecommunications and Defence Systems of the Philips group, supply cameras for aerial surveillance and strategic aerial photography from helicopters and jet fighters. A subsidiary of Philips supplies, in turn, radioaltimeters for use in Mirage III and Mirage F-1 fighters which are built under licence in South Africa.[58]

The electronic industry of the United States is well developed and expansive, and that is why its activity in South Africa can be expected. Many of the electronic companies figure prominently among the top military contractors and operate at the same time subsidiaries in South Africa. Standard Telephone and Cables (STC), is one of the largest electrical manufacturing concerns in the country. It used to be a subsidiary of ITT but in 1978 it was sold to a South African partner. According to one estimate STC, which also participates in the local production of the Mirage fighters, sells about 70 per cent of its turnover to various government departments. In much the same way the South African General Electric, which initiated its operations as early as 1898, is dealing extensively with the South African government and without any doubt some of these transactions have military implications. Motorola South Africa, which is 40 per cent owned by the U.S. company Motorola Inc., is specialized in the production of radio electronics and produces, for instance, two-way radios for the South African police.[59]

It is no wonder that West German electronics firms are also participating in the South African economy. In particular Siemens and AEG-Telefunken are involved in telecommunication engineering which is of special importance to the military. These companies are supplying, for example, electronics for speed boats constructed at Durban, for the installations at the Drumpel military base in Namibia as well as to the armoured cars used by the South African police and military. The most significant undertaking by the West German electronics companies is probably the radar surveillance system Project Advokaat. This project was started in 1969 by the initiative of the Armaments Board, which also financed it, and it was completed in 1973. The surveillance system is composed of a number of stations in various parts of the country, including the illegally occupied Namibia. The headquarters of the Project Advokaat are located at Silvermine, in the vicinity of Cape Town, where the headquarters of the South African navy are also situated. This radar network is also linked with the corresponding NATO installations.[60]

In addition to the electronic firms from major industrialized countries of the West Israeli firms are also active in South Africa, partly because of the special political relations between these two countries. Hi-Distributors, which is a South African firm, is producing look-out towers for counterinsurgency purposes under a licence from Israel. Tadiran Israel Electronic Industries, which is the largest producer of military electronics in its own country, has founded together with South African Galan Group a joint venture near Pretoria. Tadiran is producing, among other things, batteries which are especially important for military walkie-talkies and manpack radios.[61]

In this connection it is not possible to pay any detailed attention to the role of the transnational computer industry in the South African military sector. Sufficed to say that most leading international computer companies, such as IBM, Control Data Corp., Honeywell, Burroughs, International Computers and Sperry Rand, are active in South Africa through various subsidiary arrangements. At the same time the role of computers has also increased in the transmission and processing of information within the police and military establishments. Computers are, for example, necessary in the modern aircraft and missile industry as well as in the operation of various kinds of radar and surveillance networks.

The quantitative and qualitative growth of the South African military establishment has been largely based on the foreign military and semi-military technology supplied by the TNCs. South African military and civilian authorities have naturally realized both the positive and negative aspects of this dependence which is probably most visible, for the time being, in electronics and computer industry. It is out of the question to try to cut down the linkages with the transnational capital and technology, but on the other hand political dangers inherent in these dependence relations have to be minimized. This has been implemented by encouraging licence production, by strengthening the domestic industry and by converting subsidiaries of TNCs from the outward orientation closer to the domestic capital either through acquisitions or by various legislative measures.

The strengthening of the domestic arms industry is a part of a new total national strategy which contains a combination of political, economic and military measures aimed at thwarting external and internal pressures on the privileged position of the Whites. This strategy has been mainly planned by General Magnus Malan, at present the Minister of Defence and a close confidant of the Prime Minister P.W. Botha. Malan's influence is a sign of the growing role of the South African military in controlling and guiding the development of the political and economic system of the country. This is reflected both in the actual decision-making and in the organizational rear-rangements implemented by the Botha government. This tendency has gained prominence especially after the South African intervention in Angola in 1975-76, which could be used as an argument for the increasing dangers posed by the political and military developments in the region to the South African national security.

The total national strategy is, roughly speaking, composed of a more lenient neo-apartheid policy vis-á-vis the Blacks, although the basic tenets of the racial discrimination remain and are even strengthened, the strengthening of the economic and military base of the country and finally the formation of a regional constellation of states under the South African leadership. The new strategy is based on a kind of siege mentality, under which the population is mobilized to respond to the threats and to accept sharp increases in military spending as well as the participation of the military in the political processes. The total national strategy is, in other words, a marriage of military preparedness, economic and technological capacity, fortress mentality and the regional consolidation of power.[62]

5.3.   Egypt

Egypt is located at the intersection of many diverse strategic, political and economic interests. Its role is connected to the developments in the Arab countries of Northern Africa, in the Horn of Africa as well as in the Middle

East and the Persian Gulf. All these factors have considerably influenced the direction of the military and foreign policy of Egypt, although the conflict between Israel and the Arabs, whom Egypt has in a sense represented as a frontline state, has had the most profound effect. To survive in this conflict Egypt has armed heavily by armaments purchased abroad, often financed by its Arab brothers, and by embarking upon the domestic production of arms. Egypt's military policy has been thus dictated by its exposed geographical location, its resolution to confront Israel and its position as the advocate of the collective Arab hatred against Israel.

The Western unwillingness to provide the Nasser regime with arms led to the Soviet initiation of military aid to Egypt in 1955. During the next twenty years the Soviet Union delivered Egypt military aid worth more than three billion dollars. For a long time Egypt was a leading recipient of the Soviet military assistance. The weapons were provided in fairly advantageous terms; the prices were subsidized, the credits were characterized by low interest rates and relatively long grace periods and some of them were paid by cotton exports. It has been estimated that the grant element in the Soviet arms aid to Egypt amounted to some 40 per cent. In spite of these relatively favourable terms the Soviet aid increased the debt burden of Egypt, and it was unable and later on unwilling to repay its debts.

During the latter half of the 1950s the Soviet Union mainly delivered outdated weapons, but since the early 1960s the provision of more modern weaponry was started. The modernity of weapons became an increasingly central factor after the 1967 war when the Soviet Union started a huge effort to compensate the arms which Egypt had lost in the battlefield. It received, for instance, the same type of air defence and other equipment as the Soviet Union's own forces. This conclusion can also be extended to most of the missiles, e.g. the new SA-3, delivered to Egypt. During the 1973 war the Soviet Union continued to resupply the Egyptian forces and at its peak the airlift consisted of 100 daily flights to Arab countries.[63] After the war Egypt's policy started to change, however, and it gradually detached itself from the Soviet Union and turned to the West, particularly to the United States as far as political and military affairs were concerned.

The value of arms imports by Egypt has been estimated as follows:[64]

Table 48.   Arms Imports by Egypt in 1969-77, Millions of Dollars at
             Constant 1976 Prices

	1969	1971	1973	1975	1977
Arms imports	169	487	1074	379	190
The share of arms imports of total imports, per cent	17	39	94	9	4

During 1973-77 Egypt imported $ 1 200 million of its total arms imports of $ 1 748 million from the Soviet Union. The next most important suppliers of arms to Egypt were France ($ 180 million) and the Federal Republic of Germany ($ 140 million).

The Egyptian arms imports peaked, for natural reasons, in 1973 after which a certain decline has been visible. The decline is partly due to a kind of intermediary period during which Egypt turned from the Soviet Union to the United States. It initiated major arms deliveries to Egypt only in 1978. These deliveries have included squadrons of modern fighters as part of the U.S. arms packages to the Middle East. Recently it has been disclosed that the United States will sell Egypt advanced F-15 fighters produced by McDonnell Douglas. In addition, the U.S. military aid program to Egypt, which will amount to four billion dollars over five years, will include Raytheon Hawk anti-aircraft missiles, M-113 armoured personal carriers produced by FMC and McDonnell Douglas F-4 Phantom jets.[65]

In spite of the considerable reliance on imported arms Egypt has also a tradition of domestic arms production. The Helwan aircraft factory was established in the 1950s to develop and produce jet training and combat aircraft. Originally this factory produced De Havilland Vampires under licence, while simultaneously developing several prototypes of fighters. The production of HA-200 fighters was started in 1960. In the 1950s the factory employed some 5 000 persons, both workers and engineers, while the present figure is apparently in the vicinity of 4 000 employees. A measure of

174

horizontal integration in the Egyptian arms industry was sought for by the establishment of the Helwan engine factory to develop and produce engines for the aircraft. The engine factory is said to employ about 250 engineers.

Sakr factory has specialized in the development and production of unguided rocketry since 1953, although it has also made some attempts at developing guided surface-to-surface missiles as well as bombs and other munitions. The factory employs 5 000 people in total. Kader factory is the smallest among these four arms factories, but is active in several programs, including Gomhouria primary trainer for the Egyptian air force and Waleed armoured personal carrier based partly on Magirus Deutz technology. Since the early 1950s these factories have formed the skeleton of the Egyptian arms industry. Its progress was, however, slow for several reasons. The dependence on foreign technology was relatively pronounced. The HA-200 fighter, for instance, was based on the Spanish Hispano HA-200 Saeta and a total of 200 of them were produced at Helwan under licence between 1960-69. The factory also became involved in the design of the supersonic HA-300 fighter. Both of these planes were originally designed and developed by Willy Messerschmitt, while he was working in Spain in the 1950s.[66]

The Egyptian arms programs were plagued by both lack of sufficient technological skills and lack of capital. This resulted in a situation in which the programs had to be cancelled or slowed down because of the shortage of funds. The industry could offer, however, a certain technological capacity which was used in the 1960s mainly in maintaining and refining Soviet military equipment. Thus the Sakr factory was gradually converted to manufacturing a broad range of Soviet artillery rockets; 'in most cases, these items have simply been copied from equipment supplied by the Soviets in the past to Egyptian forces, without any formal licensing agreements. The Helwan engine factory shifted to produce spare parts for engines powering the aircraft supplied by the Soviet Union to Egypt.[67]

Egypt thus became increasingly dependent on Soviet military technology. This tendency was reinforced by the fact that the West virtually boycotted Egypt and denied the transfer of arms and military technology to it. The loosening of relations between the Soviet Union and Egypt after the 1973 war changed, however, the situation. Egypt turned to new sources of arms, ranging from the United States through Western Europe to China. The regional alternative was manifested in the establishment of the Arab Organization of Industrialization (AOI), which took place in 1975. The idea of the joint Arab military industry originally surfaced in 1972 at the meeting of the Heads of General Staffs from 18 Arab countries. The plans established there were ambitious and envisaged the allocation of two per cent of the GNP by each Arab country to this endeavour.

In 1974 the Arab Defence Council proposed a more modest collective allocation of $ 1.2 billion for joint military production. Finally only four Arab countries, viz. Saudi Arabia, Qatar, the United Arab Emirates and Egypt, determined to participate in the AOI, which was orginally known as the Arab Military Industries Organization (AMIO). The Egyptian contribution was to provide six arms factories, including those mentioned above, for the project, while the three other countries made a pledge to provide the initial capital of $ 1.04 billion. The AOI was thus based on a certain division of labour, integrating the Egyptian infrastructure, technology and labour force - which the other participants did not have - with the capital from oil-exporting countries. The operational aims of the consortium included the production of weapons at lower prices, the exportation of the potential surplus to other Muslim countries, in particular to Pakistan, and the transformation of Egypt into a major producer and exporter of weapons.[68]

Egypt did not have, however, sufficient technological capacity at its disposal and that is why the AOI had to turn to transnational arms manufacturers, in particular in Western Europe, to acquire this technology. Although most of the deals, involving both the imports and licence production of arms, were struck towards the end of the 1970s, the pattern manifested itself much earlier. In 1974 a project was agreed between Egypt, Saudi Arabia, France and Great Britain on the licence production of WG-13 Lynx helicopters at the Helwan factory. The participating firms in this contract, the orginal value of which amounted to 110 million francs, involved Westland and Société Nationale Industrielle Aérospatiale (SNIAS).[69]

From this starting point the cooperation between the West European transnational arms manufacturers, including in fact most of the leading companies in the field, and the AOI intensified and resulted in several contracts. They were divided rather evenly between French and British corporations, whose relations were characterized by a mixture of cooperation and rivalry. The French government tried to improve the competitive position of its 'own' companies by marketing their systems on several fronts through high-level political contacts with the Egyptian political leaders.[70] In this competition the U.S. companies were pushed aside and their role was in fact restricted to production of military vehicles. Table 49 contains a summary of the main features of the projects concluded between transnational arms manufacturers and the Arab Organization of Industrialization.[71]

Table 49.   Main Characteristics of the AOI Projects

Joint venture	Product	Established	Total value	Ownership
Arab-British Helicopter Co.	280 helicopters, WG-13 Lynx	n.a.	£ 330 million	AOI 70 %, West-land 30 %
Arab-British Engine Co. (ABECO)	750 GEM-engines for WG-13 Lynx	Febr. 1978	$ 205 million	AOI 70 %, Rolls-Royce 30 %
The Arab-French Aircraft Company	160 Alpha Jet fighters	Sept. 1978	n.a.	AOI, Dassault-Bréguet/Dornier
Arab-British Dynamics Co.	Several thousands of Swingfire anti-tank missiles	Dec. 1977	$ 75 million	AOI 70 %, British Aircraft Corp. 30 %
Arab-French Engine Co. (AFECO)	Larzac and Snecma M.53 engines for Alpha Jets	Nov. 1978	n.a.	AOI 70 %, Snecma 30 %
Arab-Electronics Co.	Military electronics	1978	n.a.	AOI 70 %, CSF-Thomson 30 %
Arab-American Vehicle Co.	12.000 jeeps	1978	$ 30-35 million (estimate)	AOI 51 %, American Motors Corp. 49 %

A salient characteristic of all these projects is that they are based on joint ventures in which the AOI has a controlling majority. These projects depend on the other hand almost completely on the technology transferred by participating TNCs. The application of this technology to the production conditions prevailing in Egypt requires the participation of technical experts from corporations involved. Thus Snecma provides the AFECO project with 35 technical specialists, which is 90 per cent of the total need.[72] More important has been, however, the willingness of the AOI to train its own managerial, technical and production personnel to guarantee the realization of the long-term aim of autonomy in arms production. Thus in 1978 alone some 2 500 persons completed their training in the United States and Western Europe including

> finance, airframe design, gas turbine design, propulsion, flight controls, metallurgy and structure. Both education institutions and industry are involved in this program. The Harvard Business School is providing some of the management finance training in the United States, for example, while such European firms as British Aerospace, Rolls-Royce, Westland and Snecma are providing technical training.

Thus provision of training services has been integrated with the supply of technology and finance to the projects undertaken by the AOI.[73]

For training purposes the AOI has also been funding the Arab Institute for Aerospace Technology which is located in Cairo and assisted in its operation by the U.S., French and British experts. Technical Studies Institute of Saudi Arabia at Dhahran is also providing courses in aerospace engineering. These courses are mostly arranged under the aegis of the government-to-government contract between Great Britain and Saudi Arabia. This contract wa signed in 1973 and in 1977 it was extended for another four years.[74] These examples show to our mind that the training in the Arab military industries and military establishments is highly dependent on foreign skills and knowledge. This is in fact understandable for the reason that practically all weapons systems originate in foreign suppliers which are thus in the best position to provide training and other necessary services.

Aircraft. Already in the 1950s and the 1960s the Egyptian military factories had produced trainers and fighters under various licence arrangements. With the establishment of the AOI, technologically more advanced projects were initiated. The negotiations on the co-production of Alpha Jet trainer close-support aircraft and Mirage 2000 fighters were initiated in 1976 and the contract for Alpha Jets was concluded in September 1978. Alpha Jet is a joint product of Dassault-Bréguet and the West German Dornier. According to the contract 160 Alpha Jets in total should be manufactured at Helwan, although few of them will be delivered complete at the beginning. According to the original plans the factory should have been later adapted to assemble Mirage 2000 fighters. The first Alpha Jets were expected to begin rolling off the AOI production lines in 1980-81 and the first Mirage fighters, which were planned to replace the aging Mig-21 fighters, in 1982.[75]

Westland established with the AOI a joint venture, called the Arab-British Helicopter Co. to produce locally 280 WG.13 Lynx helicopters. According to the contract the first helicopter would have been fully assembled in 1979, while the maximum rate of four helicopters per month would have been assembled in October 1981. In the beginning the implementation of plans proceeded rather smoothly: Westland received the bulk of the total contract of $ 115 million and the production of the first 20 helicopters started in early 1979. These helicopters were produced in Great Britain, but the next 30 vehicles would have been assembled in Egypt from the components imported from Westland factories in Great Britain.[76]

Engines. There is usually a rather high degree of integration between aircraft producers and engine companies; collaborating aircraft and engine manufac-turers are supporting each other in the competition for specific deal vis-à-vis other coalitions of companies. This is also visible in the AOI projects where the organization resorted to the licence production of engines as a part of both the fighter and the helicopter contract. This is no surprise as such because developing countries usually have major problems in the production of aerospace engines and in fact none of them is self-sufficient in this respect.

The Arab-French Engine Co. was established for a fixed period of 20 years, with a provision for extending its activities up to 10 additional years, to produce Larzac turbofan engines for Alpha Jets. The two French companies involved, i.e. Turbomeca and Snecma, provide management and technical personnel for the endeavour. In due time the production line of Larzac was planned to extend to the Snecma N-53 turbofan engine for Mirage 2000 fighters as well as for the potential AOI military aircraft based on indigenous design.[77] Rolls Royce engineers have been, in turn, assisting with the overhaul and repair of the Tumanski turbojets which power Mig-21 fighters supplied by the Soviet Union.[78]

A separate joint venture, Arab-British Engine Co., was established to produce 750 GEM turboshaft engines, originating in Rolls Royce, to power Lynx helicopters. The company is transmitting expertise for the assembly of GEM engines at Helwan. The first 150 engines had to be delivered, however, directly from the Rolls Royce factory at Leavesden, England, with assembly work gradually shifting to Helwan. The contract presupposed that Rolls Royce would train Egyptian manufacturing workers in Great Britain and would also send technical and supervisory personnel to Egypt during the initial phases of the project.[79]

Missiles. The only missile project which has been explicitly connected with the AOI programs is the production of several thousands of Swingfire anti-tank missiles by the Arab-British Dynamics Co. It is a joint venture between the AOI and the British Aerospace Corp., which concluded the $ 75 million contract in December 1977. According to the contract the first Swingfire missile should have been delivered from the production line in September 1979.

Another missile venture, although only indirectly related to the AOI, is the decision of the Egyptian Army to start the licence production of the French Crotale missile. This missile technology is transferred by Thomson-CSF and Matra. Crotale is - like Shahine, a version developed for use in Saudi Arabia - a mobile missile system mounted on a single vehicle and capable of operating near the front line. Egypt has also been planning to acquire improved Hawk and Roland missiles.[80]

Electronics. In the AOI framework Saudi Arabia concluded a joint venture, Arab Electronics Co., with Thomson-CSF. This venture will build a manufacturing facility at Kharj, 50 miles south of Riyadh, which will produce avionics and other sorts of military electronics. One of the first products which the

Arab Electronics Co. has planned to manufacture is a navigation radar under licence from the British Decca Navigator Co. for use in Westland's Lynx helicopters to be built by the AOI. The products of the Arab Electronics Co. are expected to form the backbone of the Saudi surveillance radar and communications equipment needed to control and coordinate their air defence network. An interesting feature in this joint venture is that the technology needed will not come from the French partner only, but licences have been sought also from a number of other leading arms manufacturers.[81]

Thomson-CSF has in general acquired a considerable share of the electronics market in Egypt. The most recent manifestation of this is the huge $ 1.8 billion deal concluded by the Egyptian government with Thomson-CSF and Siemens, whose share of the contract amounts to $ 1.1 billion, on the development of the telecommunications system of the country.[82]

The collapse of the AOI. The peace treaty between Egypt and Israel led to an economic boycott by the great majority of Arab countries against Egypt. In the military field this decision of the Baghdad summit, held in November 1978, culminated in the announcement by the Saudi Defence Minister, Prince Sultan bin-Abdel Aziz, that the AOI and associated joint ventures would be disbanded by July 1, 1979, all investments would be ceased and all outstanding contracts would be cancelled immediately. Saudi Arabia decided to withdraw all its funds from the AOI and a special committee was formed to oversee its liquidation. The dissolution of the AOI was not, however, due only to the Camp David agreement, but in the background one could also see other underlying disagreements which have been based on the competing organizational, financial and military interests of Egypt and the other participating Arab states.[83]

The withdrawal of Saudi Arabia and other oil exporters from the AOI resulted in a financial crisis, because Egypt did not have resources to continue the support of the projects. Although precise information is lacking it seems that most AOI projects have been killed, but some new approaches have simultaneously been considered. This has meant financial losses to at least some of the participating TNCs, but they will be partly compensated by the new orders from, for example, Saudi Arabia and Qatar.[84] Egypt has held hundreds of millions of dollars in production equipment and machinery without returning them to Saudi Arabia. By relying on these resources President Sadat has announced that the activities of the AOI will be continued in a new form as the Egyptian Organization for Military Industrialization.

U.S. transnational arms manufacturers have shown some interest in the cooperation with Egypt and proposals for co-production have been made. The reliance on the United States as well as on the U.S. corporations would alleviate the financial problems faced by the arms production in Egypt. In total $ 4 billion will be transferred to Egypt over a five-year period as military aid and credits, connected to the implementation of the Camp David agreement. Egypt will receive $ 1.5 billion of this money for the fiscal year 1979 through fiscal 1981. In fact teams of Pentagon specialists visited Egypt during 1979 to explore how some of the funds allocated for Egypt could be used in shoring up the Egyptian military industry.[85]

Egypt has become, by its own initiative and by the pressure of developments, an important U.S. ally in the Middle East. It is sending weapons and military advisers to pro-Western countries in Africa, training muslim rebels from Afghanistan and providing military facilities such as the Wardi Kenna airfield, to the U.S. forces. The United States has, in turn, done its best in supporting the stability of the Sadat regime as a part of the overall military and political strategy in the Middle East.[86]

One of the consequences of the Arab boycott against Egypt has been that the U.S. arms manufacturers start replacing their West European cousins. The Egyptian military industry will increasingly shift, as the entire country has done, to utilize the U.S. technology and capital. So far the only U.S. company operating in the military sector of Egypt has been American Motors, which has committed itself to producing 12 000 jeeps for the Egyptian army. The decision of Egypt to continue the production activities started in the AOI framework is understandable for the reason that there are now some 15 000 high-skill jobs and a new transnational channel to obtain advanced military technology and funds.

Egypt cannot however operate the Helwan and other factories alone and that is why it has to rely on foreign sources of technology and capital. If West

Europeans do not have enough money to continue the activities without Saudi support, Egypt must start courting the U.S. transnational corporations. It is in fact rather easy because of the close military and political relations now existing between the U.S. and Egyptian governments. A consequence of the visits by the U.S. experts to Egypt is the plan to start the production of Northrop F-5 jets and Bell 214ST helicopters in Egyptian factories. They would replace the production of Alpha Jets and Lynx helicopters.[87]

Such contracts are only logical after the statement by President Sadat that Egypt would 'turn to the American people for help' to compensate the negative effects of 'Saudi policy of bribery' which has persuaded Arab countries to break relations with Egypt.[88] The cancellation of the AOI contracts with a number of West European companies was a rather serious blow for most of them, because these companies had already experienced difficulties in the loss of the Iranian market. These cumulative effects have increased pressure to seek for alternative markets in the Middle East and elsewhere.

From the standpoint of the Egyptian economy the production of arms has no doubt enhanced the technological skills in the factories concerned. Although the lofty aim of the AOI was to achieve an autonomous capacity to produce weapons and military technology there was no evidence, partly because of the short time of operation, that the degree of independence had in reality increased. On the contrary the reliance on foreign military technology, controlled by transnational corporations, was substantial. This was not only the case with the engines and electronics, which are the 'normal' bottlenecks, but the dependence was much more general in its character.[89] On the other hand there is very little evidence that any technological spill-over from the military to the civilian industry had operated. The AOI factories have been rather effectively isolated from the civilian industries and they have indeed been more of bridgeheads of foreign technology, both during the Soviet and AOI periods, than integral parts of the domestic economy.

5.4.   Iran

As a "forward defence area" of the West and as a member of CENTO military alliance, Iran has had a priority status in Western strategy. Until 1967 it was a major receiver of U.S. military assistance, but in November 1967 the U.S. declared Iran a developed country, terminated economic aid and initiated the termination of military aid by 1969. In 1950-78 Iran received $ 766.7 million U.S. military assistance.[90] After 1967 Iran started to pay its increasing arms purchases with oil revenues, and at that time it also tried to diversify its foreign dependencies. In February 1967 it concluded an agreement to exchange Soviet military equipment - nonarmoured vehicles, troop carriers and anti-aircraft guns - for Iranian natural gas and other raw materials. Iran also purchased arms from France, Italy, the USA and Britain.[91] In 1967, the Shah declared: "Our independence is now firmly established".[92]

Until the mid-1960s Iranian military equipment was rather simple and aimed mainly at the maintenance of internal security. But at the end of the 1960s Iran became more concerned with the security in the whole Persian Gulf area. With this growing concern, the Shah started to build up his army, navy and air forces for operations in the Persian Gulf, particularly to guard Iran's oil installations. Imports of modern Western weapons systems started, e.g. jet fighters were purchased from the U.S., helicopters from Italy and from France later on, missiles from the U.S., the UK and Italy, and naval vessels from the UK and the US.[93]

Although the U.S. arms supplies increased rapidly, critical voices against the arms deals went unheard and were suppressed by defence personnel or representatives of the armament industry. The U.S. Agency for International Development objected to McDonnell F-4 sales on the ground that Iran needed the funds for development. Senator Fulbright, the Chairman of the Foreign Relations Committee, said in the hearings in 1967:[94]

> I have been in Iran and it is a most desolate country. There are very few rich people, but the majority could easily turn to revolution. I think you are doing a great dis-service to them loading them down with these arms.

In the 1970s Iran continued to build up the military capacity; e.g. in 1970 the defence expenditures rose by 50 per cent. The real arms boom started, however, in 1972.[95] After the British withdrawal from the Persian Gulf area, President Nixon promised to provide the Shah with virtually any conventional weapon he desired. Several factors can be seen in the background of this decision. First, the British had withdrawn from the Persian Gulf area. Thus Iran assumed the role of a regional policeman. Secondly, this was a period when the Nixon doctrine was launched. The purpose of this doctrine was to decrease the direct military presence of the U.S. troops abroad and increase the military capabilities of important countries; particularly the creation of regional power centres (or 'new influentials') was to become essential in the new, indirect military strategy.[96] Thirdly, the end of the Vietnam War was in sight. Many arms manufacturers had increased their capacity during the war, and there was a risk of overcapacity crisis. After the rapidly rising oil revenues since 1973, Iran became one of the largest arms importers of the world and finally number one. Arms imports thus became a way of "recycling" petrodollars.

After 1973, the strategic role of the Persian Gulf area increased rapidly. The fact that Iran was ready to assume the role of the regional policeman was welcomed in the West, as expressed in a research report by the Atlantic Council:[97]

> The changes in Iran require a new assessment of the problem of security in the Persian Gulf. The Shah's ambitions outran his capabilities, yet his policies and actions in the region were not without positive results: Iranian forces helped Oman to control the rebellion in Dhofar province which was being fueled by the Soviet-supported regime in South Yemen; Iran helped Oman to assure the security of the Strait of Hormuz, the narrow and vulnerable point on the oil route from the Gulf to world markets; Iran's forces provided a balance to the Soviet supplied Iraqi forces and helped to safeguard the security of smaller Gulf states against possible pressure from Iraq; Iran cooperated with Saudi Arabia, the leading state on the other side of the Gulf; and the Shah's plan for a security organization of Gulf states, although premature, was a constructive proposal that brought those states together for the discussion of common problems.

The U.S. Arms Control and Disarmament Agency has estimated Iran's arms imports from different supplier countries during 1973-77 as follows:

Table 50. Arms Transfers to Iran in 1973-77 by Major Supplier, Cumulative Values in Million Current Dollars

Supplier	$ Million 1973-1977	Per cent
United States	5 425	77.4
Federal Republic of Germany	400	5.7
Soviet Union	390	5.6
United Kingdom	350	5.0
Italy	150	1.4
Canada	80	1.1
Others	110	1.6
Total	7 005	100.0

Source: World Military Expenditures and Arms Transfers 1968-1977. U.S. Arms Control and Disarmament Agency, Washington 1979, p. 156.

The growth of Iran's arms arsenals has been rapid. Starting with poorly equipped military establishments in the 1960s, Iran had acquired 427 supersonic aircraft, 1 200 main battle tanks, more than 700 surface-to-surface missiles and more than 700 helicopters by 1975. The weapons imported by Iran were most sophisticated: McDonnell Douglas's F-4 Phantom, Grumman's F-14 Tomcat, Northrop's F-5, Lockheed's P-3 C Orion anti-submarine aircraft, as well as the most controversial of all: Boeing's E-3C AWACS aircraft (Airborne Warning and Control System). Military transport aircraft was bought from VFW-Fokker and Lockheed (Hercules). Iran also ordered General Dynamics's F-16 fighters but these deliveries did not start before the collapse of the Shah's regime.[98] As can be noted the Shah bought most sophisticated models; he did not want to stay behind the NATO countries as far as armament sophistication was concerned. In an interview with the British journalist Anthony Sampson the Shah explained:[99]

> I hope my good friends in Europe and the United States and elsewhere will finally understand that there is absolutely no difference between Iran and France, Britain and Germany. Why should you find it

absolutely normal that France will spend that much money on her army, and not my country?

It was not always the Shah who took initiatives for new purchases. At least in the case of AWACS aircraft the order was just as much pushed by the Pentagon, who made the offer to keep the aircraft's production line open until the European NATO countries reached decisions on their purchases. The price of seven AWACS aircraft for Iran was $ 1.2 billion, consisting of $ 718.7 million for the aircraft and $ 510.2 million for spares, maintenance and support, site survey and training.[100]

When Grumman sold 80 Tomcat to Iran, the deal was worth more than $ 1 billion for the company (in 1975). The spares, ground support equipment, training and maintenance cost about a half of the sum, while the other half was for the planes. For Grumman the deal was most welcome, since the company had financial difficulties at that time.[101] In addition, the Shah spent about $ 1 billion more on engines and weaponry.

The political authorities in the United States were well aware of the unrealistic nature of Iran's purchases with regard to Iran's technological capabilities. A Senate Foreign Relations Committee report in 1976 stated that "Iran will not be able to absorb and operate within the next five to ten years a large proportion of the sophisticated military systms it has purchased from the United States unless increasing numbers of American personnel go to Iran in a support capacity".[102]

The purchases of a large number of foreign aircraft led to the establishment of Iran Aircraft Industries (IACI) in 1970 with the assistance and 49 per cent participation of Northrop Worldwide Services. The company's main tasks were overhaul, repair, manufacture of components, modification and some assembly of Iran's aircraft and engines. IACI occupies two 170 000 m^2 sites at Mehrabad airport, Tehran, and employs 3 000-4 000 persons, of whom about one third are foreigners. The equipment needed by the company is predominantly imported from the US and maintenance is organized along USAF lines. Lockheed was also a contractor in IACI's expansion program (Peace Log). It had a $ 138 million contract for providing a logistics system for the Iranian Air

Force. IACI was planning to become a licence producer of spares and a co-producer of aircraft engines, and eventually a manufacturer of airframes, too. The Northrop company, a minority owner of IACI, did its best to promote business with Iran, e.g. in 1976 the company promised the Iranian government to help in oil marketing if Iran bought F-18 Cobra of Northrop and McDonnell Douglas.[103]

Most of Iran's helicopters came from Bell Textron either directly or through the licence producer Agusta. Again the orders were sometimes very large, e.g. in 1973 489 helicopters for $ 720 million. The deal concerning 50 large Chinhook helicopters, which are produced by Agusta with Boeing's licence, was a typical arms-for-oil deal since in exchange Iran agreed to sell 5 million tons of crude oil to Italy. Agusta has later said that Iran and Libya are its main export customers, and the Chinhook contract was worth $ 425 million for the company.[104] The large helicopter deals were accompanied by an agreement to start assembly and licence production of Bell's Model 214 in a government factory. The cost of this program was $ 650 million in 1978, and would also have resulted in large imports of helicopter parts. Bell also had a co-development plan with Iran for a new super-transport 214, the prototypes of which were supposed to fly in 1979. The development work was going on in Isfahan facilities, 100 miles South of Tehran, where also the pilot and mechanic training schools were located. The turnkey manufacturing facility was valued at more than $ 575 million through 1985. Now that the co-development with Iran has been cancelled, Bell now continues the program alone in the USA and plans to start deliveries of the new model in 1982.[105]

The present regime of Iran has decided to keep the helicopter fleets in operation, but there are great problems with spares and overhaul work, as well as political difficulties. Iran has turned to German-Dutch VFW-Fokker to have its Sikorsky mine sweeping helicopters repaired and overhauled for patrol over the vital strait of Hormuz.[106] This inquiry brings a new aspect to the question of the implications of transnational helicopter production: such situations are possible where the different producers of the same model compete for orders. This will be the case if VFW takes the job which is lost by Sikorsky. On the other hand international production gives Sikorsky possibilities to delegate more controversial orders to its licence partner in case the U.S. authorities do not permit Sikorsky's work in the present Iran.

Iran's missile imports were more diversified than the imports of aircraft and helicopters. The main U.S. suppliers were Hughes, Raytheon, McDonnell Douglas and Ford Aerospace and Communications, but also British Aerospace and Short Brothers as well as the French Aérospatiale made major sales. Again some of the orders were very large: British Aerospace's contract for Rapier surface-to-air missile deal for $ 800 million, Hughes's 400 Phoenix air-to-air missiles for $ 250-300 million, 300 McDonnell Douglas Harpoon missiles for $ 100 million, 360 Raytheon Hawks for $ 30 million, just to mention some examples.[107]

For missiles, too, Iran had co-production programs. A joint venture Irano-British Dynamics was formed in 1976 between Iran Electronics Industry (65 per cent) and British Aerospace Corp. for the production of Rapier missiles since 1980. For BAC the program was worth £ 400 million. Another joint venture was formed between Iran Electronics Industry and Hughes Aircraft to manufacture TOW-missiles in Shiraz. Westinghouse also assisted in this project and Litton Industries planned to have the company as a subcontractor for high grade electronic components.[108]

With the vast military build-up the need for military electronics also became evident. The electronization of Iran took place on many levels: large turnkey communication and defence projects, weapons electronics, computers, services etc. A modern communication network was planned under the leadership of American Telegraph and Telephone; this program had both civilian and military functions. Ford Aerospace and Communiations was involved in the engineering of defence systems, too. In 1975, the New York Times announced that Rockwell International would install a most secret intelligence system called IBEX, capable of listening to all civil and military electronic communication in the Gulf region. The project cost was supposed to be about $ 500 million. In 1975 GTE received a contract for 2 million telephone lines and equipment, worth $ 500 million. Rockwell also had another contract for earth and air surveillance.[109]

Iran had a plan to create modern electronics industry. Numerous Western electronic companies opened offices in Iran, and many companies started joint ventures. One of the first ones was a company called Computer Terminals, which was owned by Control Data and Iranian Electronics Industries (30 per cent and 70 per cent). The company was to produce computer terminals not just for Iran but also for export markets, mostly to Western Europe.[110] The list of electronic companies who rushed to Iran after 1973 is rather long. Some examples: Litton Industries defence systems, Emerson Electric missile launchers, Computer Sciences, General Electric aircraft engines, Honeywell security systems, ITT telecommunication, IBM computers, Motorola military systems, communication equipment, microwave systems, Systems Development Corp. electronic engineering, Westinghouse military electronics, radars, RCA communication, Racal Electronics defence systems, Watkins Johnson surveillance, reconnaissance and electronic warfare applications, Electronic data systems computer services for administration (a $ 20.5 million contract).[111]

Besides armaments, weapons and associated equipment, Iran started massive plans for military infrastructure. Fifty new airports were being constructed, as well as large airspace controls for civilian and military traffic. Thirty centres for logistics were built along the coast of the Persian Gulf. Large underground halls were constructed for Phantom fighters in Dezfoul base. Many new military bases were built, or equipped with new technology. The naval command centre in Banda-Abbas was supposed to cost $ 200 million, and the Chabbahar base close to Pakistan border cost $ 60-70 milion. Numerous installations were constructed for radars, navigation and so on.[112]

There are no exact figures available on the numer of foreign personnel in Iran. In 1975 it was estimated that Iran would need some 50 000 foreign technicians, trainers and advisors for its defence by 1980.[113] In December 1978 the U.S. State Department said that 35 000 Americans had left Iran within a few weeks but it was not indicated how many of them were normal businessmen, dependents or defence personnel.[114] According to Aviation Week & Space Technology altogether 8 830 persons in American military, civil service and Defence Dept. contractor personnel worked in Iran in November 1978.[115] The number of British, Italian or German personnel is not known. The transnational military companies with business in Iran must have had thousands of persons in the country. Information has been published on some U.S. companies only: Bell

3 000, Grumman 350, Northrop 650, General Electric 24, Westinghouse 100, Lockheed 500, Boeing 350, United Technologies 200.[116] In addition, we must note that the foreign personnel had their dependents with them. So, the role of immigrants was remarkable in Iranian society and culture. It is useful to note that the foreign technical staff consisted only of people who "knew everything better" while the role of the Iranians was to follow their model. There is a basic inequality in such relationships; the local population in almost any country dislikes foreigners who come and tell them how to do things.

The rush of foreign armament industries to Iranian markets lasted for about 5-6 years and suddenly it was over.

The U.S. armament industry had a backlog of orders from Iran for $ 12 billion at the beginning of 1979, and at least $ 10 billion of it has now been cancelled. The British government had orders for $ 4.7 billion, and a report stated:[117]

> The crisis in Iran could have disastrous consequences for Britain's flourishing arms export industry, which for the past few years has prized the Shah as biggest single customer ... in all, Iran, together with Saudi Arabia, has accounted for about 60 per cent of Britain's arms export business.

The Iranian revolution will influence arms markets for a long time, particularly because it coincided with another "failure" for transnational arms industries, i.e. the fall of the planned Arab Organization for Industrialization (AOI) in Egypt. The losers are by and large not the same because the AOI was mainly a European undertaking while the military industry in Iran was mainly the market for American companies.

Iran may sell back part of the arms that it had already received.[118] Some of the arms which were still on production lines, will be offered to new customers with intensified marketing campaigns. Perhaps some companies may even consider conversion into civilian programs, because of the unpredictability of military markets. The feelings of Iran's present regime were clearly expressed by the Deputy Secretary of State Amir Entezam while he was in Washington trying to sell back the U.S. Tomcat fighters:[119]

> Instead of using the money for roads, water, bread and health, the Shah wasted money to this mad arms business. Against whom would we fight with our F-14 aircraft?

Iran is one of those cases which should be studied very carefully, when the relationships between international power politics, arms transfers, economic strategies and internal developments are being discussed and evaluated. Iran could be approached as a good lesson, which shows that there can be something basically wrong in the power-political conception of the world. Iran was a victim of power-political ideas both in international and internal relationships. In the international dimension, there was a massive penetration of Western culture, arms, companies and experts. The whole penetration contained power-political elements since those who penetrated believed that their culture and knowledge was superior.

Part of the local population, e.g. representatives of the Shah administration, joined the admiration of Western superculture, and thus acted as bridgeheads of the penetration process. Internationally, there was a power-political idea to have Iran working as a regional policeman in an important oil-producing area. Finally, there was a power-political idea of the Shah that he could rule without asking what the people felt or needed. The foreign TNCs, which extensively and intensively participated in Iran's development in the 1970s have cited the case as a "failure". A more positive approach would see the case of Iran as a good historical lesson.[120]

5.5.   India

India is a regional power centre with large area, population and influence. During 30 years of independence, it has emphasized non-alliance and autonomy of foreign policy, which is also reflected in its arms acquisition policy and policies concerning military production. Besides autonomy of decision, the regional conflicts have naturally also affected armament needs and decisions. During the last 30 years India has been involved in five military conflicts: in 1947-48 with Pakistan over the Kashmir area, in 1961 with Portugal over Goa, in 1962 with China at the border, in 1965 again with Pakistan over Kashmir and the borders, and in 1971 with Pakistan over East Pakistan, which ended up with Indian intervention and formation of the new independent state of Bangladesh. International tensions are intertwined with the internal problems and huge development needs of these societies. Thus, non-alliance and autonomy, regional instabilities and internal development needs form the conditions of Indian armament policies.[121]

Until about 1960 India imported mainly British weapons. The reason for this was experience: the Indian military was used to and trained for British weapons. During the 1950s India and Pakistan together accounted for about half of the British exports of major weapons, while during the period 1960-72 their share fell to 23 per cent. Some French and Canadian weapons were imported, too, but no arms or military aid from the US or the Soviet Union were accepted.[122] While Pakistan joined the Western military alliances CENTO and SEATO, India emphasized non-alliance.

In 1960-64 major changes in armament policies took place, due to the three military conflicts. During the conflict with China, India asked for military assistance from the United States, NATO and the Soviet Union. It started importing their weapons on both commercial and aid terms. After the war with Pakistan a change in the arms acquisition pattern took place again. As the West was not able or willing to supply arms on sufficiently favourable terms, India increasingly came to rely on Soviet supplies.[123] With arms imports for over $ 1.6 billion in 1961-71 India was the sixth largest arms importer in the Third World after South Vietnam, North Vietnam, Egypt, South Korea and Turkey. The Indian subcontinent showed characteristics of a regional arms race, since the Indian and Pakistani arms imports were closely correlated.[124]

In the 1970s the Indian arms imports were divided as follows:

Table 51.   Indian Imports of Major Weapons by Main Supplier Countries in
             1973-77, Million Current Dollars and Per Cent

Supplier country	Arms imports 1973-1978	Per cent
Soviet Union	1 100	85.1
United Kingdom	40	3.1
Poland	40	3.1
France	30	2.3
United States	22	1.7
Federal Rep. of Germany	10	0.8
Czechoslovakia	10	0.8
Others	40	3.1
Total	1 292	100.0

Source: World Military Expenditures and Arms Transfers 1968-1977.
           U.S. Arms Control and Disarmament Agency, Washington D.C.
           1979, p. 156.

Note: ACDA calculates the values of Soviet arms on the basis of
           prices of corresponding Western arms. Indian arms imports are
           also difficult to estimate because of the extensive practice of
           licence production.

As can be observed from the table, the Soviet Union was the leading supplier
of arms to India in the 1970s. The largest single deals were 100 MIG-21 M
fighters which were delivered in 1973-79 and 150 MIG-21 bis fighters,
delivered in 1977-78. The MIG-series are designed by Mikojan and the Soviet
Union also granted a licence for their production in India. Other major Soviet
supplies were Iljusin anti-submarine and patrol aircraft, Kamov helicopters,
various types of missiles (sometimes in rather large quantities), various naval
ships and armoured vehicles. The role of the socialist countries is further
strengthened by the delivery of Polish jet trainers and Czech armoured
vehicles.[125]

Until 1977 the Western supplies consisted of Westland helicopters, Britten
Norman's light transport planes, Short missiles as well as Hawker Siddley's

(now part of British Aerospace) Gnat and HS-748 aircraft, which are also produced with licence in India. The Western powers did not grant any licences for missiles at this time, while part of the Soviet missiles were provided with licences.[126]

Toward the end of the 1970s - i.e. after the period covered by Table 51 - the Indian arms import pattern again changed. After the large MIG-deals the relative share of the Soviet Union has declined, while the Western share has risen. In 1978 India decided to buy Jaguar fighters, produced jointly by British Aerospace and Dassault. The project was worth $ 1.8 billion. It was envisaged that India would import about 40 Jaguars from BAe, assemble 45 and manufacture about 45 more in India. The deal was, however, reconsidered after the Congress party came to power in January 1980. At the time of this writing it seems likely that India will increase the number of outright purchases and cancel the indigenous part of the deal. One of the main reasons is that a Jaguar built in India is twice as expensive as a Jaguar purchased from Britain.

The Janata government also ordered 30 Sea Harriers from BAe to be delivered later on. The Gandhi government has cancelled part of these purchases, too. The role of Western arms supplies was further strengthened by continuing sales of Westland and Short Brothers; also the British Vickers sold 1 000 tanks with a licence. These tanks are called Vijaynta in India. France has also increased its sales in India. Aérospatiale (SNIAS) has sold 239 helicopters with licences for production and Matra has sold missiles with licences. Dassault, a partial supplier of Jaguar, has also sold Alize fighters; in addition, it has offered India the rights to manufacture the sophisticated Mirage 2000 as well as Mirage F1. To complete the picture of Western arms supplies we may refer to the sales of Boeing transport aircraft and West German submarines.

Latest developments have, however, again lifted the Soviet share in Indian arms imports. In 1980 India, in its largest-ever purchase, signed a $ 1.6 billion agreement to buy Soviet weapons. India asked for sophisticated T-72 tanks, four squadrons of MIG-23s, missile-equipped patrol boats and surface-to-surface missiles. As far as the tanks are concerned, India will probably buy 200 T-72 tanks and later produce an estimated 600 more under licence. The present Soviet credit is repayable over 17 years and carries a low interest rate, according to newspapers. Previous Soviet arms credits to India carried a 2 per cent interest rate and were repayable over 10 years.[127]

On the basis of this information we can conclude that after the period of strong dependence on Soviet supplies India increased imports of British and French weapons and weapon systems, but recently again increased Soviet supplies. It is also notable that some British and French industries, which have expanded their market shares in India in the 1970s (Westland, SNIAS, Dassault and Matra) are also major suppliers for Pakistan.

Since there is, to some extent, a regional arms race going on between India and Pakistan, it seems to be the same companies who make money out of it. On the other hand it must be added that the total import pattern of Pakistan differs from that of India, particularly because of the large Chinese supplies.[128]

It is not unique in the history of arms trade in the Indian peninsula that the same suppliers provide weapons for rival parties. The same problem existed in the mid-sixties when the political situation was tense because of the war:[129]

> By the mid-sixties, Congress was becoming more worried by the effects of arms sales in the Third World, partly as a result of the Indo-Pakistan war of 1965, where American arms (together with those of other countries) were used on both sides. Pakistanis in Patton tanks fought Indians in Sherman tanks, and both armies were flown in American transports. The United States soon embargoed the supply of arms to both sides (though later relenting to supply 'non-lethal' arms), but the American role in the war aroused sharp recrimination: 'The arms we supplied under this policy', said J.K. Galbraith, the former Ambassador to India, 'caused the war ... If we had not supplied arms, Pakistan would not have sought the one thing we wanted above all to avoid: namely the military solution.'

Although India imports 74 per cent of the total South Asian weapons and was the sixth largest Third World importer in 1978, it has always emphasized the role of indigenous arms production to promote its non-alliance and self-reliance.[130] This aim is clearly expressed by the Indian Ministry of Defence:[131]

The main thrust of defence production is towards the twin objective of modernization of arms and equipment and achievement of progressive self-reliance and self-sufficiency.

India's indigenous arms production consists of fighters, light trainers, smaller warships, military electronics, small weapons and ammunition. In addition the country has extensive licence production of all weapons categories. In fact, India is a state which has both large imports and large production of weapons. The division of labour between imports and national production seems to be that major and most complex weapons systems are imported while lighter and less complicated weapons are produced at home. This general notion must be qualified, however. India is very consciously trying to become able to produce more complex weapons itself. This is the reason why licences are often demanded in connection with purchases (e.g. MIG). India maintains a large scientific and technical apparatus, with the aim to become autonomous in complex military technology too. Compared to the developing countries in general it allocates a great deal of money to military R&D. It is of particular interest in this connection that India has also invested in the research and production of special materials for military production (like special steels and alloys) - a weak point in the military production of the developing countries in general.[132]

The leading producer of weapons systems is government-owned Hindustan Aeronautics Ltd., which is engaged in aircraft, aeroengine, ancillary systems and accessories manufacture. HAL employs over 40 000 persons, and the reported sales in 1977 amounted to $ 158 million. HAL produces fighter and training aircraft, of which 6 models are based on indigenous designs (e.g. Marut, Kiran). Many essential parts of these indigenous models are, however, imported. The engines are imported from Rolls Royce (UK) and Avco Lycoming USA). Weaponry and electronics are often imported, too.[133]

HAL is also one of the leading licence producers in the Third World. At present its licence production includes Lama and Alouette helicopters (SNIAS), Gnat-trainers (BAe), HS-748 transport planes (BAe) and MIG-fighters (Mikojan).[134] Extensive licence production is a result of Indian demands in all armament imports: it wants licences, a high degree of indigenous work, transfers of technology and know-how, and participation in the development and design processes to increase HAL's designing capacities. Finally, India also wants the right to export parts made in India. Only companies reacting positively to these demands are welcomed as partners in international arms transfers.[135] When India decided to buy Jaguar aircraft, it demanded that 75 per cent of the work should be done in India. BAe also agreed to buy Indian-manufactured spares once the production has started.[136]

HAL has recently decided to invest $ 60 million in new plants, equipment and particularly numerically controlled machine tools over the next few years.[137] Therefore many efforts are made to secure work in the future; particular attention has been paid to Indian designing capacity. International co-development of new weapons systems has high priority, since in that process foreign design know-how is being transferred to India. French SNIAS has agreed to develop a new armoured helicopter jointly with HAL. It will be powered with Turbomeca's engines (France), and it will fly in 1981.[138] HAL has discussed possibilities for joint development of civil transport aircraft with the German Dornier and Dornier has agreed to train 75 HAL engineers for the project. Because Dornier was responsive to the Indian demands, it was chosen as a partner instead of the U.S. Beech, which did not want to transfer designing know-how. Also the German MBB has shown interest in Indian aircraft design.[139]

India has presented similar demands for indigenization to the Soviet Union. When it comes to MIG-21M, India produces 75 per cent of the plane. In the case of the more sophisticated MIG-21 bis, India has demanded a high share of Indian work as well and plans to manufacture spares and avionics also for export to the Soviet Union. The Soviet Union has been very restrictive in sales of spares to third countries, however, although India has been willing for third country exports. Both Egypt and Indonesia have turned to India for MIG spare parts but they have been turned down; on the other hand, India was able to sell spares to Iraq in 1977.[140]

Two divisions of HAL are engaged in engine production, but so far they are strongly dependent on foreign technology. The Koraput division builds Soviet Tumanski engines for HAL-built MIG-21M fighters. The other division at Bangalore builds Turbomeca's engines for helicopters built with Aérospatiale's licences. The same division has three licences for Rolls Royce engines which are used in aircraft built with British licences. The Bangalore division is promoted by India's Gas Turbine Research Establishment, which has worked for many years to develop new, totally Indian engines, but this program has had problems.[141] Indians have also demanded that the Soviet Union should provide them with adequate technology for the production of the latest generation of jet fighter engines. They have also wanted to manufacture engine spares in India, instead of sending Soviet engines to Moscow for repair.[142]

In the field of military electronics India has tried to develop its own capacity. Bharat Electronics manufactures communication equipment for defence purposes, wireless transmitters, radars etc. 3 000 scientists and 5 000 technicians are employed in nearly three dozen laboratories, i.e. Bharat is a large complex even by international standards. Its programs include missiles and rockets, aeronautics and avionics, electronics, radars and naval equipment.[143] Bharat Dynamics produces Soviet Atoll-missiles with a licence. It also has licences from the French Matra for air-to-air missiles and from SNIAS for antitank missiles. Bharat has also become a partner in the international vertical division of labour.[144] The Swiss company Oerlikon-Bührle has sold Bharat Electronics a licence to build parts for fire control radars. The parts are then exported to Switzerland where the final production and assembly of the whole system takes place. The Swiss TNC then exports these radar systems in large quantities. Bharat has said that it has similar arrangements with U.S., British, German and Australian companies. It is evident that in this case the low wages in Indian industry are an incentive for the involvement of the company in the international production scheme of transnational armament industry, the result being a role of an international subcontractor.[145]

Despite the advances within electronic industry Indian weapons are often equipped with electronics produced by foreign TNCs. Particularly British and French firms supply electronics for Indian weapons. This situation is an indication of the fact that despite large efforts India has not been able to proceed to the most complex fields of military electronics. This does not surprise anybody; how could a newcomer India achieve such a level when even the most important military technology in Europe and in the U.S. is produced by a few TNCs only with enormous state funding. On the other hand the dependence of India on foreign military electronics is also an automatic result of the licensing system: foreign weapons are imported as packages, and the foreign suppliers want to produce the most complex parts of the weapons themselves instead of transferring technology abroad. The Indian share in production consists of less advanced and labour-intensive parts. The TNCs want to enjoy their monopoly of the most advanced military and civilian technology to preserve their competitive edge vis-à-vis potential new rivals.

In this connection it is relevant to observe that the United States has recently announced that it will be ready to sell highly sophisticated military electronics to India. This announcement came after the U.S. had published its intention to supply Pakistan with large quantities of arms after the Soviet intervention in Afghanistan. India has been willing to buy items like guidance systems for aircraft, missiles and so-called smart bombs, and it would probably allocate $ 200 million to these imports.[146]

Electronic industry is one of the high-priority areas of Indian industrial policy.[147] This is logical since India has skilled labour power, designing capability and technically qualified personnel - in this respect India differs from, e.g. South East Asian countries, whose electronic industry is rather based on large unskilled labour reserves. The existence of qualified but comparatively cheap labour power in India has, however, already led to subcontracting in some cases, as the example of the Swiss connections with Bharat shows. It is quite possible that a similar situation arises in the aircraft industry. By exploiting Indian dependence on TNC technology the foreign companies can start subcontracting practices with India. Such a situation is not commensurable with the goal of self-reliance, expressed repeatedly in official statements. The economic results within the electronic industry do not necessarily promote self-reliance, either.

According to Economic and Political Weekly, the import content of Indian electronic industries is so high that foreign exchange outflows exceed the export earning.[148]

The will to participate in the technological arms race on all fronts has also resulted in ambitious Indian space programs. India has developed rockets, launch vehicles and experimental satellites of its own.[149] Foreign technology is needed, however. The civilian spacecraft for weather, TV relay and communication purposes is built by Ford Aerospace and Communications.[150] With the Soviet Union India has built two scientific satellites but further information is not available. In 1983-84 India intends to launch a resource-sensing satellite. In July 1980 India launched Rohini satellite with the SLV-3 rocket, which can be in principle modified into an intermediate-range ballistic missile. India has officially denied, however, the allegations that it is starting to develop IRBMs for military use.[151]

Indian armament industry can be seen as an example of the difficulties that arise when a developing country tries to follow the technological arms race, or even participate in it. Several important problems can be noted. The first one concerns the R&D capacity, so scarce in the developing countries. When India has decided to mobilize a large part of R&D capacity for military purposes, the resources are taken away from other sectors. The Indian Defence Research and Development Organization and related military research projects employ more scientists, engineers and technicians than private industry as a whole. Arms production absorbs 200 000 people, most of them highly qualified.[152]

The second problem concerns the degree of autonomy and self-reliance with regard to foreign suppliers. The fact that foreign designs and licences are bought already tells of dependence. After the production rights have been achieved, the share of indigenous work in the total value of weapons can be used as an indicator of dependence or independence. The bigger the indigenous share, the more self-reliant armament production. There are different possibilities: e.g. indigenous design with plenty of foreign parts and components or foreign design with plenty of indigenous components.

The development work for Indian fighter/ground attack aircraft HF-24 Marut started in 1958. In 1972, after 14 years of development and production, the foreign content was still 30 per cent.

The production of the Soviet fighter MIG-21FL was started in 1964. In 1972 the Indian share was 40 per cent. A better result was achieved in case of the British-Indian Gnat, the Indian share being 85 per cent. At the beginning of the

1960s India decided to have an indigenous battle tank. The British firm Vickers Armstrong sold the design of a modified British Chieftain tank. The first prototype was completed in 1963, and the first Vijaynta tank was ready in 1965. In 1968, after 66 tanks had been delivered, the indigenous content was 43 per cent. In 1972, after 400 tanks had been completed, the Indian content was 68 per cent. In missiles, built with a licence (Aérospatiale), Bharat factory is able to produce 70 per cent of the value. The Indian shipbuilding industry is considered very strong in the Third World. The Indian share of the first Indian-built frigate was 53 per cent. The second frigate Himgiri, which was delivered in 1975, was 75 per cent Indian. In sum, none of the large weapons systems are totally Indian so far. The foreign component often consists of weaponry, electronics or engines, which are hence the critical stages in Indian domestic arms production.[153] Dependence on foreign designs is also clear. The more complex weapons India wants, the more difficult it is to achieve self-reliance.

The third large problem is connected to production costs in Indian armament production. In 1971 SIPRI compared the prices of domestically produced aircraft and equivalent imported aircraft. It showed up that all aircraft were more expensive to produce locally than to import from abroad.

Table 52. Costs of Locally Produced and Imported Aircraft in India, $ Thousand

	A Total production cost	B Cost of importing equivalent aircraft	A/B (%)
HJT-16 Kiran (basic jet trainer)	340	200	170
MIG-21 (supersonic fighter)	1 520	830	180
HF-24 Mark I (supersonic fighter)	940	600	160
Alouette (helicopter)	270	170	160
HS-748 (transport)	1 490	1 000	150
Gnat[a] (fighter)	380	200	190

Source: The Arms Trade with the Third World, SIPRI, Uppsala 1971, p. 738.

Note: [a] 1956 price.

The main reasons for the high prices of domestic production were large material costs, inefficient use of labour, the prices of imported components, and the general problems resulting from the special character of weapons parts, machinery, testing equipment and so on. One important reason may also be that the foreign TNCs charge higher prices for parts in licence production than in sales of finished weapons.

Another serious problem for India is caused by the foreign exchange costs of armaments, particularly aircraft production. The study by SIPRI noted in 1971 that foreign payments caused by three licence programs were larger than would have been the costs of imported weapons:[154]

Table 53.   Foreign Exchange Costs of Aircraft Production in India,[a]

$ Thousand

		US $ thousand;	$1 = Rs 7.5
	A	B	A/B
	Foreign exchange cost of production	Imported cost of purchase	(%)
MIG-21	1 020	530	192.5
Alouette	250	170	147.1
Gnat	110	200	55.0

Source: The Arms Trade with the Third World, SIPRI, Uppsala 1971, p. 739.

Note: [a]This table is based on the following information: a) All the materials used to produce MIG-21 and Alouette are imported, b) 20 per cent of the materials used to produce Gnat are imported, c) 50 per cent of the non-material costs are imported; this comprises imported capital equipment, and direct charges such as licensing fees, tool replacements, etc. It is an estimate, and may well be too low.

Unfortunately no price comparisons like the ones in the above tables are available concerning today's aircraft production. We can assume, however, that the same factors that caused the disadvantages of licence production in 1971 are also present at the moment.[155] As was already mentioned, a Jaguar produced in India is twice as expensive as the one imported from Britain. In fact, the problems may have become very large in the Third World in general, because the practice of licence production has become very common. Licence payments are not the only factor causing foreign exchange costs. A more important factor is that arms technology is sold as packages, and the licence producer buys several intermediary inputs which are very expensive.[156]

5.6.   Summary

From the point of the TNCs the participation in the military build-up of the developing countries is a part of the company strategy. If the marketing is not successful with traditional exports the next stage is to transfer technology in such a way that the position of the company is strengthened in a given market vis-à-vis the competitors. The company may also be forced to sell technology; for example Brazil does not allow imports of light aircraft, and Piper would have lost the whole market if it did not agree to transfer technology to Brazilian aircraft industry. Regional marketing considerations and economic advantages offered by subcontracting may also promote internationalization of a transnational arms producer in a developing country.

For the developing countries the choice of the high-technology model of military production leads most probably to a cooperation with a foreign partner because that is the shortest way to get technology. The examples of Iran and Egypt show that in the initial stage of new military production the dependence on foreign technology, personnel and - in case of Egypt - financing is very intensive.

After getting the production technology and after a certain learning period, the aim is to gradually increase the local content of production and decrease the role of foreign TNCs until total independence is achieved.

The countries studied in Chapter 5 have not achieved military self-reliance. India and South Africa have had a most conscious policy for autonomy of military production but both depend on foreign TNCs in certain critical areas like electronics and military engines. Not even Israel - which has not been analyzed here - has achieved totally independent technology in these respects although the technological level of its industry is otherwise very high.

Excluding the dependence on TNCs in certain key areas the developing industries have managed to increase the share of indigenous work and thus increase their self-sufficiency to a certain extent. Particularly Indian and South African arms production has advanced in this respect, and Brazil is making efforts in the same direction.

The Indian example shows, however, that indigenization of arms production requires enormous costs from a developing country, and a 100 per cent independence may never be achieved. For almost 20 years India has produced fighters, but it had to rely on Jaguar rather than its own designs when new planes were recently needed. Thus the 20 years, experience did not result in autonomous production capacity. Yet the Indian R&D capacity is probably the largest in the Third World and the labour force is highly skilled. The fact that there are more R&D personnel in military projects than in private industry as a whole tells of the enormous costs of military production.

Another paradox of indigenous military production is that although it is started to save foreign exchange it may end up with increased foreign exchange costs, due the high prices of foreign inputs, licence fees and related payments. To cover these costs developing producers start considering exports, but they cannot compete with high-technology products and thus the export chances for the most expensive weapons are limited, as shown by the export efforts of India. On the other hand there are also examples of export successes, for example Brasilian armoured personnel carriers.

6 Transnational corporations, armament process and development

With regard to the relationship between militarization and development we may adopt two different approaches; things can be viewed either in a synchronic or a diachronic manner. The synchronic approach aims at classifying the countries by the degree of their integration into the world military and economic order, while the diachronic approach attempts to trace the phases of involvement into the military network of the world. In the synchronic approach roughly four categories of countries can be distinguished.

The first category consists of those mainly developing countries which do not rely in their security policy to any conspicuous extent on arms; hence they have less need to import them. The second, and apparently the biggest category of nations is composed of those societies which acquire most or all of their military hardware from abroad, although they may themselves have the capability to produce small arms and ammunition. The third group of countries contains, in turn, those countries which are participating in the international military-economic division of labour through various types of licence and co-production arrangements. They have thus a certain capacity to produce weapons systems at home, even though that would hardly be possible without the technological and financial contribution of transnational corporations and governments of industrialized countries.

The integration into the global network of military production does not decrease the need or the inclination to import arms. On the contrary, these two forms of internationalization of the armament industry appear to be complementary in many cases. This state of affairs is reinforced by the fact that the dependent domestic production of arms normally increases, because of the type of development model chosen, the need to import, for example, the more sophisticated components of the military technology needed in the production process. Finally, the fourth category is one which is hardly met in reality; an independent, indigenous technological and financial capacity to produce weapons to fulfil the perceived security needs.

This, admittedly rough, categorization of countries is useful because the nature and magnitude of the economic costs of militarization differs from one case to another. In the first group the relative lack of military programs means that no major burden is imposed on the economy of the country. In the second category the costs incurred are mostly related, to use our subsequent classification of problems, to the distortion of the trade profiles as well as to the financial complications. The importers have to find, in other words, money to pay for the arms consignments ordered. This normally happens in two ways: either by boosting the exports or by borrowing money from abroad. Naturally the financing of arms imports also has domestic allocation effects which we shall discuss in Chapters 6.1. and 6.2.

The decision to launch arms-production projects opens a qualitatively new future, including the integration of these projects into the prevailing techno-logical and economic realities of the world. The domestic production of arms naturally has an impact both on the trade profile and the financial aspects, but in addition to that it also leads to the misdirection of the production process, both in the developed and the developing countries. This consequence of the armament processes has been commented upon by several authors some of whom may even accord the military dimension a primary role.

> From a historical point of view, the process of acculturation initially manifests itself in the military sphere, where the overwhelming superiority of the industrialized countries since the 19th century has obliged the Third World to borrow Western technology. It then spreads gradually to other spheres of life of a society, and it is in this way that the aspiration to the model of consumption of the indus-trialized countries becomes generally accepted, and it is not possible to satisfy the demand of such a model but through technological borrowing, usually taking the form of the massive and indiscriminate import of the products of technology,. and not of a global and sustained effort to acquire a command of technology. Whether they are military or whether they consist of capital equipment for the production of consumer goods, the equipment imported by the Third World is in no sense a transfer of technology. At most they constitute a transfer of productive capacity, the excessive cost of which is apparent only over a long period and blocks the dissemination of progress locally, and the egalitarian and profitable insertion of the country into the circuits of international trade.[1]

An important aspect of the domestic production of arms is that, at least in the initial stages, it does not remove the country from the trade and financial problems - because of the continued import of arms as well as components for the locally manufactured systems - but adds new burdens in the form of the misdirection of the industrial capacity and industrial policy. In this sense the burdens due to the military programs are cumulative rather than discrete in character.

It would be erroneous to conclude that the four categories described above are the stages through which all or close to all countries have to move over time. In some cases this indeed happens, but there are apparently some which tend to stay in a fairly stable manner in one of the categories. This is most probable in the first and second alternatives, because the initiation of the domestic arms industry implies a qualitative break with the past and an effort to start moving to the fourth category with indigenous capacity to produce arms and military technology. In any case in many developing countries the imports of foreign arms represent the first phase of the military build-up.

Some of these countries move to the second phase, which is characterized by the switch into the licence production of arms whereby imported parts are assembled in the purchasing country. In the third phase the arms importer may start producing some parts locally, adding gradually the domestic content of the final product. In some cases the local producer may also agree to become a subcontractor for the weapons supplier. From this situation it is only a short step to the co-production of weapons systems which may, of course, assume several alternative forms, both in terms of organization and technological orientation.[2] In that case, the developing country concerned starts taking part in the vertical division of labour within the transnational armament industry. Transnational corporations involved can, for instance, take advantage of the lower labour costs in the developing industry. It is typical of this stage that the developing country, and its industry, supplies less sophisticated components, while the TNCs keep producing technologically more advanced parts.

In the fourth phase the demand for more indigenous production is manifested in a gradual increase in the local share of the value of the weapons system. The remaining percentage may contain, however, critical dependencies on foreign technology such as engines and electronics. In this phase the production is probably so expensive and the required investments so large that the producing country starts considering the expansion of arms exports to cover part of the costs by sharing them with the potential purchasers. This is also a way of trying to avoid the financial dependence which is an almost obligatory outcome of the domestic production of arms in developing countries. The role of the arms exports is seen in the fact that those developing countries which have the most extensive domestic production of arms are also the leading suppliers of arms among the Third World countries (in addition to being major importers).[3]

The last phase would then be totally indigenous armament technology, where TNCs are no more needed and the armament industry of the developing country starts competing for markets with the leading industrialized countries, particularly in the Third World. No developing country has yet reached this phase, but evidently this is the goal of the leading military producers among this group of countries. For instance India and South Africa are relatively independent arms producers.

One may raise, however, serious doubts whether this 'goal' will ever be achieved. The global tendency appears to be that the self-sufficiency and viability of the armaments economy of even the leading military powers, in particular in the West, is decreasing. It has to adjust to the emerging tendencies in the international division of labour in which the guiding hand of the TNCs is more apparent. Considering this prospect it would be illusory to imagine that the developing countries producing arms could avoid its impact.

The shift from the arms-import phase into the position of an arms producer has naturally a much more intensive impact on a developing society. The countries starting new military production become dependent on foreign, TNC-controlled military technology, because they do not have enough local technology to build on. The relevant costs are partly due to the licence fees and royalties as well as - and in fact to a much higher extent - to various intermediary inputs which have to be purchased either because of the lack of domestic capacity or the provisions contained by the technology contract. The domestic production of arms has naturally a much more profound impact on the technology and industrial policy of the country than the mere importation of arms. In Chapter 6.3. we shall aim at a more detailed analysis of the economic as well as non-economic costs involved in the military production programs.

6.1.   Arms Imports and Development

The main form of armament process in the developing world continues to be the import of weapons and weapons systems from the industrialized part of the world. These weapons are mostly manufactured by the TNCs of the largest producer countries, although smaller producers in medium-sized or small countries should not be neglected, either.

In 1978 the value of world arms trade was estimated at $ 20 billion, of which 70 per cent consisted of arms transfers from industrialized countries to developing countries. In 1979, the value of world arms trade has been esti- mated as high as $ 25 billion dollars. Assuming that the share of the imports to the LDCs has been roughly the same 70 per cent, the arms transfers to the LDCs were $ 17.5 billion in 1979.[4]

During the period 1970-78, the Third World imports were distributed among various regions as follows:

Table 54.   Major Arms Importing Regions in the Third World 1970-78, $ Million at Constant 1975 Prices

Region	Arms imports 1970-78	Per cent of LDC total imports
Middle East	27 284	50
Africa	9 039	17
Far East	8 912	16
South America	4 691	9
South Asia	4 051	7
Central America	732	1
Third World total	54 537	100

Source: World Armaments and Disarmament. SIPRI Yearbook 1979, London 1979, pp. 170-171.

212

As can be noted the Middle East has absorbed half of the total arms imports of the Third World, with Iran as the largest single importer, followed by Israel, Saudi Arabia and Syria. It used to be the conflict between Israel and Arab countries which fuelled the arms imports of that region. After 1973, the oil producing countries joined the group of large importers, mainly to protect their resources by military means and to increase their prestige.

During the 1970s 17 per cent of arms supplies went to Africa. The liberation wars in the former Portuguese colonies, various conflicts in Sub-Saharan Africa and in the African Horn area, the military build-up of South Africa and Northern Africa spurred imports in the 1970s. The role of South Africa is dominant, however, since it has accounted for over half of all the arms supplies to Africa.

The end of the Indo-China War in 1974-75 did not decrease arms imports to the Far East, as might have been expected. On the contrary, South Korea, the new unified Vietnam, Taiwan, Thailand, Malaysia, Indonesia and Singapore have allocated large funds to arms imports as well as to armament production. The war between China, Vietnam and Kampuchea in 1978-79 has no doubt given new stimulus for armament investments in the whole region. In South Asia, the traditional rivalry between India and Pakistan causes arms imports, and has also led to increased arms production and purchases of licences. In Latin America, as was already discussed in Chapter 5.1., the armament rivalry between Brazil and Argentina dominates the circumstances in the whole continent.

In each region, some few countries dominate the armament build-up, either because they want to show their regional power with arms or because they are involved in regional conflicts. The largest number of heavy importers can be found in the Middle East, where also the largest absolute sums of money are spent on arms by particularly Iraq, Iran, Israel, Saudi Arabia and Syria. South Korea, India, Libya and Cuba are top arms importers in their regions, while the top positions are shared in Sub-Saharan Africa (between South Africa and Ethiopia) and in South America (between Brazil and Argentina). The role of regional armament leaders is clearly visible in SIPRI's arms import data:

Table 55.   Rank Order of Third World Importing Regions and Major Importing Countries, 1978

Importing region	SIPRI value of imports (1975 $ million)	Percentage of Third World total	Five largest recipient countries	SIPRI value of imports (1975 $ million)	Percentage of region's total
Middle East	6 583	47	Iraq	1 423	22
			Iran	1 393	21
			Israel	1 377	21
			Saudi Arabia	1 081	16
			Syria	626	10
Far East	2 366	17	S. Korea	1 357	57
			Vietnam	262	11
			Taiwan	209	9
			Thailand	129	5
			Indonesia	74	3
Sub-Saharan Africa	1 600	12	Ethiopia	365	23
			S. Africa	330	21
			Sudan	160	10
			Rhodesia	92	6
			Nigeria	91	6
North Africa	1 158	8	Libya	694	60
			Algeria	223	19
			Morocco	213	18
			Tunisia	29	3
South America	1 069	8	Brazil	371	35
			Argentina	265	25
			Peru	152	14
			Venezuela	151	14
			Ecuador	68	6
South Asia	1 019	7	India	750	74
			Pakistan	118	12
			Afghanistan	77	8
			Bangladesh	73	7
			Sri Lanka	2	0.2
Central America	192	1.3	Cuba	98	51
			Bahamas	48	25
			Mexico	20	10
			El Salvador	8	4
			Panama	6	3
Total Third World imports	13 948				

Source: World Armaments and Disarmament. SIPRI Yearbook 1979, London 1979, p. 183.

Figures for arms trade are never very exact.[5] Nevertheless, they indicate with sufficient accuracy general patterns and structures. In the above table we can see that the largest importers are countries which 1) are in a threatened position, 2) have critical natural resources (like oil or phosphate), 3) have ambitions for a regional power position. Many of the largest importers can be considered semi-industrialized (e.g. Israel, South Korea, Brazil, Argentina) while others are rural, underdeveloped societies with very limited purchasing power.

The arms imports have several economic effects on the importing societies. Some of them can be approached by more or less inaccurate statistical information while other effects are more qualitative in character.

The first problem is connected with the distortion of trade profile caused by arms imports.[6] If we imagine that the costs of arms imports consist of the mere prices of weapons systems - which is not, of course, the case - we can relate the arms imports to the total imports, and get an idea of the total import capacity devoted to military priorities. A closer picture can be achieved by relating the arms imports to the imports of capital goods, i.e. SITC category 7. International trade statistics do not report arms imports at all. It can be assumed that some military transfers are hidden in various SITC subcategories; on the other hand some countries totally exclude arms from their trade figures, to make their statistics look better.

Table 56. Arms Imports, Total Imports and Imports of Engineering Products (SITC 7) in Selected Countries 1977, Million of Current Dollars and Per Cent

Country	Arms imports	Total imports	SITC-7 imports	Arms imp./ total imp.	Arms imp./ SITC-7 imp.
Middle East					
Iraq	1 100	4 052	2 663	27	41
Iran	2 400	13 750	6 535	17	37
Israel	1 100	5 788	975	19	113
Saudi Arabia	925	17 412	6 457	5	14
Syria	575	2 685	942	21	61
Far East					
Korea	280	10 811	2 991	3	9
Republic of Vietnam	262[a]	n.a.	344	n.a.	76
Taiwan	180	8 522	n.a.	2	n.a.
Thailand	50	4 616	1 393	1	4
Indonesia	60	6 230	2 402	1	2
Sub-Saharan Africa					
Ethiopia	430	352	173	122	249
South Africa	130	6 270	3 314	2	4
Sudan	20	1 059	456	2	4
Rhodesia	10	n.a.	n.a.	n.a.	n.a.
Nigeria	10	11 095	4 335	0	2
North Africa					
Libya	950	5 258	2 126	18	45
Algeria	280	7 171	3 307	4	8
Morocco	200	3 199	1 247	6	16
South America					
Brazil	120	13 257	3 290	1	4
Argentina	40	4 162	1 568	1	3
Peru	430	1 880	602	23	71
Venezuela	90	9 810	4 338	1	2
South Asia					
India	460	6 033	1 350	8	34
Pakistan	200	2 447	851	8	24
Central America					
Cuba	80	n.a.	1 492	n.a.	5

Sources: World Military Expenditures and Arms Transfers 1968-1977, U.S. Arms Control and Disarmament Agency, Washington D.C. 1979, pp. 118-154, Bulletin of Statistics on World Trade in Engineering Products-1977, Economic Commission for Europe, United Nations, New York 1979, pp. 32-41.

Note: [a] Year 1978.

The figures in the above table are artificial in many ways, particularly because arms sales figures are never very precise and their role in international trade statistics remains hidden.

Taking these reservations into consideration, the table gives no uniform picture of the role of arms imports in international trade profile. Only one tendency is clear: the larger the absolute size of arms imports, the higher its share in the total imports and SITC-7 imports in general. The share of arms imports in the total imports was particularly high in the Middle East, Ethiopia and Peru in 1977. In India, Pakistan, Morocco and Saudi Arabia the share of arms imports varied between 5 and 10 per cent of the total imports, while in Korea, Taiwan and Brazil even the rather large arms imports did not account for more than 1-3 per cent of the total imports. The comparison of arms imports with capital goods imports again shows the general tendency according to which large absolute amounts of arms imports are connected to large shares of SITC-7 imports. Thus the implication could be that countries with large arms imports cannot afford very large SITC-7 imports.

The second problem caused by arms imports is a financial one. Large arms imports create a financial burden to any importing country due to the high costs of weapons, but the problem is particularly severe for the developing countries with difficulties in generating the necessary funds. The most common practice is to buy arms on credit after commercial arms transfers have by and large replaced military aid by grants.

All the major arms suppliers have various arrangements by which government credits can be expended and guaranteed. In the United States the main form of financing are loans provided by the Federal Financing Bank in the Treasury Department and guaranteed by the Defence Security Assistance Agency in the Department of Defence. The bank was created in 1974 as part of the effort by the Congress to shift from military grants to sales. The loans granted in 1975-76 carried 6.2 per cent interest rates, but in 1979 an interest rate of 9.5 per cent was adopted.[7] It is rather difficult to say what share of the arms sales of the United States, for example, is financed through the public credit sources and what share is paid in cash or borrowed from private banks. It is evident that rather few purchasing countries are able to pay cash - perhaps only some oil-producing countries can do it if they so decide.

Since the middle of the 1970s the U.S. President has been authorized to use some two billion dollars for foreign purchases of weapons from the United States. Almost half of these credits have been earmarked, however, for Israel, which has also received more advantageous terms for its credits.[8] It can be estimated that on average 20-30 per cent of the U.S. arms supplies abroad are covered by these public credits. This leaves, however, considerable room for manoeuvre for the private banks, too, whose share, in relative terms, may have increased since the middle of the 1960s,[9] but not during the 1970s. When we speak of absolute contributions by private banks the conclusion is different to a certain extent: because of the considerable rise in the world arms exports the financing needs have increased and the international banks have come to fill this gap. This is a consequence of the more general tendency for private banks increasingly to finance economic activities of developing countries and not only finance but also develop 'their own methods for appraisal and their own personnel for the economic, social and political auditing of Third World borrowers'.[10]

The financing practices of the Soviet Union are not known at the moment. Earlier it used to supply a considerable part of its arms exports as grant aid, or with very easy credit terms, e.g. for 10-12 years at only some 2 per cent interest rate. Also barter deals were used, e.g. Egypt and Syria paid for at least part of their arms imports with cotton. In the first half of the 1970s, the Soviet Union increasingly started to demand hard currency cash payments particularly from countries able to pay.[11] According to some estimates, India also had to pay with hard currencies although it had difficulties in payments, and had a huge deficit with the Soviet Union.[12]

France and the United Kingdom have a practice comparable to the U.S. one, i.e. Departments of Defence promote arms sales and government credits are available, but information of the size of these funds is lacking. It is only known that credit terms are one of the main means by which the main supplying countries compete in arms markets. Thus they have offered loans to the LDCs rather liberally.

Although public credits are available to the developing countries, they evidently do not cover all arms sales. Some military projects are also so large that a financial consortium has to be formed of bilateral funds, multilateral organizations and private banks to raise enough money - an example of this is the Egyptian communication contract in 1979 where such a consortium was necessary.

Knowing the high prices of weapons, those cases must be very rare when a developing country pays for arms in cash. Thus the bulk of $ 17.5 billion arms imports in 1979 is included in the foreign debt of the LDCs. By comparison, we may recall that the combined deficit of the LDCs was about $ 45 billion in 1979. Thus, the size of the 1979 arms bill of the LDCs is about 40 per cent of the combined deficit of the LDCs, although we cannot identify the share of the deficit directly or indirectly caused by arms imports. It is only known that the largest borrowers are often countries which are also large arms importers, e.g. Argentina, Brazil, Iran and South Korea.[13] The arms import policy is, however, only one component in the overall international economic strategy, and it is the total strategy rather than mere arms imports which cause the financial problems.

There are, however, also cases where arms imports can be considered a main reason for a country's weakening financial position. In Tables 55 and 56 we can observe the relatively large arms imports of Peru. It is Peru that has been quoted as an example of a country in which arms imports have seriously aggravated the debt problem. In 1976 Peru spent some $ 600 million on arms; this sum accounted for one-third of Peru's exports. In 1977 the value of arms purchases by Peru amounted, according to one estimate, to $ 350 million. At the same time Peru has had considerable difficulties in servicing its foreign debt. In 1977 the public debt amounted to $ 5 billion and the debt to foreign private banks was $ 3 billion. When the service rate, i.e. payments for debt service as a ratio of the total exports was as high as 36 per cent, we can conclude that large arms deals did not only add to Peru's difficulties but were one of the main causes.[14]

Peru's problems might have been alleviated, however, by the fact that a considerable portion of its arms imports came from the Soviet Union. Up to

1977 Peru's purchases of Soviet military equipment have been estimated at $ 900 million, which has been largely financed by the Soviet credits. Recently Peru decided - inspired by the soaring metal prices and the Chilean decision to purchase 70 Mirage fighters - to acquire 48 Sukhoi jet fighter bombers from the Soviet Union. The new purchase is worth $ 140 million, which will be paid over 12 years with a three-year grace period and the interest rate at two per cent a year.[15]

A somewhat more general finding can be obtained from a study by Swedish researchers who resorted to a number of regression analyses to find more general explanations for the debt burden of the LDCs. The analysis concerned two separate periods, 1968-70 and 1971-73. The results of the investigation showed that in both these periods there were two factors most capable of explaining the variation: GNP as a measure of the size of the economy, and arms imports. Approximately half of the debt burden is explained by the GNP and arms imports. A diachronic analysis provided weak evidence for the fact that the degree of indebtness precedes arms imports. Such a result could possibly be interpreted as increased economic resources at the disposal of the country through foreign loans. These resources are then partly allocated to the payment for arms and military technology.[16]

To determine with somewhat greater precision the financial implications of growing arms exports we may quote the thinking of a defence planner. The increase in the U.S. military sales to a country will, according to this model, lead - in addition to a number of political and military consequences - to the decrease in the foreign exchange resources of the recipient, to the slow down in its economic growth and to the reduction of civilian imports, both from the United States and elsewhere.[17] A net consequence of this process is the necessity of the recipient to borrow money to cover the loss in the foreign exchange resources and to finance the civilian imports which have been deprived by the purchase of military goods. In fact the civilian imports may experience reductions in spite of the new credits arranged to finance military purchases.

Seeing from the Third World the growing indebtedness of the developing countries, we must put this into perspective and observe that a great proportion of the Third World debt is borne by those countries which have embarked upon the road of industrialization and which try to catch up with the industrialized countries. A heavy debt burden is thus an aspect of the development model chosen.[18] Some of these countries have also decided to develop their arms industry as an integral part of their overall economic and industrial strategy. By integrating their arms production with the international division of labour they also join the debt game. This is to say that the domestic manufacture of arms introduces new elements into the indebtedness of the country concerned, beyond the debt implications of the financing of arms purchases alone.

The domestic arms industry thus increases the probability of becoming involved in a debt crisis. The crisis would probably be a combination of the development crisis and the debt problems caused by the growing import requirements, to borrow Göran Ohlin's terminology.[19] Ohlin states that the development crisis is characterized by the financing of long-term projects by short-term credits without sufficient supervision. This is not, however, a necessary characteristic of the indebtedness connected with the military production. Following our earlier statement we may conclude that the import requirements are in a more central position. The transnational integration of the military industry and the need to buy various kinds of intermediary inputs, ranging from raw materials to technology, lead to a situation in which these import requirements are an essential and almost indispensable part of the industrial and economic strategy chosen. To somewhat oversimplify one may conclude that in these circumstances there is no way to avoid the growth of the debt burden as a consequence of the establishment of the armament industry.

In general the defence sector is consuming rather that producing resources. Thus the third problem of arms imports is their unproductive nature. In an explanation of financial problems arms imports are not like any other capital imports because arms do not generate any new production in the purchasing country while other capital imports usually do so. The problem was formulated by a UN study as follows:[20]

> It is increasingly often pointed out that imports for military purposes generate no income and no exports with which to service the added debt further aggravating the long-term effect on the balance of payments. For some developing countries facing acute debt-servicing problems, the balance-of-payments aspects of the costs which the

worldwide character of arms race imposes on all countries, is particularly salient.

The fourth problem concerns the possibility of <u>misdirection of production</u> structure as a result of arms imports. Because arms imports must be paid somehow, the result may be that the structure of the whole production in the importing country is modified with the aim to be able to finance arms imports. Thus, industrial structure may be directed to supply parts and components for arms suppliers. The mining sector may be mobilized to supply raw materials for foreign military production; actually in some cases developing countries have paid for part of their arms imports with raw material supplies.

The fact that many important raw material producers of the Third World import arms from the same industrial countries to which they sell raw materials points to such an exchange. The foreign trade patterns of, for instance, the Philippines, Zaire, Peru, Brazil, Malaysia, Nigeria, South Africa, Jamaica, Zambia, Bolivia, Thailand and oil producing states could be approached from this perspective, particularly in the longer run. Research into these exchange patterns is far from sufficient, however. Therefore we can only point to two hypotheses, which call for more research. The first one suggests that some LDCs mobilize their raw material production to finance arms purchases. The second hypothesis is that the leading industrialized countries primarily aim at extending their military-political controls over the military apparatuses of the important raw material producing countries. Naturally, these hypotheses by no means exclude each other.

Since the agricultural sector is the dominant one in many developing countries, arms imports increase the pressure to produce commercial agricultural commodities (cash crops) for foreign markets with the aim to get foreign exchange for arms imports. Since many developing countries suffer from severe malnutrition problems, the widening cash-crop production of e.g. coffee, spices, tea and cocoa threatens the satisfaction of the basic needs of the local population. Thus all these different ways to raise foreign exchange may end up in large purchases of weapons which are kept in military bases and generate no new production.[21]

The fifth consequence of sophisticated arms imports is related to the longterm impact of imported military technology. The weapons of the industrialized countries are designed for an industrial society, but when they are exported to developing countries they end up in entirely different circumstances compared to the ones they were designed for. The developing countries importing sophisticated arms do not import only particular weapons, they import an industrial model of warfare, which requires plenty of technical staff, heavy infrastructures, large logistical machinery and so on. In other words, they may import war machines which do not correspond to their level of development. Besides, the basic idea of many weapons of industrial countries is to decrease the role of men and increase the role of weapons - a conception which contradicts the situation in many developing countries which have large human resources but a small number of technically educated personnel.

For logistics, the importing countries need a large number of spare parts. According to American estimates it takes an inventory of 70 000 spare parts to keep a squadron of F-4 Phantoms operational under wartime conditions.[22] The import of this type of weapon systems thus leads to continued dependence on spare parts. The importing countries are very seldom capable of overhaul and repair; the result is the purchase of such services from the supplying country and company. The necessary facilities like repair halls, test apparatus and so on will have to be constructed. Arms importers will also have to prepare themselves for the retooling of their expensive weapons several times during the life-time of the weapon, because of the technological changes. If they do not do this, their weapons get old in 5-10 years because their performance lags behind new developments. This is particulary so in military electronics.

6.2.   Armament Process of the Poorest Countries

Purchase and production of weapons is an economic and social burden for any country, but it is a particularly heavy burden for the poorest developing countries which would urgently need all their resources for development programs and satisfaction of the basic needs of the population.[23] In addition, these countries need aid and cooperation from the industrialized countries to meet their severe development needs.

We have tried to elaborate the relationship between arms build-up and development in this particular group of countries. Before going any further, we would, however, like to point out that in principle the poorest countries need security just as much as every other country, to be able to carry out their development tasks. In the best case they would live in a peaceful, stable region and would guarantee their security by political means, by friendly relations with other countries and by making progress in their development programs so that internal security is also achieved.

The poorest countries do not always live in peaceful surroundings, however, and they start arming themselves despite lack of financial and other resources. Some countries face internal security problems, which are most often related to social inequality and growing domestic contradictions. Those cases are not rare when a small elite tries to fortify its privileges with military means and repression. Also tribal, ethnic, religious and related disputes as well as disputes over territory and borders create armament pressures. Some of the poorest countries may also have strategic importance because of their geographical location or possession of strategic commodities, whereby the major industrial powers may show their interest by offering arms and cooperation for such countries. Finally, the nature of political struggle may take violent and military forms in countries where the direction of future social development is uncertain, and social contradictions create tensions. The formation of liberation and guerilla troops in such circumstances usually leads to purchases of counterinsurgency weapons for the regime. Paradoxically, this type of countries acquire arms not despite poverty but precisely because of poverty.

The opposite case is, however, also possible: that the poorest countries do not arm themselves because they are so poor, and cannot buy arms or very much else, either, from the international market. It is possible that some poorest countries are saved from the general process of militarization because they are small, maybe distant, isolated, do not have strategic resources or location - in other words they are uninteresting from the point of view of international power politics. As an example of strategic vs. non-strategic countries we could compare the military developments in Angola and Guinea Bissau after their independence from Portugal in 1974. Why did Angola face a civil war and interventions while Guinea Bissau was left alone in peace? Perhaps one reason could be that Angola is big, strategically located and rich in resources, while Guinea Bissau is very poor, small and uninteresting for the bigger powers. From the point of view of militarization it was an advantage to be small, poor and uninteresting.

Students of militarization have suggested that the share of military expenditures of the state budget is a better measure of defence burden in society than military expenditures compared to the GNP. This is due to the fact that usually a rather low percentage of the GNP (e.g. 2.0 - 2.5 %) can mask a much higher share of military expenditures in the national budget.[24] The national budget share also indicates the priorities of the governments. Bearing in mind that data on military expenditures may not always be very exact, and that cross-country comparisons may not be justified due to different statistical criteria used, the military expenditures of the poorest countries looked as follows in 1977:[25]

Table 57.   Military Expenditures of the Least Developed (LLDC) and Low-Income (LIC) Countries as Percentage of the GNP and State Budget in 1977

Country	MEX/ GNP %	MEX/ budget %	Country	MEX/ GNP %	MEX/ budget %
Yemen, DR	7.6	34.4	Mozambique	3.1	11.7
Chad	4.2	30.9	Somalia	7.3	10.5
Mali	3.9	26.3	Kenya	2.5	10.4
Pakistan	6.1	26.1	Benin	1.6	9.7
Burma	3.7	25.5	Central Afr.		
Uganda	3.3	20.9	Empire	1.9	9.5
Ethiopia	3.9	20.5	Bangladesh	1.7	8.3
India	3.2	17.7	Togo	2.3	7.6
Burundi	2.0	17.6	Nepal	1.1	7.4
Upper Volta	2.5	16.1	Haiti	1.0	7.4
Tanzania	4.1	15.7	Zaire	1.7	7.0
Afghanistan	2.0	15.4	Malawi	1.7	6.3
Indonesia	3.4	14.7	Niger	0.9	5.1
Madagascar	2.7	12.8	Sierra Leone	1.0	3.9
Rwanda	1.7	12.5	Sri Lanka	0.7	2.0
Mauritania	7.3	12.1	Gambia	0	0
Sudan	3.9	11.9	Botswana	0	0

Source: World Military Expenditures and Arms Transfers 1968-1977. U.S. Arms Control and Disarmament Agency, Washington D.C. 1979, pp. 32-69.

Note: No data is available of Bhutan, Comoros, Guinea, Kampuchea, Laos, Lesotho, Maldives, Western Samoa, Vietnam or Yemen.

Given that all the countries in the above table are very poor, we can note that the relative burden of military apparatus is by no means evenly distributed among the countries concerned. The shares - particularly the shares of the state budgets - are very high in some countries which live in the middle of regional tension, or which participate in a regional arms race like Pakistan and India. On the other hand the shares are also high in some countries which face no international threats. In countries of this type the only reason for high share must be the internal political reasons and the high internal priority attached to the military by the regime. It is also useful to observe that some of the poorest countries do not allocate very large funds to the military apparatus themselves because they receive military assistance from the leading military powers. In the above table the shares of, e.g. Zaire, Sudan and Kenya are very low compared with the size of military apparatus they have.

When the allocation of funds to military purposes in the poorest countries is discussed, it is also useful to recall that in general the _relative_ economic burden caused by the military is about the same in the poorest countries as it is in the leading military powers. In the Federal Republic of Germany the military expenditures accounted for 3.4 per cent of the GNP and 22.4 per cent of the state budget; the shares are comparable to those of India and Ethiopia. In France the shares were 3.9 and 18 per cent, in Italy 2.7 and 8.3 per cent, in the Soviet Union 13.3 and 52.6 per cent and in the USA 5.4 and 25.1 per cent in 1977.[26] Thus the burden of the poorest countries does not essentially differ from the burden of the leading armament centres in relative terms. What makes the difference is the absolute size of the military apparatus, and the problem of absolute poverty in connection with heavy military burdens in the poorest countries.

If we then turn to look at the arms imports of the poorest countries we again observe the large differences among the countries. Some countries are heavy importers while others import very little or even no arms at all.

Table 58.   Arms Imports, Total Imports and Net Receipts of Official Development Aid by Least Developed Countries, 1977[a] ($ million and per cent)

Country	Arms imports/ total imp., % 1974	Arms imports/ total imp., % 1977	Value of arms imp., 1977	Net ODA[b] 1977	Arms imports/ODA % 1977
Afghanistan	33	n.a.	60	100	60
Bangladesh	2	n.a.	20	763	3
Benin	3	n.a.	10	49	20
Botswana	0	n.a.	10	47	21
Burundi	0	7	5	48	10
Central African Empire	0	0	0	42	0
Chad	0	n.a.	n.a.	83	n.a.
Ethiopia	4	122	430	114	377
Gambia	0	0	0	22	0
Guinea	13	n.a.	n.a.	22	n.a.
Haiti	0	n.a.	n.a.	86	n.a.
Laos	250	n.a.	30	32	94
Malawi	0	0	0	80	0
Mali	0	19	30	113	27
Nepal	8	0	0	80	0
Niger	0	n.a.	n.a.	96	n.a.
Rwanda	0	0	0	96	0
Somalia	47	n.a.	80	255	31
Sudan	3	2	20	221	9
Tanzania	1	10	70	340	21
Uganda	5	n.a.	5	22	23
Upper Volta	0	0	0	110	0
Yemen	5	n.a.	30	249	12
Yemen, Dem. Rep.	10	n.a.	20	100	20

Sources: World Military Expenditures and Arms Transfers 1968-1977. U.S. Arms Control and Disarmament Agency, Washington D.C. 1979, pp. 118-154, Development Cooperation. DAC 1979 Review, OECD, Paris 1979, pp. 171-173 and 244-245.

Notes: [a] Development aid by centrally planned economies excluded.

[b] ODA = official development aid.

In the above table it is easier to say what cannot be observed than what can be observed, because the trade statistics as well as arms trade statistics are extremely deficient. If we assume that the arms import statistics by and large indicate the level of arms imports - but not the exact amount - we can note that the clear armament leader is Ethiopia, which is involved in military conflicts both across borders and within borders in Eritrea. Ethiopia is followed by Somalia, Tanzania and Afghanistan though a clear difference is noted. Because of the imperfect statistics, it is impossible to compare arms imports with the total imports in the least developed countries.

It is notable that the only systematic data available are those of the official development aid supplied by the industrial market economies. In fact these countries keep much more precise records of their development aid than of the arms they supply to the poor countries. When inaccurate arms trade figures are compared with accurate development aid figures, we can observe that arms imports clearly exceed development aid in the Ethiopian case - the reason being that the table does not cover development aid by the socialist countries at all. In Laos also the arms import figure approaches the development aid figure but here, too, the comparison is not too informative because the ODA figure concerns aid given by the capitalist countries while the arms are imported from the socialist countries.

Actually the only reasonable comparisons can be made in cases where both arms imports and development aid come from the West, and also in these cases it is only the ODA figure that is reliable. Bearing these reservations in mind, we can note that arms imports are small compared to ODA in Bangladesh, Central African Empire, Gambia, Malawi, Nepal, Rwanda and Upper Volta, while the arms imports account for a higher share of ODA in countries like Botswana, Burundi, Mali, Somalia, Sudan, Tanzania, Uganda and Yemen.

In discussions concerning the allocation of development aid funds it has sometimes been suggested that development aid should not be given to poor countries which acquire arms, or in general allocate large funds to military apparatus. This problem is not a simple one, however, because the poorest countries do have a right for both security and development and legitimate claims should of course be respected.

If the poor countries clearly prefer political means to solve regional conflicts, and if their development programs make progress as far as the satisfaction of the basic needs of population is concerned, and if the army is under political control, the relationship between development allocations and allocations to military purposes is probably also politically defined and enjoys legitimacy among the population. If, however, the army grows at the cost of the population, and armaments make it easy to apply military means to solve political and social contradictions, and finally, the army assumes social autonomy with no control whatsoever, repressing the population, then the "security" needs and development needs are in clear contradiction and deserve international attention as well. In each case the empirical judgements are problematic, but it should be borne in mind that the army and armaments should never be studied in isolation from the general social, political, economic and cultural context. The international community can also act as a mediator in regional conflicts and contribute to political solutions, whereby the international pressures for armament process are decreased and scarce funds consequently allocated to development purposes. In internal conflicts the chances are less because of the national sovereignty and the principle of non-interference in the internal affairs of other countries.

Because the financial resources of the least developed countries are so limited or even non-existent, the foreign powers transferring arms to these countries usually have to grant assistance or find someone else to finance the transfers. Within the last few years the Soviet Union has supplied large amounts of major arms to Afghanistan, Ethiopia, Laos and the Democratic Republic of Yemen exclusively, and tanks to Tanzania which, however, has mainly relied on Western suppliers. China has supplied major weapon systems to Bangladesh and Guinea.

The rest of the least developed countries (LLDCs) have received arms from the Western powers. Their aircraft consists mainly of light planes for transport and counterinsurgency purposes. This means that beneficiaries from these transfers are in most cases not the largest transnational aircraft producers but companies which produce light aircraft. For example SNIAS from France, NZAI from New Zealand, Britten-Norman and Short Bros. from the UK, De Havilland from Canada, Embraer from Brazil, SIAI Marchetti from Italy and

FFA from Switzerland can be mentioned as supplying companies to the poorest countries. In some cases, the poorest countries have also bought more sophisticated aircraft. For example, Dassault and British Aerospace have sold 15 Jaguar planes to Chad; Dassault has sold 24 Mirage fighters to Sudan and Northrop has sold F-5 planes to Sudan and Yemen. Lockheed has supplied its large Hercules transport aircraft to at least Sudan and Somalia. In general the US is not a dominant supplier of arms to the poorest countries at all, but France, the United Kingdom, Italy and minor arms producers like Canada and Switzerland have been the leading suppliers. Single arms deals with the LLDCs are usually not very large.

There is also, however, a group of leading armament importers among the poorest countries. Afghanistan and Ethiopia have been heavily armed within last few years, the supplier being, as already mentioned, the Soviet Union. The Western powers, on their part, have supplied large quantities of arms to Somalia and particularly Sudan. Sudan is particularly interesting because in statistics it does not look like a heavy arming state at all, while in the light of arms trade registers its arms acquisitions are considerable. The explanation for this contradiction is most probably the fact that the Arab countries have financed a large part of Sudan's imports and these imports do not show up in Sudan's military expenditures or arms import figures published in 1977. The Arab countries in the Middle East have often very poor conditions for agriculture, and they have invested heavily in Sudan's agriculture to develop it into their "bread basket" to decrease their dependence on Western food supplies. It is therefore logical that they also participate in Sudan's military build-up particularly because Sudan is geographically close to several regional tension areas, particularly the Horn of Africa.

As far as imports of major arms are concerned, the least developed countries are not heavy importers - yet - by international standards. This general finding must be specified, however, since there are some growing armament centres in this group. It should also be noted that imports of small arms can just as well contribute to militarization and repression, and this trade is not covered by arms trade statistics. Rifles, mortars, bombs, grenades, small jeeps and related equipment can cause enormous suffering to the population and it is precisely this type of equipment which is often used by these countries. It is also easy to buy them from international arms traders - the "death merchants" - in case leading military powers refuse to supply them.[27] It is also easy to smuggle this type of equipment, while major arms - if smuggling is tried - must be smuggled in pieces, which is not always easy. Therefore it can very well be that there is a small-scale, hidden armament process going on which is not registered or noted by concerned institutions or scholars.

Some of the poorest countries are also able to produce small weapons or ammunition in their local factories. At least Guinea and Sudan have plants for which technology has been supplied by the FRG, and Nepal has a munitions factory supplied by Indian military assistance. As a heritage of colonialism some countries also have facilities for shipbuilding and repair (e.g. Aden) but it is not known whether they are now in military, or in civil use.

In general it is the "second poorest" group of countries - those which qualify as low-income but not as least developed - which is much more heavily armed than the very poorest group. Some of these countries are influential in a regional context, or have natural resources or strategic location - all these factors are relevant from the standpoint of arms build-up and militarization. These factors are also connected to the general transformation in the North-South axis as suggested in Chapter 1.

In international transfers of major arms, this group of countries looked as follows in 1977:

Table 59.   Arms Imports, Total Imports and Net Receipts of Official Development Aid by Selected Low-Income Countries, 1977[a)]

($ million and per cent)

Country	Arms import/ total imp., % 1974	Arms import/ total imp., % 1977	Value of arms imp., 1977	Net ODA 1977	Arms import/ODA % 1977
Burma	3	0	0	102	0
India	4	8	460	1 128	41
Indonesia	1	1	60	514	12
Kampuchea	n.a.	n.a.	0	0[b)]	0
Kenya	3	1	10	165	6
Madagascar	0	n.a.	5	61	8
Mauritania	0	10	20	165	12
Mozambique	n.a.	n.a.	20	80	25
Pakistan	5	8	200	545	37
Sierra Leone	0	0	0	26	0
Sri Lanka	0	0	0	187	0
Togo	0	n.a.	10	64	16
Vietnam	n.a.	n.a.	10	248	4
Zaire	5	8	50	261	19

Sources: World Military Expenditures and Arms Transfers 1968-1977. U.S. Arms Control and Disarmament Agency, Washington D.C. 1979, pp. 118-154, Development Cooperation. DAC 1979 Review, OECD, Paris 1979, pp. 171 and 244-245.

Notes: [a)]Development aid by centrally planned economies excluded. The countries selected for the table belong to the low-income groups defined by IRBD and UN but do not qualify for the internationally defined LLDC group.

[b)]Kampuchea's net ODA received from all sources was $ 0.3 million in 1977.

Burma, Sierra Leone and Sri Lanka were not interested in arms at all in 1977, and also their cumulative arms import values for 1973-77 are minimal.[28] As far as Kampuchea is concerned, the table does not reflect the present situation which is characterized by foreign troops, civil war and largely unknown transfers of arms to the combatants.

The second largest arms importer category in the above table is composed of Kenya, Madagascar, Mauritania, Mozambique, Togo and Vietnam, but Vietnamese imports have rapidly risen after the table was constructed. According to SIPRI the Vietnamese arms imports were $ 262 million in 1978, i.e. more than 25 times the value given by ACDA for 1977.[29] Madagascar and Mozambique have imported their arms from the socialist countries, while France has been the dominant supplier of arms to Mauritania and Togo. In fact Togo's rather large arms imports deserve closer attention: a small poor country, located in Western Africa between Benin and Ghana.

According to available sources, Togo has tried to achieve some sort of air superiority in the area, by acquiring most modern fighter and training aircraft. Five Dassault/Dornier's Alpha Jets, 5 Dassault's Mirage-5s and 5 Panavia's supermodern Tornados belong to Togo's imports, together with SNIAS/MBB transport aircraft and Embraer's EMB-326 GB, which is suitable for counter-insurgency purposes.[30] As far as it is known, there are no international conflicts around Togo which would create the need for heavy arms imports; so, the only reason can be either the fear for future political developments in the area or a strong prestige attached to sophisticated aircraft.

In this group of countries, India and Pakistan are the leading arms importers. However, we have already discussed their relationship in Chapter 5.5. In this connection it is sufficient to note that the two rivals belong to the lowest income group in the Third World, and it most certainly is critical for their vast development needs that they participate in the arms race. The same can soon be said of Vietnam, unless the degree of tension decreases in Indo-China. The relationship between arms imports and development aid also suggests that the larger the arms imports, the higher the usual share of official development aid.

For some countries in this group it is also possible to compare arms imports with imports of engineering products to see whether the pattern in the poorest countries differs from the pattern of wealthier developing countries, presented in the previous chapter, in Table 56 on page 216.

Table 60. Arms Imports and Imports of Engineering Products (SITC 7) by Selected Low-Income Countries 1977 ($ million and per cent)

Country	SITC 7 imports 1977	Arms imports 1977	Per cent
Burma	149	0	0
India	1 350	460	34
Indonesia	2 402	60	2
Madagascar	82	5	6
Mozambique	132	20	15
Pakistan	851	200	24
Sri Lanka	96	0	0
Togo	85	10	12
Vietnam	344	10	3
Zaire	312	50	16

Sources: World Military Expenditures and Arms Transfers 1968-1977. U.S. Arms Control and Disarmament Agency, Washington D.C. 1979, pp. 118-154, and Bulletin of Statistics on World Trade in Engineering Products 1977. Economic Commission for Europe, United Nations, New York 1979, pp. 32-33.

In 1977 the arms import shares of India and Pakistan were the highest ones when compared with the SITC-7 imports. On the other hand the import shares were also high in Mozambique, Togo and Zaire, and in the two last named countries the shares are certainly much higher now - in Togo because of the highly sophisticated aircraft imports and in Zaire because of the internal conflicts, which have presumably increased the level of arms imports.

The fact that some of the poorest countries do not participate in arms races at all and are able to allocate their funds to essential development needs shows that the militarization of the poorest countries with the help of foreign powers is by no means a historical necessity. It is clearly the political conflicts in regional and internal contexts which spur the militarization process.

Where such conflicts do not exist, life is peaceful and funds can be allocated for development. It is also remarkable that some of those countries which have managed to stay away from the militarization are relatively isolated and live, so to say, on their own. Particularly Burma and Sri Lanka can be noted as examples of benefits of isolation as far as the risk of militarization is concerned.

Many low-income countries also produce arms. Excluding India, which was already discussed in Chapter 5.5., there is some arms production in at least the following low-income countries:

Table 61.   Arms Production of Selected Low-Income Countries

Country	Fighter aircraft	Light aircraft	Heli-copters	Missiles	Naval vessels	Small arms, ammunition
Burma					x	x
Indonesia	x	x	x		x	x
Madagascar					x	
Pakistan	(x)	(x)	x	x	x	x
Sri Lanka	x				x	
Vietnam		x				x
Zaire				x		?

Source: Peter Lock and Herbert Wulf, Rüstung und Unterentwicklung. Aus Politik und Zeitgeschichte. Beilagen zur Wochenzeitung das Parlament, B 18/79, 5, Mai 1979, p. 17.

(x) = production planned.

All production in the above table is based on licence agreements and technology is provided by the leading military powers. Burma has received technical assistance from Italy and the Federal Republic of Germany for small arms plants and from Yugoslavia for shipbuilding. Indonesia produces military aircraft under licences from Pazmany (USA), PZL (Poland), CASA (Spain) and Aermacchi (Italy). The Indonesian helicopter licences are provided by MBB (FRG) and SNIAS/Westland (France, UK). In shipbuilding Indonesia may already be capable of indigenous designs, but more complex equipment has to be imported. In small arms production Indonesia has licences from several foreign companies, but information on the present licence agreements is not available. The official Indonesian policy is to become self-sufficient in arms production.[31] Experience from other countries (cf. Chapter 5) shows, however, that this policy usually leads to greater dependence on foreign technology in case self-sufficiency is sought for high-technology major weapons.

Besides India, Pakistan is one of the leading arms producers among the low-income countries. It has also declared self-sufficiency in arms as its goal. Because it wants sophisticated technology, the policy has led to a number of licence agreements in all weapons categories. Aircraft licences are provided by the Swedish Saab and the U.S. Cessna, and helicopter licences by the U.S. Hughes and the French SNIAS. Hughes plans to sell helicopters built in Pakistan to the Middle East. Pakistani missile licences have been sold by MBB (FRG) and China; according to SIPRI the MBB-designed anti-tank missiles are now 100 per cent indigenous as far as components and production are concerned. Pakistani shipbuilding has already indigenous technology, and warships have been sold to e.g. Saudi Arabia and Abu Dhabi. Bombs are also indigenous, while small arms production has been assisted by German (Rheinmetall, Walter, Hecler & Koch, Meissner) and Chinese technology.[32]

The goal of military self-sufficiency is mainly the result of two reasons: several arms embargoes declared in connection with military conflicts and the strong arms production of India, to which Pakistan has responded with a similar goal. Pakistan has offered Arab countries armament know-how, and has carried out maintenance and service activities for their weapons. Dassault has also granted Pakistan rights for its Middle East service as part of an offset deal.[33]

The present state of Vietnamese military production is not known. During the war in the 1960s and in the 1970s North Vietnam was able to provide rather simple but efficient weapons, and under the present circumstances this production has most probably been strengthened.

The general conclusion regarding the armament build-up in the low-income countries is that the same supplier countries who emphasize the need for progress in development efforts and satisfaction of basic needs also provide a large number of weapons and technology for military production. So far the development aid is bigger than arms exports to these countries but if all arms technology agreements are included in the calculations, it is possible that military transfers exceed external development inputs. It is impossible to verify this opinion, however, because information regarding arms technology agreements and their economic details are never published.

6.3.   Armament Technology and Development

The empirical analysis carried out in this study strongly indicates that considerable changes have taken place in the armaments industry during the last 10 to 15 years. The armament industries in the leading industrialized countries have had a pioneering role in this development, but gradually also a number of developing countries have been incorporated into the emerging international military order. The transformation of industrial systems is reflected in three major changes: 1) technology is increasingly science-related, i.e. the relationship between science and technology has become more intimate, 2) technology has grown more complex, and 3) technology has contributed to a new division of labour, both on a national and international scale.[34] A further tendency is that technology has become more commercial; it is a commodity by which firms and nations increasingly compete with each other. The patent system is a central means of protecting the private ownership of technology.

The more modern the technology is, the more visible these features are compared with the traditional or standard-modern technology. The military sector is no exception to this general trend. The armament industry has also become much more intensive in research and development (R&D) which has, in turn, led to the employment of fewer people who are often highly-skilled engineers and technicians. It is no exaggeration to say that the present wave of militarization is driven by the development of military technology which is supported by various political, economic and bureaucratic interests. There are a number of differences between the United States and the Soviet Union in this respect, though from a technological perspective they appear to be narrowing.[35]

Many analysts of the armament industry in the West maintain that there is a relatively high degree of spill-over or spin-off from the military innovations to the civilian sector. This point is argued by references to the vague borderline between military and civilian technologies, in particular in the aerospace industry. According to this view the interpenetration of these two sectors has contributed to technological breakthroughs in both of them. A related point is expressed in the conclusion that technological developments in aerospace research, development and production up-grade the development in related civilian industries such as electronics.[36]

The validity of this conclusion is often refuted by saying that the military applications have grown so specialized that they have very few useful applications in civilian life. The estimates of the share of military inventions applicable in the civilian sphere appear to vary between 20-35 per cent.[37] These percentages seem to reinforce the view that military R&D has preciously few civilian uses. A couple of caveats have to be made, however. First, the resource factor is at least as essential as the technology factor. It is true that technology has grown more complex, but its inapplicability in the civilian production is not only due to that. Probably a more potent reason is the disproportionate allocation of resources to the military R&D, which prevents the development of science- and technology-related components in the civilian industry. This is in fact detrimental in the long run even for the military industry because its technology base is much more dependent on a healthy civilian technology than vice versa.

A further factor in this equation is that in spite of patents and other forms of monopolies, civilian technology is disseminated more freely through commercial channels than military technology, which is effectively guarded by secrecy and vested bureaucratic interests. This tends to hamper the spread of military innovations into the civilian field. A related explanation would be also valid for the Soviet Union, in which interaction between research centres and the industrial system, in terms of the application of science-related innovations, is considered to be rather slight.[38]

For a number of reasons the spin-offs from military to civilian applications of technology seem to be relatively slight in the developed countries. In the developing countries military production is often regarded as a high-skill sector which encourages the overall technological development of the country. It may even be considered a central strategy in the upgrading of its economic and technological potential which would, in turn, improve the opportunities to compete in the export markets of both civilian and military goods.[39] This sort of reasoning, although rather wide-spread, is deceptive because the entire conception of spin-offs is inapplicable in most developing countries as they do not have a coherent industrial structure.[40] Only in a developed production structure, characterized both by backward and forward linkages, could spin-offs between the military and civilian industries operate in a meaningful manner; and, as argued above, even there considerable difficulties arise.

Increasing reliance on R&D has considerably raised the costs of a weapons system, which has created a need to further the economies of scale. This aim can be promoted by selling arms by which the production numbers can be increased and the R&D costs distributed more evenly. The significance of this point can be seen in the fact that the higher the ratio of development to production costs the worse off is the producer with the smaller total market.[41] In practice this means that smaller producers have, of course, a greater pressure to export their products to recover the advantages of the economies of scale. The export drive is an illustration of the internationalization of the armaments industry. As analyzed above this is, however, only one form of internationalization and it has been in fact complemented by institutional arrangements such as direct investments and co-production, often under the aegis of transnational corporations.

To put it crudely, the international armaments industry is characterized by three emerging and by now to a certain extent established tendencies, viz. internationalization, technologization and commercialization. They are not contradictory, but tend rather to reinforce each other. A common denominator to these tendencies is concentration, which is both a precondition for the tendencies described above and in some cases a consequence of them. This is the framework within which the developing countries have to operate in striving for the construction of their own arms industry. In this policy various economic incentives may have a certain role, even though in most cases it would be cheaper to import weapons than to produce them at home. In fact political and military considerations seem to determine the decisions of developing countries to launch the domestic production of arms.[42]

We have analyzed earlier in this study the impact of arms imports on the trade profile and the financial situation of the purchasing country. In this section the aim is to explore the economic and technological consequences of the domestic arms production. This exploration may be started by a brief note on the relationship between technology and organization as they are closely intertwined: a given type of organization is producing technologies peculiar to it, while they are shaping the organization of the recipient in the transfer process. Technology has, in other words, its social carriers; transnational corporations, government agencies and national entrepreneurs. In the case of military technology, governments and their agencies have a more conspicuous role than in the transfer of civilian technology. This is, of course, due to the specific role of the state in national security policy. In addition to that, public authorities are needed to finance large-scale and often immensely costly military programs which may be implemented by a coalition of transnational corporations, government agencies and domestic capital. It is self-evident that military establishments have a special position as carriers of technology into a country as well as in its use.

Earlier we divided developing countries into three groups on the basis of their involvement in the international armaments industry (see pp. 208-211). Here we are interested mainly in the third and fourth groups, which are already involved to varying degrees in the domestic production of arms. In particular we try to illustrate the impact of this activity on the overall economic and technological development of a country. It is apparent that the initiation of domestic arms-production programs require the existence of a certain industrial base, from which resources can be drawn. There is, however, hardly any one-to-one relationship between the overall industrial base and the domestic production of arms because a nation can naturally forego the option of building a military industry. That is why an empirical examination of this relationship is justified.

Herbert Wulf and his colleagues have empirically defined the major arms producers. They have arrived at the following list, given in rank order: Israel,

India, Brazil, Yugoslavia, South Africa, Argentina, Taiwan, South Korea, Philippines, Turkey, Indonesia, Egypt, North Korea, Pakistan and Singapore.[43] From our analysis we have excluded Yugoslavia, Israel and Turkey because they are relatively industrialized and predominantly European countries. All the remaining countries are also producing several weapon categories, although only India, Brazil and to a lesser extent South Africa as well as Argentina, Taiwan and South Korea have more extensive, and at least to some degree indigenous base for military production. Applying strict criteria only India and Brazil can be considered members of our fourth category.

The industrial capacity of developing countries can be estimated by the way in which they meet their demand for capital goods. In this respect these countries fall distinctly into three groups: 1) capital goods are domestically manufactured, 2) they are partly covered by domestic manufacturing, and 3) they are mainly imported as fully assembled equipment. An essential difference between the first and the third categories is that those belonging to the former group have their capital-goods industries linked backwards to their raw materials and intermediate goods production as well as linked forwards to the manufacturing of consumer goods. They have, in other words, a measure of coherence in their industrial structure, which is lacking in the countries importing their capital goods. They are at the mercy of the international market, while the countries in the second category fall in between (though they probably are closer to the first category).

This picture can be qualified by observing that the capacity of most advanced developing countries to produce capital goods is limited to standard-modern technology, while they are still dependent on the import of highly-modern technology, to use the concepts applied by M.R. Bhagavan. The crucial difference between these types of technologies is that highly-modern technology is both science-related and research-intensive. That is why its social carriers want to control and even monopolize its applications, while standard-modern technology is more evenly, though by no means equally, distributed between countries at various levels of development.[44] It is a kind of natural law that developing countries undergoing the process of industrialization try to stretch their hands to highly-modern technology of which military technology is a good example. This effort is a consequence of their policy of accelerating

242

industrial development and asserting their sovereignty though the construction of domestic arms production.

The cross-tabulation of the importance of domestic military industry and the level of industrialization as measured by the production of capital goods yields the following result (the arms-production variable is dichotomized between major producers and the rest of the developing countries):

Table 62.   Industrial Capacity of Developing Countries and Their Role in the Arms Production

	Major arms producers	No major arms producers
Countries producing their own capital goods	Argentina, Brazil, China, India, North Korea and South Africa	Chile (P), Mexico (P)
Countries partly producing their own capital goods$_{45}$	Egypt, Pakistan, Philippines, Singapore, South Korea and Taiwan	Colombia (P), Cuba, Hong Kong (P), Iran (P), Malaysia, Peru and Venezuela (P)
Countries importing their capital goods	Indonesia	All other developing countries

The symbol P in parentheses indicates that the country concerned has a potential capacity, measured by the strength of the manufacturing sector and the available manpower, to produce more advanced weapon systems.$_{46}$

The table shows that there is a relatively high positive correlation between the strength of the industrial base and the development of the major arms industry. By combining the categories of industrialized and semi-industrialized countries, although it is to some extent unjustified, we arrive at the following broad classification:

- Major arms producers with a relatively developed industrial base (12 countries)

- Countries with a relatively developed industrial base, which are not major arms producers (9 countries)

- Major arms producers which do not have an industrial base (Indonesia)

- Countries which do not have an industrial base and which are not major arms producers (all the other developing countries).

These classifications could have also been made otherwise, by applying different criteria and different divisions. The typology illustrates, however, the predominant tendencies in arms production in the Third World.

Most developing countries are not producing arms for the simple reason that they do not have economic and technological preconditions, consisting of the industrial base and the availability of manpower, to launch military programs. According to our analysis Indonesia is the only country which has done so. Its industrial structure is scattered and oriented to non-durable consumer goods. Thus there is no real basis for the indigenous production of arms, partly for the reason that until the 1960s the economic and industrial development of the country was slowed down by rising military expenditure. Future development plans (so-called Repelita plans) presuppose, however, the construction of a viable and balanced industrial structure by focusing on capital goods.[47] An estimation of the development costs of the Indonesian military establishment is complicated by the fact that the official defence budget covers only 40-50 per cent of the real expenses. The deficit is financed by the state-owned oil company, Pertamina, as well as by the companies - ranging from shipping lines to timber concessions - controlled by the regional military commands.[48]

According to our analysis more than half of the developing countries possessing sufficient industrial infrastructure have in fact initiated major arms-production programs. This correlation is reinforced by the fact that the countries among the top arms producers also have an exceptionally strong capital-goods industry. They can be, however, separated from each other in at least one respect: in India and South Africa the arms industry is aiming at self-sufficiency while in Brazil, and in Israel for that matter, the military industry is firmly integrated into the international division of labour and hence the role of transnational corporations is also more prevalent.[49]

Some developing countries have made a deliberate choice of not initiating major arms production programs, although some of them - as Table 62 shows - would have sufficient industrial potential to do so. Their activities are confined to some isolated projects. These countries would be interesting objects of further studies and would illustrate the apparent multitude of reasons why the production option has been foregone. Their economic and industrial development could also be systematically compared with those countries which have embarked upon a large-scale military production. Mexico, Venezuela, Chile, Peru and Malaysia in particular would be interesting cases for research.

After having explored the distribution of the developing countries in different categories on the basis of their industrial development and intensity of arms production it is time to move to a more detailed analysis of development consequences of the armaments industry. This approach is naturally applicable only to those countries in which a large-scale capacity to produce arms exists. In them a constant dialectical process operates: by trying to eliminate dependencies embodied in the arms purchases and develop a self-sufficient arms industry, a new set of dependencies is in fact created.

While the old dependencies distorted the trade profile and resulted in financial difficulties, the new dependencies created by arms production direct the development of the entire economy, its industrial structure and manpower. These dependencies are created by the asymmetries of the international system. The asymmetries are particularly strong in the science-related, highly-modern fields, in which the developed countries have a definite edge. These asymmetries tend, furthermore, to be cumulative in character; technological asymmetries, for example, tend to coincide with the financial ones.

Many studies suggest that the extent of military spending correlates positively with the rate of economic growth.[50] In these analyses the economic growth is regarded, however, only as a quantitative phenomenon and its qualitative and structural dimensions are largely neglected. Furthermore, the causal relationship is often interpreted in a misleading manner. Instead of resulting in higher growth rates of the economy the increase in military capability itself is made possible by the economic expansion. Although this is rather a restatement of the correlation, and not a new explanation, this point of view deserves closer attention because of its apparent plausibility.[51]

The coincidence of economic growth and militarization have without any doubt strong allocation effects within the country. This combination tends to lead to a society which is developing in an unbalanced manner, i.e. its structural heterogeneity is great.[52] The growth is normally concentrated in those sectors in which there is, or at least is supposed to be, an abundance of advanced technology, human skills and capital, and which are integrated into the international or regional centres of power. The domestic production of sophisticated arms belongs as a rule to this part of the industrial system, while one of the functions of the military establishment equipped by the arms so produced is to protect the continuity of this unbalanced industrial pattern.

Technology-intensive and externally-oriented parts of the national economy are bridgeheads, which prosper at the expense of the rural areas and the urban poor.[53] This allocation effect should be studied in more detail, in addition to the boosting of export income and foreign borrowing, as a method of financing weapons purchases. The bridgeheads or enclaves are also channels, through which transnational corporations penetrate into the country. The most modern technologies they try to keep, however, in their own reservoir. In the military field this is indicated, for instance, by the dominance of a few transnationals in the production of engines and electronics.

Besides transforming the industrial structure the technological dependence on international armaments corporations also has financial implications. The purchase of technology is often immensely expensive, partly because of the royalties and licence fees, which have to be paid, but even more these expenses are due to various clauses in the technology contracts concluded. They may force the recipient to buy, for instance, various intermediary goods or components from the owner of the technology at the prices dictated by it. There is some evidence that the costs of these clauses are in fact much greater than those due to licence fees.[54] This state of affairs contributes in its own part to the situation that domestic arms production programs do not normally result in any savings in foreign exchange costs, but rather tend to have contrary effects.

In the production of capital goods, multipurpose machinery is needed, whilst the production structure in semi-industrialized and non-industrialized countries requires specific-purpose equipment. The use of multipurpose equipment, most often imported, cannot be entrusted to unskilled workers, but presupposes the existence of proportionately high numbers of skilled workers, technicians and engineers.[55] This kind of composition in the labour force is available in industrialized countries, but can seldom be found in developing countries in spite of their embryonic training programs. As the military production is based more on the multipurpose machinery than the average civilian industries one of its consequences is the lopsided use of manpower:

> In comparison to civil production, larger numbers of qualified personnel are absorbed in the production, operation, and maintenance of arms. Since qualified labour is generally a scarce factor in peripheral countries, the importation or local production of modern weapons necessarily intensifies existing bottlenecks in civilian sectors. On the other hand, the military and arms sector absorbs relatively few unqualified or semiskilled personnel, who are available in abundance and are therefore under- or unemployed. The reason for the low demand for unqualified personnel in arms production is the great complexity of weapons and the constant introduction of new types.[56]

Thus the low employment effect of the arms production in developing countries is due both to the general properties of modern technology (complexity as well as research-intensiveness) and to the specific characteristics of the qualitative arms race (constant introduction of new types).

Manpower problems are not only visible in the production phase, but also in support and maintenance. The largest number of skilled maintenance personnel is required for modern aircraft, but all industrial weapons need plenty of skilled personnel to be operational and to be repaired when they break down. These so-called back-end problems have considerably increased with the change in the technological sophistication of weapons systems imported or locally produced by developing countries. These back-end problems have to be solved if the new systems are expected to be really and not only nominally operational.[57]

The extent to which support and maintenance requires skilled and trained manpower in different military sectors is estimated in the following table:

Table 63.   Maintenance Man-Years Needed for Armoured Vehicles, Warships and Aircraft in 1970

	Armoured vehicles	Warships	Aircraft	Total
Egypt	3 075	634	5 466	9 175
India	2 175	717	4 632	7 524
North Korea	1 600	658	4 110	6 368
Brazil	150	849	5 142	6 141
Israel	2 120	187	2 976	5 283
Argentina	90	705	3 672	4 467
Pakistan	1 455	423	2 400	4 278
Iran	1 995	319	1 782	4 096
Taiwan	n.a.	1 176	2 772	3 948
Iraq	1 445	122	1 800	3 367
Syria	1 225	143	1 416	2 784
Indonesia	n.a.	1 503	1 272	2 775

Source: Gavin Kennedy, The Military in the Third World, London 1974,
pp. 293-301.

The figures from the above table may not be quite exact, but they indicate,
however, the scale on which the maintenance of weapons absorbs skilled
manpower in certain developing countries. The maintenance of aircraft
requires most of the manpower, 62 per cent in the cases listed above. The
figures from the table describe the situation in 1970, and thus the ranking of
the countries may have changed since then. Particularly Iran and Saudi Arabia
would now rank higher due to their massive arms imports in the 1970s.

The lack of industrial infrastructure and skilled personnel to repair, service
and maintain the military equipment has made it necessary to resort to foreign
specialists in training and technical matters. The scale of U.S. training and
technical assistance projects is indicated by the fact that in 1975 U.S. firms
and the Department of Defence were implementing military projects worth $
296 million and involving about 2 500 specialists, if only ten largest projects in
all Third World countries are taken into account. By 1977 the value of the

projects had risen to $ 695 million and the number of personnel to some 4 300 technicians. These persons were in fact only a part of the total number of U.S. technicians in Iran, which was said to amount to some 15-20 000 people. In Saudi Arabia the value of contracts grew during the same period from $ 362 million to $ 856 million, and the number of personnel from 2 245 to 2 331. Other countries with whom the U.S. firms and military authorities have concluded training and technical assistance programs include South Korea, Taiwan, Kuwait, Turkey, Greece, Zaire, Egypt and Jordan.[58]

The lack of skilled personnel may lead to a situation in which a large part of the defence - particularly if it is modernized very rapidly - is run by foreigners, not by locals. When Iran and Saudi Arabia started their enlarged military programs in 1973, and decided to build a modern defence system in the shortest possible time, the result was that a large part of the defence system was actually run by foreigners. A modern air defence system is perhaps the ultimate example of dependence on foreign technology and personnel. In a publication by British Aerospace, these activities are called "defence support services" and the company gives the following description:[59]

> The provision of comprehensive Defence Support Services to overseas nations has become a very important facet of BAe's business and, in the years ahead, promises to make even more substantial contributions to Britain's export earnings. Valued at many hundreds of millions of pounds, the contracts cover not only the supply of aircraft, missiles and other equipment but also extensive programmes of flying and ground training, civil engineering and construction, maintenance and repair, logistics and all the intricate infrastructure of support services needed to establish and maintain a modern air defence system. Today, for example, British Aerospace has over 2 000 UK personnel in Saudi Arabia and Oman. Many areas of British industry outside British Aerospace itself benefit from these contracts: for instance, the Saudi Arabian defence contract - now valued at well over £ 300 million - involves the co-ordination by the support department at Warton Aerodrome, Lancashire, of the purchase and delivery of products from some 700 suppliers in the UK.

The infrastructure includes a wide range of installations, some of which, like roads and telecommunication, can also be of value to the civilian population, provided they are rich enough to use them. Infrastructure for military use, as required in connection with arms imports and production of major arms, include high quality airports equipped with modern air control technology, shelters and hangars for weapons systems - possibly even underground as in

Iran - heavy roads and bridges for motorized ground forces in tanks and armoured vehicles, military bases with modern security systems - including protection from terrorist or guerilla groups - and so on.

It is not possible to describe these developments in quantitative terms, because no systematic empirical data exist. As an example we shall below summarize developments in Saudi Arabia during the last few years. Saudi Arabia has not so far invested in arms production but relies on arms imports for its defence. These imports have, indeed, a most intense impact on Saudi society, and all the changes have taken place in a very short time since 1973:[60]

> In earlier times a large part of the Saudi population was not mobilized into military activities. Now the army has been promoted into an important social institution, indicating a general trend toward militarization of the Saudi society. The army is presented as a good route for a young Saudi man to "become a good Saudi". In 1979 the army was changed into a national conscription system.
>
> The Saudi military spending has risen very rapidly. The defence budget for 1978 was estimated to be more than $ 14 billion of which about $ 8.4 billion was spent on foreign, mainly American hardware and services. Saudi defence spending per capita was $ 2 000, among the highest in the world. The largest single project is no doubt the King Khaled Military City near the Iraqi border the value of which is estimated at $ 8.5-10 billion. It is being constructed for 70 000 inhabitants, of whom 30 000 will be soldiers on active duty. Recently the Ministry of Defence and Aviation presented plans for another giant $ 10-billion military city for 90 000-100 000 troops south of Riyadh. Other large military construction projects are at Tabuk in the northwest near Israel, Khamis Mushayt in the southwest near Yemen, as well as multi-billion dollar military academies, naval facilities and support facilities for the kingdom's three F-5 squadrons and F-15 bombers. King Khaled Military City, KKCM, is based on the idea that the city would not only be a huge military base and camp but the army could also carry out various social activities. Perhaps the "theory of the modernizing soldier" is present in this project, because the military is supposed to train a capable indigenous workforce for various development projects. Young Saudis could come to KKCM, pick up an occupation and learn languages.
>
> Because of the huge manpower needs, the Saudis have frequently turned to foreign personnel not only for technical assistance but also for manpower. Thus, South Koreans have been enlisted to maintain Saudi naval facilities in the Eastern Province, and Taiwanese and Pakistani technicians form a sizeable presence within the Royal Saudi Air Force. In addition, Yemenis have been recruited for some of the more menial tasks at military bases.
>
> The largest and most important military presence, however, is

American. They form the technological backbone of the Saudi armed forces. The U.S. aid ranges from assistance to the air force, to help in creating a multibillion-dollar naval expansion program. Many technicians from cancelled Iranian training programs have now moved to Saudi Arabia. Arms imports from the U.S. are so large that, according to a U.S. Army analyst, the kingdom is "so dependent on long-range U.S. follow-on training and support that such programs nearly approximate a treaty". The Royal Saudi Force has at the moment 171 combat aircraft, including 45 F-15 fighters (McDonnell Douglas), 60 F-5E fighters (Northrop) and 16 British-built Lightning F53 fighters. After the collapse of the Shah's regime in Iran and fighting between the two Yemenis, the U.S. has increased its arms supplies, including 12 F-5 fighters, 100 armoured personnel carriers, two Hercules transport planes (Lockheed), and two radar recon-naissance planes.

The foreign companies which supply the weapons usually take re-sponsibility for maintaining them, too. Thus Lockheed is maintaining the kingdom's squadrons of C-130Es, C-130-Hs and KC-130Hs sup-plied by the same company.

Thus the penetration of modern technology into Saudi Arabia has by far exceeded the technological capacity of the country. It remains to be seen whether the Saudis are willing to pay for all the rising economic and cultural costs of dependence on foreign technology and the massive foreign penetration of their society. One cannot avoid the conclusion that the national culture and traditions are in danger of being destroyed in the process of this change.

In fact Saudi Arabia is an example of a country in which a contradiction is developing between the indigenous social structure and the requirements of modern technology. This is because every technology contains a certain social structure, in this case a capital-intensive approach to production, which is incompatible with the original structure. This state of affairs leads to a tension between the old and the new and accumulates a potential which may finally result in a revolutionary change of the system. Especially in the Persian Gulf area these types of changes may be destabilizing from the standpoint of the entire region and even the relations between great powers.[61]

The tension between the traditional social structure and the requirements of modern technology is partly due to the need for foreign inputs, both human and material, in the development process. In most countries the emerging arma-ments production is based on the model of import-substitution industrialization. This does not mean, however, that the armaments industry would rely mainly on domestic resources, but that transnational corporations have crept into the country and started to produce for the local market. The import-substitution model, instead of leading to self-sufficiency, has multiplied the involvement of TNCs in the economy and has in fact diversified their activities from the extractive to the manufacturing sectors. Constantine Vaitsos has summarized this tendency in the following statement which also emphasizes the relative importance of import substitution compared to export promotion by transnational corporations:

> The area in which the TNCs continue to play their most important role in the distribution of industrial operations internationally will be that of import-substitution manufacturing activities of developing countries. Despite increased and well-publicized TNC exports from the Third World during the present decade, the share of local sales in the total volume of operations of manufacturing foreign affiliates in developing countries has been increasing. The model of foreign direct investment in manufacturing continues to be basically an import substitution model. This is particularly so in Africa and Latin America, but it is also true in South-East Asia.[62]

In arms production the situation is somewhat different, because the marketing opportunities are not as predominant as in civilian manufacturing, but in spite of that related tendencies are also visible there.[63]

This point is in fact only a restatement of the conclusion that the autonomy of military production in developing countries is in many respects illusory. This does not concern only the arms industry based on the promotion of exports, but also - even though to a somewhat lesser extent - the import-substitution strategy. It is apparent that the latter strategy is possible only in relatively big countries where there is a sizeable internal market, while the smaller countries developing their arms industries have to rely on exports to recover a part of the development and production costs. This would indicate that, besides external dependence, the economies of scale would be the central problem in the arms production in the Third World. This problem could be partly removed by resorting to regional cooperation. In principle this could be a remedy, but the only available experience from the Third World, viz. the Arab consortium, strongly suggests that the problems of external dependence - not to speak of the political intricacies involved - cannot be easily removed.

Furthermore, there are relatively few subregions in the Third World which would be able to promote internal collaboration in this particular field. The emergence of regionalist tendencies is no doubt more visible and perhaps also more acceptable in the civilian than in the military sectors. This is shown by the opposition mounted against the military cooperation within ECOWAS.[64] This does not, of course, exclude the possibility that somewhere else, for instance in the ASEAN region, programs for military co-production would be initiated.

Too strong a concentration on economies of scale would lead, however, to somewhat erroneous conclusions, because the real problems are elsewhere. Independent of the industrialization strategy the <u>dependence on foreign technology</u> appears to remain. Neither the export-promotion nor the import-substitution strategies have been able to remove it, though the latter model may have better opportunities to attain this end in the long run. The situation seems to be that the technological independence can only be achieved by allocating an almost unacceptably high proportion of domestic resources to this purpose. If this path is chosen the programs of economic and social development would naturally suffer.

6.4.   Alternative Approaches

In the Third World equality with the developed countries is sometimes sought for through the acquisition of highly sophisticated conventional weapons and even nuclear explosives. The view that the Third World should give up the acquisition of modern weaponry has been regarded, with some justification, as neocolonial and patriarchal. The consequence has been that a number of developing countries are gradually overwhelmed by military arsenals, either imported or produced at home, or both. A fact giving credibility to this point is that in 1973-1977 the developing countries imported in total 3 181 supersonic combat aircraft of which 1 670 came from the Soviet Union, 996 from the United States and 300 from France. In addition to that, the developing countries imported during the same period 504 surface combat naval craft; 207 from the United States, 132 from the United Kingdom, 55 from the Soviet Union and 45 from France.[65]

This section of our study explores the possibility that developing countries could develop alternatives, short of unilateral disarmament, to the present hegemony of military technologies and doctrines originating in the industrialized part of the world. The premise is thus that as developing countries cannot match developed ones in the quantity and quality of arms, in spite of some claims to the contrary, they have to find out alternative ways of guaranteeing their security and welfare.

6.4.1.   Alternative Security Doctrine?

In the Clausewitzian tradition political decisions should guide the development of military doctrines and military technology. Without belittling the significance of political considerations, it is becoming increasingly evident that military technology is a powerful factor in shaping the military doctrines. In one sense technology sets the limits within which the doctrines can vary. Within these limits the doctrine can, on the other hand, guide the development of military technology. Technologies and doctrines mutually reinforce each other within a political environment, the specifics of which determine the precise character of this interaction.

The growing role of technology has several implications for developing countries. They are dependent on the import of arms or on the acquisition of equipment for the domestic military industry. At the same time they also are acquiring, however, specific modes of organization and military doctrines from the developed countries. Developing countries become dependent in a double sense when they try to accommodate their strategy and tactics to take new technologies into account:

> This is not necessarily bad; however, it cannot help but confuse military planning and raise questions about operational effectiveness. Possession of a new technology is not equivalent to the possession of a new military capability. This technology must be incorporated into the existing military structure. If it cannot, then the structure must be changed (which could entail considerable disruption) or the technology should be abandoned.[66]

Developing countries have thus major difficulties in adopting new military technologies and concomitant military doctrines into the force structures.

These problems, I submit, would become especially evident when the military organization so structured faced an adversary, an industrial army from the developed part of the world.

It is true that the mere balance-of-power considerations between the opponents are not sufficient in the prediction of the outcome of the battle, though they may play an important role in the escalation of the crisis. A case study of the Bangladesh crisis in December 1971 shows that India's overwhelming military superiority was not the decisive factor in the outcome of the conflict. Pakistan's military inferiority was no doubt a factor in its defeat, but far more important was, according to the authors, the lack of political will and cohesion. An illustrative fact is that in the air war Pakistan was dominant in spite of its inferior technology.[67]

Care should be taken, however, in the generalization of this conclusion to the far more asymmetrical relations between major developed countries, which are responsible for most military interventions, and developing ones. In this sort of asymmetrical situation new conventional military technologies permit massive coordinated attacks against the defender. In fact these technologies may encourage the employment of limited offensive strikes by which the adversary is subdued.[68]

On the other hand it has been claimed that precision-guided weapons, which are relatively inexpensive, make it easier to defend a small country and inflict considerable harm, both in economic and military terms, to the offender. In a more symmetrical relationship, which seldom prevails between developed and developing countries, this conclusion is apparently valid. It has to be qualified, however, by a couple of additional observations. First, the development and procurement of precision-guided weapons requires advanced electronic systems, which are seldom available in developing countries. It has been one of the main findings of this study that electronics, both civilian and military, is an area in which the dependence relations are the most critical, and developing countries have hardly any means to overcome them in the short run.

Furthermore, the attacking side can develop countermeasures by which the military significance of precision-guided munitions can be eliminated. It is close to self-evident that in this sort of electronics race a developing country, even though it might possess PGMs, tends to be the loser. One remedy to this problem would be the dispersion of defensive battlefield units to allow greater mobility and a potential for concealment. In the circumstances it would be more difficult for the aggressor to succeed in destroying a defender's forces.[69] This solution provides in fact a key to the reorganization of the military policy and doctrines guiding it. Reorganization is needed for the simple reason that developing countries will not be able to match the military-industrial capacity of industrialized countries and that is why they need a less vulnerable defence system.

An alternative defence system, which has been proposed, is based on a type of militia in which people are actively participating. Defence is in other words in the hands of the population itself, and not of the elitist army possessing sophisticated weapons systems as a means of coercion. A 'people's army' would rely on lightly armed infantry units which are mobile and decentralized. The number of military targets would therefore be decreased and their nature altered: the aggressor would, in other words, have fewer invasive options. In fact the question is of a guerilla strategy which is designed to defend a certain territory, but first of all a certain group of people which considers the territory worthy of defence.

Herbert Wulf has compared this kind of defence system with the traditional armed forces in the following manner:[70]

Table 64.   Alternative Security Systems and Doctrines

Dimension	Technocratic army	People's army
Weapons and equipment	Capital-intensive modern carrier systems: tanks, aircraft, and fighting ships, mobile tank divisions; partly locally built and assembled	Simple: anti-aircraft and anti-tank missiles, light infantry weapons; mainly local production; diversified supply lines; marine equipment for coastal protection
Armed forces	Professional army: specialized troops in army, navy, air force	Militia system, personnel intensive, new organizational forms, geared to serve also economic functions
Mobilization	Permanent mobilization of the professionals, limited reserves	In peacetime limited mobilization; in wartime total mobilization of the population
Command and structure	Hierarchical, centralized	Democratic, decentralized
Strategy	Defensive and offensive including potential for pre-emptive strikes	Defensive, reactive, territorial defence to prevent occupations

The main point here is that a people's army is preferable for several reasons: it is more democratic, based on the will of the people to defend themselves and also concordant with a self-reliant model of development.[71]

A typical counter-argument would be that 'the proof of the pudding is in the eating'. In other words the defence system based on a people's army should also work in practice and be able to repel the aggressor:

> As in many other branches of politics, the question that matters in strategy is: will the idea work? More important, will it be likely to work under the special circumstances under which it will next be tested? These circumstances are not likely to be known much in advance of the moment of testing though the uncertainty is itself a factor to be reckoned with in one's strategic doctrine.[72]

It is indeed true that the conditions of struggle are not usually known very well in advance and hence the taste of the pudding is difficult to anticipate. There are, however, several historical examples which show that the militia system can well resist the aggressor. The success of early colonial armies in their expansion can be explained by the fact that they seldom encountered guerilla tactics and could hence, with the aid of their superior weapons and organization, defeat the masses of warriors.[73]

The wars of liberation after World War II tell a somewhat different story. The organization of people's armies and the application of guerilla tactics created such an efficient resistance against the aggressor that it could not reach the political objectives without considerable military losses. This does not mean, however, that an industrial or a technocratic army cannot win a guerilla war. The evidence of the Algerian war of independence is worth recalling here. Hartmuth Elsenhans has shown that the French counter-insurgency was rather effective judged by the military criteria, and in the long run could have conceivably crushed the liberation army.[74] The protracted nature of the war worked, however, in favour of the Algerians. France became internationally more and more isolated and domestic opposition against the war grew increasingly strong and vocal. The war was lost by France for political reasons and not on the battlefield. This conclusion can also be extended, with some reservations, to the U.S. involvement in Vietnam.[75]

These experiences underline the significance of other factors than mere military strength. Organization, political will and, of course, international circumstances are important in determining the outcome of a war. It seems to us that the military struggle between Polisario and Morocco is another example, though in some respects a very special one, in which a semi-industrial army is not able to overcome a mobile and decentralized military establishment which is enjoying support both from its people and from external powers.

The mobile warfare of the Moroccan army has met some military success and it has been able to secure the control of major population centres in Western Sahara. Morocco has not been, however, able to defeat the Polisario guerillas in the deserts; they are in fact controlling some 75 per cent of the entire territory. The outcome has been a military stalemate which has contributed to growing social and economic pressures within Morocco, though the anti-war opposition is still weak. Internationally the Polisario has been relatively successful, both within the OAU and elsewhere, in gathering increasing political support and recognition.[76] The case of Western Sahara is yet another example of the possibilities which an alternative defence strategy contains from the standpoint of weaker parties in a military conflict.

The wars also have, however, their military aspects. One characteristic of the people's army is apparently that the population is exposed to heavy sacrifices if the aggressor is exploiting in full its firepower and air superiority. The invasion of the Ethiopian army into Eritrea indicates that a militarily superior aggressor can occupy a country, force the guerilla army to withdraw and destroy the society and its people of whom many become refugees. If the military asymmetries are big enough the people's army and its supporters can be also defeated, although the victory can never be complete as the revival of the Eritrean struggle against the Ethiopian army shows.

No defence system is perfect and hence their merits and demerits must be looked at in comparative perspective. With some hesitation we may conclude that in an asymmetrical military conflict, a reliance on a decentralized people's army better guarantees the security of a country. Its advantages include the possibility of avoiding a complete defeat which is much more probable in a war waged by an industrial army under the umbrella of a 'total strategy'. Furthermore the militia system is flexible in the sense that it enables a combination of territorial and social defence. The traditional strategy is solely geared to the defence of the territory, while the reliance of the militia on the population adds a social dimension to a defence struggle. It also has to be recalled that a non-violent defence, which is thoroughly social by character, could be better combined with a military system based on a people's army.

The people's army is by no means an ideal solution. Its efficiency can be doubted for the reason that it may result in considerable physical sacrifices. It also requires a workable organization, which has to be able to function in a decentralized manner in difficult and unexpected circumstances. The people's army is, in other words, a political solution to the problems of defence and does not rely so much on technical remedies which are characteristic of the industrial armies. This fact has, however, a number of implications to be kept in mind. The political implications of the people's army may hamper its development because the leaders may not trust the citizens sufficiently to equip them with arms. The possibilities of implementing this kind of defence system may also vary from one country to another depending on their relations with their neighbouring countries.

To our knowledge there has been relatively little instrumental discussion in developing countries on the shift to a full-scale militia strategy, with the exception of the countries which themselves waged a guerilla war against an aggressor or a colonial power. Discussion has been in fact more active in Western Europe where the traditional military strategy is increasingly chal-lenged partly because its logical outcome would be a nuclear war. To avoid this frightening alternative several West European writers have emphasized the need for new strategic concepts. They should be built upon a relatively strong conventional defence which is composed of a decentralized system of modules which are of varying character and weight.

These modules would contain mobile and effective techno-commandos which could inflict considerable damage on the aggressor but could avoid major, decisive battles in which they would probably be defeated. This strategy is based, in other words, on protracted warfare (non-bataille) which would give time to the decision makers to consider the situation. It may even be hypothesized that this sort of territorial or area defence would for this very reason make a nuclear threshold higher in a European war. The dispersion of military capabilities and troops would also deprive the adversary of the major targets against which nuclear weapons could be effectively used. In practice this argument would, for instance, be against tank concentrations which have anyway become more vulnerable because of the development of precision-guided weapons.[77]

The kind of territorial defence which has been described above, has been implemented to varying degrees in Yugoslavia and Switzerland and in certain respects also in Finland and Sweden. It appears therefore to be a defence system suiting best neutral and non-aligned countries which are not affiliated to military alliances. It is a bit misleading to speak of a territorial system of defence because it has also a strong social component as described above. That is why it might be more advisable to speak of a strategy of inoffensive deterrence to quote Bert Röling's phrase. This strategy is a 'military posture strong in resistance but almost incapable in offensive power':

> The advantage of the doctrine of inoffensive deterrence is not only that the principle can be applied in different grades of intensity, but also that it can be applied locally, in a restricted theatre of possible military confrontations.

In many respects the strategy of inoffensive deterrence is the only available approach to smaller nations, given the constraints on their resources: 'by adopting the strategy of inoffensive deterrence, small countries make a virtue out of necessity'.[78]

There are no a priori reasons to exclude the defence system based on inoffensive deterrence from the arsenals of developing countries, although some of them are developing their doctrines in almost opposite directions. In fact the 'labour-intensive' military establishments of developing countries, the relative scarcity of advanced military technology and the high costs of its acquisition as well as the political need to develop defensive approaches instead of aggressive ones would speak in favour of a variant of an inoffensive strategy or the people's army.

The decision to opt for an alternative defence system also has implications for the type of military technology acquired. It has been repeatedly emphasized in this report that the military technology of great powers is normally evaluated by technical performance characteristics such as speed, accuracy and payload. This kind of technology may not even work in developing countries because of the lack of sufficient industrial base, skilled manpower or the availability of spare parts. An example of these problems is that in 1965 Pakistani troops were unable to operate the automatic control needed to fire the guns of their Patton tanks which no doubt hampered their operations.

Another example can be taken from the war between Iraq and Iran both of whom have very modern and technically sophisticated weapons systems obtained mainly from the Soviet Union and the United States, respectively.[79] Until at least early October 1980 the war was waged without external support.

As these two powers are relatively equal in military terms neither of them could attain a victory but the war gradually evolved into one of attrition. Iraqi ground forces were somewhat more intrusive than the Iranian army, but could not score any crucial victory. The Iranian air force was, on the other hand, more capable of bombing strategic targets in the adversary's territory and could hence respond to the attacks made by the Iraqi air force.

The combination of these dimensions of warfare yields a military stalemate in which neither party can advance in a significant manner. The fighting results in physical and human losses, but because of the relative military symmetry they are not excessive. The problems of the availability of spare parts and technical skill tend to slow down the tempo and scope of the warfare. The restraint shown by the great powers has greatly contributed to this tendency, although Iran, for instance, has been able to purchase spare parts from the private international market.

The acquisition of an advanced military technology may not in other words increase correspondingly the military power, defined as the ability to attain specific political and strategic objectives, but may even reduce it:

> It is evident that the techniques of force are only one element in the determination of military power and that theories which fail to take into account the social organization of the military, the relations of force, and the social basis for technology are inadequate.[80]

This being the situation the military and political power of a developing country may not be necessarily reduced by a shift to an alternative defence conception based on the inoffensive deterrence and the people's army. It would also increase the opportunities to meet the demand for weapons and military technology from the local sources, because the sophisticated technology - imported from the metropoles of the world - would not be needed to the same degree. In that way the emergence of military-industrial enclaves highly dependent on foreign inputs could be slowed down. The military establishment and the military industry would be concordant, both in structure and doctrines, with the local society and the factor endowment of the economy without depriving them of the ability to develop and also defend themselves.

We may again be running the danger of idealizing the situation, because there are constant pressures to direct the economy towards a technology and capital-intensive - and capitalist-intensive, for that matter - path of development which would also normally result in resorting to an industrial army.[81] The alternative is, of course, to resist these pressures and make deliberate, conscious choices concerning the direction of the development and defence policy of the country.

6.4.2.   Guidelines for the Reorientation of the Armaments Industry

It has been argued above that the main characteristics of the present world military order are its hierarchical structure and consequent asymmetric dependence patterns. The world military order can be in fact divided into three or possibly four layers which are both analytically and empirically separate from each other. At the highest level there are the great military powers which largely dictate the qualitative dynamics of armaments production in the world, including that of the smaller industrialized countries which seldom have a comprehensive and viable defence industry of their own. The third layer then consists of developing countries which can be further divided, if so desired, into two groups; those which have embarked upon the domestic production of arms and those which rely on arms imports.[82]

It is reasonable to state that in global terms the civilian and military industries form their own vertical sectors which are less integrated with each other through a spill-over process than by the overall industrial dynamics of the leading industrialized countries. This appears to be a reason for the gap between the civilian and military industries being bigger in developing than in industrialized countries.

In a historical perspective, various stages of industrial cycles have produced their characteristic weapons systems.[83] Thus the rise of the steel industry was a precondition for the extensive naval procurement before World War I, and the present rise of electronics is a precondition for electronic warfare. According to some predictions the 1980s will see the development of a massive telecommunications industry, the rise of which could facilitate the solution of the conflict between protectionist and free-trade industries which is now coming to a head in major capitalist countries. The rise of the telecommunications industry would also lead to the further development of a new generation of weapons such as precision-guided munitions (PGMs) and automated battlefields as well as many other systems based primarily on electronics and other components of the telecommunications industry.[84] If the earlier regularities in the horizontal arms race are combined with these emerging tendencies one may submit that the 1980s will see the production of weapons systems typical of the telecommunications and electronics era also in those developing countries which have relatively advanced domestic arms industries. This prospect would mean a further culmination of the economic and technological problems which the armaments industry is facing today.

The outcome would probably be that instead of achieving a high degree of autonomy in their defence industries, developing countries would rather become dependent on the new military technologies of industrialized countries, especially in the field of electronics. This would also further widen the gap between the civilian and military industries in the Third World.

To prevent these developments from taking place, strategies and guidelines must be outlined to reorient the armaments industries. In industrialized countries the most important single task is to slow down military research and development which is the major factor behind the technological arms race and its spread to practically all parts of the world.[85] This measure would also decrease in the longer run the procurement funds and hence release resources from military to civilian purposes. A part of these resources should be transferred to developing countries, especially to the least developed ones, to assist them, for instance, in their industrialization programmes.

Hence the process of disarmament in industrialized countries would produce positive results in developing nations in two ways. First, they could receive more resources through various channels of development cooperation and, secondly, the global dissemination of military technology would slow down. It is not, however, sufficient to consider only the measures which should be taken in the centre, but the need to transform industrial structures in the periphery should also be discussed. It is politically very difficult to create any multilateral intergovernmental arrangements which would govern the transfer of military technology to the Third World. In the civilian sector, arrangements to transfer better and more appropriate technology have long been planned and even implemented to a certain extent. In the military sector this approach to controlling the transfer of harmful technologies is hardly conceivable because of the number of military and political considerations involved. Consequently, the reorientation of the armaments industry must take place separately in the centre and in the periphery, although these measures in reality interact with each other.

In considering the reasons for which it is profitable to induce a process of transformation in the armaments industry one should take heed of at least two factors. The imports of weapons and military technology reduce the capacity to import civilian technology. This is shown by the fact that in the most militarized countries of the Third World, the share of arms imports of the total imports is very high, i.e. the opportunity costs are also high. In addition to the small spill-over effects, the import of military technology for the purposes of the local armaments industry absorbs resources which could have been otherwise used for the broadening and diversification of the production basis of the society. The resource absorption is also obvious in the case of manpower; the reparation and maintenance of weapons systems require technicians and other skilled or semi-skilled personnel, which would otherwise be needed in the civilian industries in order to implement the industrialization programmes. Now the growth of the military production often suppresses these emerging civilian industries by a simple negative allocation effect.[86]

A precondition for the transformation of the armaments industry in developing countries is a change in the military strategy and military doctrines. This would be reflected, in turn, in the structure and nature of the armaments industry. Instead of capital, research and electronics-intensive weapons systems, less sophisticated, more rugged multipurpose weapons of a defensive character would be produced. The thesis on the spearhead function of military technology, its assumed role in enhancing the quality and variety of civilian technology, has been proved untenable, and hence this type of reorientation in the armaments industry would in no considerable way reduce the overall technological capacity of the country. On the contrary in the alternative production pattern the spill-over process between the civilian and military sectors might be more intense than is the case in the present situation.

An important aspect of the focus on advanced military technology most often imported from dominant powers and transnational corporations is its tendency to result in security risks. The repair and maintenance as well as the operation of this technology demand higher skill levels than the country can supply. This necessitates the resort to foreign expertise which is normally provided by the supplier of the technology. It is fully conceivable that in the conditions of a political and military crisis, for which the weapons have been accumulated to protect the security of the country, military technology cannot be operated because of the withdrawal of foreign experts, sabotage carried out by them or a strike imposed by them.

The development of an alternative military technology would and should be related to the reduction of dependence on the external suppliers and would hence point in the direction of increasing self-reliance. In the course of this development the debt burden created by the purchase of arms and military technology could be reduced and the opportunities to apply political or economic pressure cut down. This is important for the reason that the growing debt burden, both in general as well as in the connection of the arms imports, is a major means of integrating developing countries with the capitalist centres of the world. In the national setting the local raw materials could be utilized more as the country concerned could decrease various conditions involved in technology contracts. In other words, so-called backward linkages could be created and in that way the armaments industry could be integrated more closely with the rest of the domestic economy.

For the time being, the emerging military industries in the Third World negate efforts towards more self-reliant development. By reorienting the armaments industry at least a measure of compatibility could be created. This strategy would be presumably opposed by a multitude of actors; among them the arms manufacturers, often transnational corporations, for which developing countries have represented lucrative marketing opportunities. One way of countering the pressures - manifested, for example, in aggressive sales and advertisement campaigns - is to pay more attention to their role in the transfer of military technology in various international codes of conducts, in particular those dealing with the transfer of technology and with the overall activities of transnational corporations. So far the transfer of military technology is completely neglected in these draft codes.

Comprehensive international reforms would also improve the opportunities to follow a more self-reliant strategy of industrialization, including that of the armaments industry. The relaxation of tension between nations would, for example, reduce the justification for continued militarization and arms sales. The implementation of basic principles of the New International Economic Order would, in turn, make the international economy more equitable and hence reduce hierarchy and vertical division of labour which have favoured the present type of armaments industry in developing countries.

The great majority of disarmament proposals advanced after World War II have concerned nuclear weapons and other weapons of mass destruction. It is self-evident that these proposals have had relevance for various industries in major military powers. This is the case, for example, in the chemical industry where the production of chemical agents for military purpose has been fairly closely related to the civilian production. It is apparent that in the chemical industry the spill-over process between the civilian and military sectors has been more extensive than in the production of other weapons systems. The nuclear industry is so much of a special case that it will not be discussed here. It may suffice to say that the civilian and military aspects are closely related in this field, and their separation is possible only by special safeguard arrangements.

The analysis of the relationship between the disarmament policy and the industrialization programs is most meaningful in the connection with the conventional weapons and forces which have been said to absorb about 80 per cent of the global military expenditures. As a consequence various initiatives to reduce the stockpiles of conventional weapons would directly affect the industrial capacity and the economic development of the country concerned. By now several tens of proposals to regulate and limit armed forces and armaments have been made.[87] One characteristic of these initiatives is, however, that they are very unspecific, and hardly touch in practice the consequences of the arms cuts. This is characteristic of official disarmament proposals in general. They normally deal only with various manifestations of the armament policies and very seldom analyze their roots and consequences.[88]

The most thorough analysis of the development aspects of the arms race and of disarmament has been carried out by a UN Group of Governmental Experts, appointed by the Secretary-General in 1975. Their report, entitled Economic and Social Consequences of the Arms Race and of Military Expenditures, analyzed, inter alia, the role of the arms race in the consumption of resources, its relationship with the economic and social development as well as the international implications of the arms race.[89] The report deals extensively with the economic role of the arms race, touching also its impact on the industrial development:

> How the actual economic performance of individual countries, public and private consumption on the one hand, and investment and growth on the other is affected by their military efforts depends on a number of factors: the level of economic development, the nature of the economic and social system, the extent and effectiveness of government planning, the volume of military expenditures, political priorities and in particular the extent to which the resources used for military purposes would otherwise have been devoted to consumption, private or public, or to investment, and many others... As regards economic development and growth in particular, the maintenance and arming of large standing military forces absorbs a volume of resources substantial enough to affect all the basic parameters involved: the volume and structure of investment, the size and composition of work force and the rate of technological change. The volume of investment which shapes the size and quality of the stock of capital is one of the basic factors determining the rate of growth. To what extent savings on military budgets would be transferred to investment depends, of course, on the economic framework, on political decisions and on the ways in which governments control the economy. Governments have means at their disposal... to redirect resources and to channel released resources towards investment. Moreover, military budgets are significantly large in comparison with current levels of investment. Some 20 per cent of the total world output is devoted to fixed capital formation, world military expenditures being equivalent to 25 to 30 per cent of this. In most countries, therefore, there is scope for significant rises in investment if military budgets are reduced. Even crude calculations indicate that the potential effects of this on growth could be substantial.[90]

We have complained above that the economic aspects of the arms control and disarmament proposals are almost entirely neglected in the official disarmament policies. A partial exception to this rule is the idea that a certain share of the reductions in military budgets should be devoted to providing assistance to developing countries. This idea was officially voiced for the first time by the Soviet Union in 1973 in its proposal to the UN General Assembly. According to this proposal, which was subsequently approved by the great majority of member states, the permanent members of the UN Security Council should cut down their military expenditures by 10 per cent and the savings should be transferred for the social and economic development of the Third World.[91] Some countries have insisted that the implementation of the Soviet proposal presupposes a consensus on what is a military budget which can be, in turn, only reached by the introduction of a system of standardized military budgets.

To improve the present situation more attention should be paid to the economic and industrial implications of the development and control of military technology. In the national context the practice of providing an industrial impact analysis of any new major weapons system should be introduced, and hence its economic implications should be made clear at the very beginning. At the international level this sort of arrangement may not work in reality. Instead, one might imagine that every arms-control and disarmament treaty, whether bilateral or multilateral, should be accompanied by the evaluation of its economic and industrial implications, and at a later stage, an indication of how the resources so released could be alternatively used. Naturally these alternative uses are even more of a national question in which context they have to be ultimately resolved.

A problem in alternative defence planning is the fact that the measurement of the economic and industrial impacts in alternative models of military production is very difficult. A number of approaches have been developed to cope with this dilemma in the present type of military production. These approaches include, for instance, various parametric studies and input-output analyses, and they can be used to determine the overall impact of on-going military production.[92] The measurement of the economic effects of alternative production arrangements is as difficult as the determination of the impact of any other hypothetical system. This being the case, the empirical decision-making, i.e. a cost-benefit analysis, relying on comparisons between different alternatives, is difficult indeed. It is not, however, impossible because present knowledge enables a rough simulation of the structure and character of the alternative defence production and the consequent evaluation of their likely economic impact.

Alternative use of the military industry is both a political and a technological process. Political decisions are needed to facilitate the initiation and implementation of technical measures of reconversion. An absolute precondition for any major transformation of the military industry is the political decision to allocate fewer resources to the military sector. This presupposes, in turn, at least a modest agreement between the main military powers that this decision is multilaterally followed; unilateral reductions of the military potential may be helpful in some respects but they do not carry very far.

National measures of reconversion together with the cuts in military spending are thus essential in the efforts to transform military industry. This does not mean, however, that nothing can be achieved in the absence of these measures. In fact by applying various gradual measures the military industry can be restructured to a considerable extent. At the transnational level one of the major aims should be switching the focus on the projects of the joint military production to the civilian undertakings.

In the present circumstances, especially in Western Europe, the civilian research projects dwindle in comparison to the transnational collaboration on military projects. To change this situation the transnational collaboration in civilian research, preferably across the traditional bloc boundaries, should be considerably increased and institutionalized.

A logical supplement to this idea would be the reconsideration of the present strategy and composition of the technology transfer. The armaments industry is rapidly internationalizing and focusing on military technology instead of mere weapons systems. By allocating more resources to the national and transnational projects of civilian research, foundations would be also laid for the transfer of more and better civilian technology to the Third World. A "better" civilian technology means here the kind of knowledge and equipment which is development-orientated, in contrast to a growth-orientated technology, and which can be used to satisfy the needs of the people and, as a precondition for this, to restructure the production system of the recipient. In concrete terms this would also mean the development of <u>alternative channels</u> for the transfer of technology, at the expense of transnational corporations.

In other words two essential changes are needed; the switch from military to civilian research, development and production as well as the switch from channels of transfer exclusively dominated by private interests to those in which <u>public authorities</u> also participate. Both of these changes have to be implemented simultaneously to really introduce new elements into the present situation. In particular the switch from channels controlled by TNCs to those supervised by public authorities is not sufficient as it does not necessarily guarantee any improvement. In fact even now, a considerable part of military technology transferred to developing countries is controlled, in one way or another, by these authorities. In this perspective the reconversion of resources from military to the civilian uses appears to be a more crucial measure.

Disengaging from the gradually emerging international military-industrial division of labour, increases the possibilities of restructuring the national defence systems and their industrial base. It has already been argued earlier in this chapter that for economic reasons it would be better to concentrate the domestic military industry on the production of such weapons systems which would use more local skills, technologies and resources and would hence avoid the adverse financial and technological effects which are caused by excessive integration with the international market in military hardware. It has also been argued earlier that the restructuring of the national defence industry should be implemented in conjunction with the transformation of military doctrine. It may not be an exaggeration to say that the attainment of the goal of self-reliance is impossible in the countries producing major weapons systems unless disarmament is realized or resources are geared to a new type of military industry. The dependence on foreign military technology perpetuates and reproduces other forms of economic, technological, and in the last instance, political dependence.

Notes and references

1.   Cf. Richard Head, Technology and the Military Balance. Foreign Affairs 4, 1978, pp.544-563.

2.   Ulrich Albrecht, Peter Lock and Herbert Wulf, Arbeitsplätze durch Rüstung? Hamburg 1978, pp. 40-52.

3.   Cf. Mary Kaldor, The Role of Arms in Capitalist Economies: the Process of Overdevelopment and Underdevelopment, in Arms Control and Technological Innovation, ed. by David Carlton and Carlo Schaerf, London 1977, pp. 322-341.

4.   Cf., e.g., Prospects for Multilateral Arms Restraint. A Staff Report Prepared for the Use of the Committee on Foreign Relations, U.S. Senate, U.S. GPO, Washington D.C. 1979, pp. 81-82.

5.   Kaldor, op.cit. 1977, p. 335.

6.   Cf. Asbjörn Eide, Arms Transfers and Third World Militarization. Bulletin of Peace Proposals 2, 1977, pp. 99-102.

7.   Katsu Kohri et al., The Fifty Years of Japanese Aviation 1910-1060, Tokyo 1961, and Peter Lock and Herbert Wulf, The Economic Consequences of the Transfer of Military-Oriented Technology, in The World Military Order, ed. by Mary Kaldor and Asbjörn Eide, London 1979, p. 210.

8.   See, e.g., John J. Johnson, The Role of the Military in Under-Developed Countries, Rand Corporation, Princeton 1962 and The Military in the Political Development of the New States, ed. by Morris Janowitz, Chicago 1964.

9.   Istvan Kende, Thirty Years, Twenty-Six Days of Peace, One Hundred and Sixteen Wars. Co-existence, Vol. 13, No. 2, 1976, pp. 126-143 and Istvan Kende, Wars of Ten Years 1967-1976. Journal of Peace Research, Vol. 15, No. 3, 1978, pp. 227-241.

10.   An intensive study of this concept and its empirical content is F. Fröbel, J. Heinrichs and O. Kreye, Die neue internationale Arbeitsteilung, Hamburg 1977.

11.   For the policies of TNCs regarding the transfer of technology, see The International Corporation and the Transfer of Technology, as well as Guidelines for International Investments, International Chamber of Commerce 1972.

12.   About the role of regional power centres see Raimo Väyrynen,

Economic and Military Position of the Regional Power Centers. Journal of Peace Research, Vol. 16, No. 4, 1979, pp. 349-369.

13. In 1973-1977, the U.S. transferred arms to 66 non-NATO countries, France to 53 countries and the UK to 44 countries. The Soviet Union transferred arms to 41 non-WTO countries, the FRG to 40 countries and Italy to 28 countries. Calculated from World Military Expenditures and Arms Transfers 1968-1977. U.S. Arms Control and Disarmament Agency, Washington D.C. 1979, pp. 155-158. From now on this publication is abbreviated WMEAT.

14. Cf. Ulrich Albrecht and Mary Kaldor, Introduction, in The World Military Order, op.cit. 1979, pp. 1-16.

15. About the social functions of arms transfers, see e.g., Kaldor op.cit. 1977, pp. 322-341.

16. For a general analysis of military relationships in the North-South context see Dieter Senghaas, Weltwirtschaftsordnung und Entwicklungspolitik. Plädoyer für Dissoziation, Frankfurt am Main 1977, pp. 223-260.

17. Cf. Albrecht, Charins et al., Militarismus heute. Wesen und Erscheinungsformen des Militarismus der Gegenwart, Berlin 1979, pp. 266-283.

Chapter 2

1. Raimo Väyrynen, Industrialization, Economic Development and the World Military Order. A report prepared for the United Nations Industrial Development Organization (UNIDO), February 1979, pp. 21-22.

2. Data from in Economic and Social Consequences of the Armament Race and its Extremely Harmful Effects on World Peace and Security. Report of the Secretary-General, United Nations, A/32/88/Add.1., 12 September 1977, pp. 50, 54, 67, 78, 84, 95, 117 and 138. In the Federal Republic of Germany the procurement budget of 1976 amounted to DM 5.8 billion of which the aircraft industry absorbed 23.6 per cent, machine building 22.9, electronic industry 18.5 and car industry 17.0 per cent. See Ulrich Albrecht, Peter Lock and Herbert Wulf, op.cit. 1978, p. 24.

3. Leonard Sullivan, Carter's New Defense Budget. Too Little, Too Late. Aviation Week and Space Technology, February 25, 1980. This journal is abbreviated AWST from now on.

4. For an analysis of the tendencies within arms industries of the capitalist countries see e.g., Raimo Väyrynen, Transnational Corporations and Arms Transfers. Instant Research on Peace and Violence (Tampere), 3-4, 1977, pp. 145-166.

5.   Cf. Interavia 7, 1979, pp. 641-645 (Future Prospects for Fokker).

6.   Le Monde, April 25, 1974 and July 13, 1979.

7.   Report on European Armament Procurement Cooperation. European Parliament, Political Affairs Committee, Document 83/1978, 8 May 1978, passim.

8.   United Nations, A/32/88/Add.1., op.cit., pp. 21-25.

9.   The World Aerospace Industry Today. IMF World Aerospace Conference, Report 3, Seattle, Washington, USA, May 22-24, 1979, p. 7.

10.   Ibid., p. 23.

11.   Ibid., p. 17.

12.   AWST, April 30, 1979.

13.   Rockwell International. Annual Report 1979, and data files of Tampere Peace Research Institute (TAPRI).

14.   Armand Mattelart, Multinational Corporations and the Control of Culture, Sussex & New Jersey 1979, p. 38.

15.   FMS statistics concern transfers based on agreements between the U.S. government and a foreign government or international organization. Transfers under military grant programmes or direct agreements between foreign government and private U.S. contractors (which require an export licence) are not included in FMS figures.

16.   Report on European Armaments Procurement... op.cit, pp. 54-55 and Julian Critchley, A Community Policy for Armaments. Nato Review, Vol. 27, No. 1, February 1979, p. 11.

17.   Dr. Ludwig Boelkow, Managing Director of FRG's largest aerospace company MBB in AWST, April 24, 1972.

18.   Allen Greenwood, International Industrial Cooperation. Nato's Fifteen Nations, Vol. 23, No. 2, April-May 1978. Mr. Greenwood is the Deputy Chairman of British Aerospace.

19.   AWST, June 6, 1977.

20.   Ibid.

21.   Interavia 6, 1979.

22.   Ibid.

23.   AWST, February 13, 1978; Aerospace Company Profiles, Co-production & Country Profiles, IMF World Aerospace Conference, Report 2, Seattle, Wash., USA, May 22-24, 1979; Business Week, July 16,   1979;

Matra exercise 1978 and other company publications; Le Monde, July 13, 1979; Jane's Major Companies in Europe 1980; Le Monde, June 8, 1979 and November 4, 1979; Interavia 6, 1979 and TAPRI data files. According to Newsweek, September 29, 1980, Matra's annual sales are already $ 3.5 billion. The rapid growth is partly due to acquisitions of other companies, but growth of production, in the military field, also explains the growth.

24.   AWST, March 3, 1980.

25.   Cf. Lawrence Freedman, Arms Production in the United Kingdom: Problems and Prospects. The Royal Institute of International Affairs, London 1978, p. 33.

26.   Aerospace Company Profiles... op.cit., p. 69; British Aerospace Annual Report 1978 and other company publications and commercials; AWST, February 18, 1980; Freedman op.cit. 1978, pp. 47-49 and TAPRI data files.

27.   Albrecht, Lock and Wulf op.cit. 1978, pp. 40-52 and AWST, April 24, 1972.

28.   Aerospace Company profiles... op.cit., p. 69.

29.   AWST, April 24, 1972. Boeing has later sold its shares, see Newsweek, March 24, 1980. According to Newsweek the share of Aérospatiale is now 12 per cent. According to The Economist, February 16, 1980, the share of United Technologies is now 26 per cent, and ITT/SEL owns 9 per cent.

30.   Albrecht, Lock and Wulf op.cit. 1978, p. 171.

31.   Erhard Heckmann, The German Aerospace Industry - Past, Present, Problems. Nato's Fifteen Nations, Vol. 32, No. 2, April-May 1978, pp. 88-95; Newsweek, March 24, 1980; Udo Mathes, Odyssee 2000. Forum - Zeitschrift für Transnationale Politik, 1/2, 1980, p. 31; AWST, June 11, 1979, November 19, 1979, December 17, 1979; World Armaments and Disarmament. SIPRI Yearbook 1979, London 1979; Aerospace Company Profiles... op.cit., p. 48-49; Le Monde, June 29, 1978; Interavia 4, 1978, and TAPRI data files.

32.   AWST, January 7, 1980, pp. 39-42. Lockheed Aircraft International, Lockheed Aircraft Service, General Electric (USA), Snecma (France), Westinghouse (USA) and Austin (USA) are responsible for the development program of Hellenic Aerospace Industries into a major service and manufacturing center.

33.   Initiatives taken by the Metal Workers Federation in the Italian Arms Industry, IDOC Bulletin, No. 10-11, Oct.-Nov. 1979, pp. 5-8 and for a survey of Italian arms production and exports ibid., pp. 13-29.

34.   World Armaments and Disarmament. SIPRI Yearbook 1979, London 1979, pp. 172-173. From now on abbreviated as SIPRI Yearbook 1979. See also WMEAT 1968-1977, op.cit., p. 133.

35.   SIPRI Yearbook 1979, pp. 90-95 and 144-147.

36.   Aerospace Company Profiles... op.cit., p. 73.

37.   IDOC Bulletin, No. 10-11, Oct.-Nov. 1979, pp. 13-29.

38.   The Arms Trade with the Third World. SIPRI, Uppsala 1971, pp. 280-281 and SIPRI Yearbook 1979, pp. 204-241.

39.   Cf. Harry F. Eustace, Selenia. Blending Technology to Meet Operational Needs. Electronic Warfare/Defence Electronics, April 1979, pp. 86-89.

40.   AWST, February 18, 1980.

41.   Michael Klare, The Italian Connection, IDOC Bulletin, No. 10-11, October-November 1979, pp. 3-4, and ibid., pp. 13-29; AWST, February 13, 1978 and March 3, 1980. The engines for Italian aircraft come from Rolls Royce, General Electric, Lycoming and the Allison Division of General Motors.

42.   Initiatives taken by... op.cit., p. 7.

43.   For a description of Spanish armament industry, see Reijo Lindroos, Disarmament and Employment. Central Organization of Finnish Trade Unions in co-operation with TAPRI, Tampere 1980, pp. 55-56. For earlier German connections of Spanish armament industry, see Albrecht, Lock and Wulf, op.cit. 1978, pp. 40-52. See also Ulrich Albrecht and Peter Lock, Multinationale Konzerne und Rüstung, in Multinationale Konzerne und Dritte Welt, ed. by Dieter Senghaas and Ulrich Menzel, Frankfurt am Main 1977, pp. 128-143 and SIPRI Yearbook 1979, pp. 100-103 and 148-149.

44.   AWST, December 3, 1979, and the Military Balance, various years, for major identified arms agreements.

45.   Afrique-Asie, No. 141, August 1977 and No. 145, October 1977. The text of OTRAG-Zaire agreement has appeared in Race and Class, Vol. 19, No. 2, 1977. See also Kallu Kalamiya, Rape of Sovereignty: OTRAG in Zaire, Review of African Political Economy, No. 14, January-April 1979, pp. 16-35; Gerd Greune, Bundesdeutsche Raketen in Zentralafrika, Forum - Zeitschrift für Transnationale Politik, No. 1/2, 1980, pp. 49-51; Flight International, June 10, 1978 and Le Monde, June 17, 1978.

46.   Thus the Israeli sources claimed that Syria was planning to participate in OTRAG's project and to obtain rockets from it; see Alan Elsner & Martin Sieft, Syrians Interested in German-Zaire Rocket. The Jerusalem Post (international edition), April 29-May 5, 1979.

47.   See John Vinocur, Zaire Orders German Firm to Halt Its Rocket Testing. International Herald Tribune, April 28-29, 1979, and Zaire Terminates Rocket Launch Site Pact. AWST, May 7, 1979, p. 18.

48. OTRAG Seeks Foreign Launch Site. Flight International, August 12, 1978, p. 456 and OTRAG: What Goes Up Must Come Down. The Economist, May 19, 1979, pp. 88-89.

49. For PGM's, see James F. Digby, Precision-Guided Weapons, Adelphi Papers 118, International Institute for Strategic Studies, London 1975. For discussion of the changes caused by PGMs, see Anne Hessing Cahn and Joseph Kruzel, Arms Trade in the 1980s, in Anne Hessing Cahn et al., Controlling Future Arms Trade, New York 1977, pp. 25-105, particularly pp. 52-58.

50. Cf. the list of current U.S. military aircraft in AWST, March 3, 1980, pp. 102-103.

51. Some Military Lessons of the War. Strategic Survey 1973, pp. 52-55; The Lessons of October, the editorial of AWST, December 3, 1973, p. 13, and Malvern Lumsden, New Military Technologies and the Security of Small and Medium-sized Countries in Europe, Current Research on Peace and Violence, No. 1, 1980, pp. 24-32.

52. For example British Aircraft industries have developed and produced 13 new military aircraft during 15 years, of which 4 have been cancelled. During previous 15 years they produced 46 new military aircraft. Sense about Defence. The Report of the Labour Party Defence Study Group, London 1977, p. 38. For discussion, see Lindroos op.cit. 1980.

53. United Nations, A/32/88/Rev.1., New York 1978, pp. 7-8. An example of a new technological step in military electronics is the new U.S. bomber Stealth, which has been developed by Lockheed. The plane is invisible for enemy radars, and calls for intensified development of better radars. See The Economist, August 30, 1980.

54. Cf. Charles M. Herzfeld, The Military R&D Process. A View from the Industry. The Bulletin of the Atomic Scientists, Vol. 34, No. 10, December 1978, pp. 33-40. The author has worked for both the Department of Defense (DOD) and ITT.

55. United Nations, A/32/88/Add.1., op.cit. 1977, pp. 140-141 and Le Monde, November 4, 1979.

56. United Nations, A/32/88/Add.1., op.cit. 1977, p. 53.

57. Prospects for Multilateral Arms Export Restraint... op.cit. 1979, p. 26.

58. Richard Hartman, Platforms and Electronics - Another Two-Way Street. Electronic Warfare/Defense Electronics, April 1979, p. 13.

59. Edmond Sciberras, Multinational Electronic Companies and National Economic Policies, Greenwich 1977, p. 42.

60. All figures from Electronics, January 4, 1979, pp. 105-128 and Interavia 6, 1979, p. 551.

61.   Sciberras, op.cit. 1977, p. 42.

62.   IBM Annual Report 1978; ITT Annual Report 1978; DAFSA - Informa-
        tions, Société de Documentation et d'Analyses Financières, Paris
        1975 and TAPRI data files.

63.   Annual Reports of the companies; 10-K-reports for the U.S. Securi-
        ties and Exchange Commission, SEC; DAFSA, op.cit. 1975 and TAPRI
        data files.

64.   Annual reports of the companies and TAPRI data files.

65.   Cf. Interavia 6, 1979, p.551.

66.   Business Week, September 10, 1979.

67.   Business Week, October 1, 1979 and TAPRI data files.

68.   Electronics, January 4, 1979.

69.   Jane's Major Companies of Europe 1980; annual reports of the
        companies and TAPRI data files.

70.   AWST, October 22, 1979, p. 75-81.

71.   Philips Annual Report 1978; DAFSA op.cit.; AWST ibid.; Global Wiew
        (a publication by Philips); Herbert Wulf, The Economic Importance of
        the Arms Industry in the Federal Republic of Germany and the
        Feasibility of Converting It to Civilian Production. Peace and the
        Sciences 2, 1979, p. 46; and TAPRI data files.

72.   Business Week, January 21, 1980.

73.   Fortune, August 13, 1979, p. 208; Siemens Geschäftsbericht 1979;
        Interavia 4, 1978, p. 303; The Economist, February 16, 1980 and
        December 8, 1979; Jane's Major Companies of Europe 1980; DAFSA
        op.cit.; Wulf op.cit. 1979, pp. 40-44.

74.   The role of planning companies in warship industry has well been
        described as follows:
            The warship today is the largest, most complicated and most
            costly of contemporary weapons systems. Its growing complexity
            over recent years has been such that the range of know-how
            required in its development is outside the resources of any single
            firm - shipbuilder, equipment, electronics or weapons manufac-
            turer. The position has, of course, been further exacerbated by
            increasingly smaller series and the extended intervals at which, in
            general, naval vessels are being ordered. The only clear solution
            to the problem has been setting up of central, independent
            planning and design organizations at the national level at least. In
            Europe a group of Dutch shipyards founded NEVESBU and in the
            UK, YARD-Yarrow-Admiralty Research and Department - filled
            the gap. In West Germany, when FRG naval rebuilding began in

the mid-fifties, the authorities decided that warship design and construction be carried out by private industry; and as technology advanced, and proper co-ordination of all sectors became essential, Marinetechnik Planungsgesellschaft was established in 1966.

See Maritime Defence, November 1979, p. 450.

75. WMEAT 1968-1977, p. 129.

76. John Lloyd, Electronics to the Fore, Financial Times, September 24, 1979.

77. Lloyd, ibid.; John Marriott, GEC-Marconi Electronics- a Profile. NATO's Fifteen Nations, Vol. 22, No. 6, December 1977-January 1978, pp. 143-144; The General Electric Company Limited. Anti-Report, Counter Information Services CIS, London (no date); Jane's Major Companies of Europe 1980; The Arms Traders. An Alphabetical and Geographical Listing of Military Exporters in the UK. Campaign Against Arms Trade, London 1980; Max Wilkinson, Electronics: All Set for Takeover Battles, Financial Times, June 22, 1979; Business Week, November 5, 1979; Defence Industry Supplement - Racal Electronics Group, Defence 1979; John Lloyd, A Merger which Could Make UK Electronics Stronger, Financial Times, January 19, 1980, DAFSA op.cit.; TAPRI data files.

78. Wilkinson, op.cit.

79. Thomson-CSF. Annual Report 1978; Military Technology 6, 1979, p. 61; Le Monde, April 7, 1978 and September 26, 1979.

80. Thomson-CSF. Annual Report 1978, p. 30.

81. Interavia 6, 1979, p. 551 and Le Monde, March 6, 1979.

82. TAPRI data files and Jane's Major Companies of Europe 1980.

83. Harry F. Eustace, Selenia. Blending Technology to Meet Operational Needs. Electronic Warfare/Defense Electronics, April 1979, pp. 86-89.

84. AWST, November 1, 1971 and June 11, 1979; Fortune, October 9, 1978; Mattelart op.cit. 1979, pp. 32-35; Fortune, September 25 and August 13, 1979; Electronics, January 4, 1979; Mitsubishi Corporation. Annual Report April 1978-March 1979, p. 12. On the possibility of Japan's future role in arms transfers, see Peter M. Dawkins, Conventional Arms Transfers and Control: Producer Restraints, in Anne Hessing Cahn et al., op.cit., 1977, pp. 107-159, particularly p. 118: "Japan already produces aircraft and tanks, and the temptation to reduce unit costs through large-scale production could lead to a major role for Tokyo in the international arms business. One possibility is that Japan will provide to second-tier producers those sophisticated subsystems - such as advanced electronics, electro-optics, special metals, and precision casting - that depend on high technologies".

85. The World Aerospace Industry Today... op.cit. 1979, p. 15, based on European Community sources.

86. The Financial Times, August 24, 1979.

87. South African built models are C-4M Kudu transport and AM-3C Bosbok Trainer, powered by Lycoming engines produced under licence by Italian Piaggio; MB-326 Impala COIN/trainer, powered by Rolls Royce engines. For documentation, see sources of Table 35. According to SIPRI Yearbook 1979, South Africa also builds Dassault's Mirage F-1C fighters under licence. Mirage family is powered by Snecma engines, which would mean that also this company supplies engines to South African industry, in addition to the companies mentioned in Table 34.

88. Cf. Financial Times, August 24, 1979.

89. The Economist, August 18, 1979.

90. AWST, June 6, 1977.

91. Ibid.

92. Jack Baranson, Technology and the Multinationals, Lexington, Mass. 1979, pp. 23-29.

93. AWST, June 11, 1979.

94. Helsingin Sanomat, August 4, 1978; AWST, August 27, 1979.

95. AWST, June 11, 1979 and August 27, 1979.

Chapter 3

1. Consequently, rumours and speculation flourish in the West which may cause overreactions because of exaggerated estimates on Soviet arms arsenals and defence spending.

2. Cf. Gerd Borst-Franz Walter, Langfristige Tendenzen im Rüstungs-wettlauf USA-USSR. Osteuropa 2, 1973, p. 98 and Head, op.cit. 1978, pp. 544-563.

3. Cf. David Holloway, Technology and Political Decision in Soviet Armaments Policy. Journal of Peace Research, Vol. XI, No. 4, 1974, pp. 257-279, particularly pp. 270-272.

4. Ibid., p. 259-261.

5. Cf. Egbert Jahn, Armaments and Bureaucracy in Soviet Society. Bulletin of Peace Proposals, Vol. 10, No. 1, 1978, p. 111.

6. Michael Checinski, The Cost of Armament Production and the Profitability of Armament Exports in Comecon Countries. Osteuropa-Wirtschaft, Vol. 2, No. 2, 1975, p. 118 and Holloway op.cit., p. 264.

7. Checinski op.cit. 1975, pp. 119-120.

8. Cf. Lindroos op.cit. 1980 and Newsweek, February 11, 1980, p. 23.

9. V. Bondarenko, Nauchno-tekhnicheskii progress i ukrelenie oborono-sposobnosti strany. Kommunist vooruzhennykh sil, No. 24, 1971, p. 15 as translated and quoted by Holloway op.cit. 1974, p. 263.

10. A.A. Grechko, The Armed Forces of the Soviet Union, Moscow 1977, p. 143.

11. Ibid., p. 159.

12. For discussion see Jahn op.cit. 1978, pp. 108--111.

13. Raymond Hutchings, Soviet Arms Exports to the Third World. A Pattern and its Implications. The World Today 10, 1978, pp. 378-389.

14. Michael Checinski, Structural Causes of Soviet Arms Exports. Ost-europa-Wirtschaft, Vol. 4, No. 3, 1977, pp. 169-184.

15. Checinski op.cit. 1975, p. 129.

16. Cf. Lindroos op.cit. 1980.

17. Checinski op.cit. 1975, p. 128.

18. Ibid., p. 127.

19. Cf. The Lessons of October. AWST, December 3, 1973 and Lumsden op.cit. 1980.

20. SIPRI Yearbook 1979, op.cit., pp. 76-77, 204, 218 and AWST, June 11, 1979, pp. 282-289.

21. AWST, June 11, 1979, p. 282 and 287.

22. AWST, March 22, 1971, June 11, 1979 and March 3, 1980.

23. AWST, June 11, 1979.

24. SIPRI Yearbook 1979, p. 144 and 148.

25. Ibid., p. 100, 148 and AWST, March 3, 1980, pp. 133, 137.

26. Checinski op.cit. 1975, p. 117.

27. Dennis Chaplin, The Subcontractors. The Soviet Union's Indirect Strategy in the Third World. Military Review, Vol. 57, No. 6, 1977, p. 12.

28. SIPRI Yearbook 1979, p. 100, 101, 142 and 148.

29. Ibid., pp. 138-139, 142, 150 and AWST, March 3, 1980, p. 123.

30. Checinski op.cit. 1975, p. 118.

31. Claude Wachtel, L'essor de l'electronique Soviétique, Défense nationale, Vol. 34, August-September 1978, pp. 146-147.

32. Ibid., pp. 140-141.

33. Barry Miller, Soviet Radar Expertise expands. AWST, February 15, 1971, pp. 14-16, quotation p. 14.

34. AWST, May 29, 1978, p. 60-61.

35. Colin S. Gray, Soviet Tactical Airpower. Nato's Fifteen Nations, Vol. 23, No. 4, August-September 1978, pp. 46-52.

36. Wachtel op.cit. 1978, pp. 143-144.

37. AWST, July 1, 1974, pp. 16-17.

38. Baranson op.cit. 1979, pp. 72-73, 92-93.

39. Ibid., p. 73.

40. Kenneth J. Stein, Export Efforts Seek Turnkey Programs. AWST, June 6, 1977, pp. 281-296.

41. The Military Balance 1978-1979, p. 55 and Angus M. Frazer, Military Modernization in China. Problems of Communism, Vol. XXVIII, No. 5-6, September-December 1979, p. 35.

42. General George S. Brown, USAF, Chairman of the US Joint Chiefs of Staff, United States Military Posture for FY 1979, Washington D.C., January 20, 1978 as quoted by Frazer op.cit., p. 40.

43. SIPRI Yearbook 1979, pp. 74-75; Frazer op.cit. 1979, p. 39 and International Herald Tribune, November 14, 1979.

44. Helsingin Sanomat, January 8, 1979.

45. SIPRI Yearbook 1979, p. 144.

46. Robert Ropelewski, China's Aerospace Market Eyed Warily. AWST, June 11, 1979, pp. 141-142.

47. Ibid., p. 141.

48. AWST, January 21, 1980.

49. David R. Griffiths, Sales Data Cleared for China. AWST, June 9, 1980, pp. 16-17.

50.   Ibid., and Philip Geylin, Guns for China. The Guardian, June 8, 1980.

51.   International Herald Tribune, July 4, 1980.

52.   Interavia 12, 1978; Newsweek, May 15, 1978; International Herald Tribune, November 14, 1979 and July 4, 1980.

53.   SIPRI Yearbook 1979, pp. 74-77; AWST, January 21, 1980, p. 17; Frazer op.cit. 1979, p. 42.

54.   Griffiths op.cit. 1980, p. 16 and Geylin op.cit. 1980.

55.   AWST, February 20, 1978 and January 21, 1980.

56.   AWST, June 11, 1979.

57.   AWST, January 21, 1980.

58.   Anthony Durniak, China Poses Problems, Opportunities. Electronics, January 4, 1979, pp. 92-94.

59.   Ibid., pp. 92-94; Frazer op.cit. 1979, p. 46 and Baranson op.cit. 1979, pp. 73-74.

60.   Ropelewski op.cit. 1979, p. 143.

61.   ITT Annual Report 1978, p. 10.

62.   SIPRI Yearbook 1979, pp. 76-77.

63.   WMEAT 1968-1977, op.cit., p. 124.

64.   Cf. Business Week, November 5, 1979, p. 74.

65.   Christian Science Monitor, January 19, 1978 and Frazer op.cit. 1979, p. 39.

66.   Ropelewski op.cit., p. 139; SIPRI Yearbook 1979, pp. 175-177, 204-241.

67.   SIPRI Yearbook 1979, pp. 148-149, 206-107.

68.   Newsweek, October 22, 1979.

69.   Business Week, February 25, 1980, pp. 14-16.

Chapter 4

1.   Arms Transfer Policy: Report to Congress for Use of Committee on Foreign Relations, U.S. Senate. US Congress, Committee of Foreign Relations, Washington D.C. 1977, p. 11.

2.   Cf. Anne Hessing Cahn, The Economics of Arms Transfers, in Arms Transfers in the Modern World, ed. by Stephanie G. Neuman and Robert E. Harkavy, New York 1979, pp. 173-183.

3.   Ibid., p. 175-176.

4.   Ibid., p. 176.

5.   Cf. Chapter 2.2.1.

6.   Cf. Chapter 2.2.2. and Lawrence G. Franko, Restraining Arms Exports to the Third World: Will Europe Agree? Survival 1, 1979, pp. 14-25, quoted from page 16.

7.   Hessing Cahn and Kruzel op.cit. 1977, p. 69.

8.   Business Week, March 24, 1980, p. 64.

9.   Franko op.cit. 1979.

10.   AWST, January 14, 1980.

11.   Cf. Steven Lydenberg, Weapons for the World. Update. Council on Economic Priorities, New York 1977.

12.   An interview on the Finnish TV, November 16, 1979. The export manager, an elderly retired officer, himself told that "for exports you have to be prepared for all sort of things - I taught the customer's daughter how to dance twist".

13.   Far Eastern Economic Review, May 7, 1976.

14.   AWST, October 29, 1979.

15.   For an analysis of military advertising in the Federal Republic of Germany, see Rüstungswerbung in der Bundesrepublik, Militärpolitik Dokumentation, Heft 9/10, Jahrgang 3.

16.   International Herald Tribune, January 26-27, 1980.

17.   Ibid.

18.   For the Dassault case, see Le Monde, October 16 and 18, 1974. For the U.S. measures against overseas payments, see U.S. Proposes System of Disclosure in Treaty on Illicit Payments, Department of State Bulletin, No. 1954, December 6, 1976, pp. 696-698 and U.S. Moves to Ban Overseas Payments, AWST, June 6, 1977.

19.   Sunday Times, February 17, 1980.

20.   The case of Space Research Corporation has been carefully documented by the BBC in a TV program in 1978. See also Michael T. Klare, South Africa's U.S. Weapons Connections, The Nation, July 28-August 4, 1979, pp. 75-78.

21. <u>AWST</u>, February 9, 1976.

22. For details, See <u>New York Times</u>, January 24, 1968, February 24, 1975, October 12, 1977 and June 22, 1978; <u>Export-Import Bank</u>, Press Release April 5, 1973 and <u>Sperry Annual Report 1978</u>.

23. Sources of this information are Michaels T. Klare, Arms Technology and Dependency. U.S. Military Co-production Abroad, <u>NACLA Latin America and Empire Report</u> 1, 1977, pp. 25-32; Michael T. Klare, La Multinationalization des industries de guerre, <u>Le Monde Diplomatique</u>, February 1977, and <u>WMEAT 1966-1975</u>, op.cit., pp. 78-80.

24. Ulrich Albrecht and Peter Lock, Multinationale Konzerne und Rüstung, in <u>Multinationale Konzerne und Dritte Welt</u>, ed. by Dieter Senghaas and Ulrich Menzel, Frankfurt am Main 1977, p. 130.

25. See Mary Kaldor, European Defence Industries - National and International Implications, <u>ISIO Monographs</u>, No. 8, Sussex 1972, pp. 31-32, and Emma Rotschild, The Arms Boom and How to Stop It, <u>The New York Review of Books</u>, January 20, 1977, p. 24.

26. See Casualties of a Cut in Arms Sales Abroad, <u>Business Week</u>, April 25, 1977, p. 34.

27. For further details see Ulrich Albrecht, <u>Der Handel mit Waffen</u>, München 1971, pp. 10-12, 163-165 and 169.

28. For more details see Ulrich Albrecht, Dieter Ernst, Peter Lock & Herbert Wulf, <u>Rüstung und Unterentwicklung</u>, Reinbek bei Hamburg 1976, pp. 54-58.

29. Claus-Detlef Lehmann, Rüstungsexport und Rüstungskooperation aus der Sicht der Industrie, <u>Wehrtechnik</u> 2, 1978, pp. 14-15.

30. For a general analysis see, e.g., Raimo Väyrynen, International Patenting as a Means of Technological Dominance, <u>International Social Science Journal</u> 2, 1978, pp. 325-327. Examples of the bans on exports include the U.S. decision to veto the Israeli plans to sell their Kfir fighters to Ecuador or the Swedish decision to sell Viggen fighters to India. The veto decision was based on the fact that both Kfir and Viggen contain a U.S. engine.

31. For a general analysis of subcontracting in the electronic industry see International Subcontracting Arrangements in Electronics between Developed Market-Economy Countries and Developing Countries, <u>UNCTAD, TD/B/C.2/144. Supp. 1</u>, New York 1975.

32. See Edmon Scibirras, <u>Multinational Electronics Companies and National Economic Policies</u>, Greenwich, Conn. 1977, pp. 41-42 and 62-63.

33. Jacques S. Gansler, Let's Change the Way the Pentagon Does Business, <u>Harvard Business Review</u> 3, 1977, pp. 110 and 115.

34. A more detailed analysis of these zones is provided by Folker Fröbel, Jürgen Heinrichs and Otto Kreye, Die neue internationale Arbeitsteilung, Reinbek bei Hamburg 1977, esp. pp. 479-551. See also Free Trade Zones and Industrialization of Asia, AMPO, Tokyo 1977.

35. See German Aerospace: Messerschmitt to Marry? The Economist, July 30, 1977, pp. 75-76, and VFW-Fokker: An Aircraft and a Company, Too Many, The Economist, October 1, 1977, p. 96.

36. See Albrecht and Lock op.cit. 1977, p. 138; Jonathan Galloway, Multinational Corporations and Military-Industrial Linkages, in Steven Rosen (ed.), Testing the Theory of the Military-Industrial Complex, Lexington, Mass. 1973, p. 272, and Raymond Vernon, Multinational Enterprises and National Security, Adelphi Papers, No. 74, London 1971.

37. See Peter Lock & Herbert Wulf, Register of Arms Production in Developing Countries, Hamburg 1977, pp. 42 and 63.

38. See A Belgian Arms Maker Bids for Browning, Business Week, August 22, 1977, pp. 27-28.

39. Paul Fitzgerald et al., Rockwell International, Pacific North-West Research Center, Eugene 1975, pp. 24-25 and 30-34, and Rockwell International. Annual Report 1974, pp. 1 and 29-30.

40. Fitzgerald et al., op.cit. 1974, p. 29.

41. Albrecht and Lock op.cit. 1977, p. 130.

Chapter 5

1. We shall not discuss here whether South Africa is a developing country or not. Its military sector has been growing rapidly, and it is a primary concern for many developing countries; both reasons justify its inclusion in this chapter.

2. Foreign Military Sales and Military Assistance Facts. Department of Defence, Security Assistance Agency, Washington D.C., December 1978, and Augusto Varas Carlos Portales and Felipe Aguero, The National and International Dynamics of South American Armamentism. Current Research on Peace and Violence 1, 1980, pp. 1-23.

3. The Arms Trade with the Third World... op.cit. 1971, pp. 689-690.

4. Anthony Sampson, The Arms Bazaar, London 1977, p. 187. A number of cases showing the US-Europe rivalry are documented in The Arms Trade with the Third World... op.cit. 1971, pp. 718-722.

5. See, e.g., Peter B. Evans, The Military, the Multinationals and the

"Miracle": The Political Economy of the "Brazilian Model" of Development. Studies in Comparative International Development, Vol. IX, No. 3, 1974, pp. 26-45. See also István Kende, Dynamics of Wars, of Arms Trade and of Military Expenditure in the "Third World", 1945-1976. Instant Research on Peace and Violence 2, 1977, pp. 59-67.

6. Foreign Military Sales... op.cit.

7. For the role of the military in Brazilian society, see Alfred Stepan, The Military in Politics. Changing Patterns in Brazil, Princeton, N.J. 1971.

8. SIPRI Yearbook 1979... op.cit., p. 183.

9. Arms Trade Registers. SIPRI, Solna 1975, pp. 107-111 and SIPRI Yearbook, op.cit., various years.

10. Washington Post, December 18, 1977.

11. AWST, February 20, 1978.

12. Peter Lock and Herbert Wulf, Register of Arms Production in Developing Countries, Arbeitsgruppe Rüstung und Unterentwicklung, Hamburg 1977, p. 42. According to Business Week, July 31, 1978, EMBRAER's sales were $ 171 million in 1978.

13. Lock and Wulf, op.cit. 1977, pp. 38-40; AWST, March 3, 1980, p. 120; Aerospace Company Profiles... op.cit. 1979, p. 68.

14. Baranson op.cit. 1978, pp. 34-39.

15. Business Week, October 16, 1978.

16. Lock and Wulf op.cit. 1977, pp. 40-41; Larry Rochtel, Brazil is Making Major Drive for Military Self-Sufficiency, International Herald Tribune, November 29, 1977, and Bob Levin, Brazil: A Call to Arms, Newsweek, February 26, 1979, p. 47.

17. Newsweek, February 26, 1979 and April 3, 1978; Flight International, February 25, 1978; Michael Moodie, Sovereignty, Security and Arms. The Washington Papers, Vol. VII, The Center for Strategic and International Studies, Georgetown University, Washington D.C. 1979, p. 52.

18. Micro Journal 3, 1978, p. 57.

19. Richard S. Newfarmer, The International Market Power of Transnational Corporations: A Case Study of the Electrical Industry, UNCTAD/ST/MD/13, 14 April 1978, passim. and B. Epstein and K.R.U. Mirow, Impact on Developing Countries of Restrictive Business Practices of Transnational Corporations in The Electrical Equipment Industry: A Case Study of Brazil, UNCTAD/ST/MD/9.

20. Lock and Wulf op.cit. 1977, p. 36.

21. Clovis Brigagao, <u>Brazil's Military Industry: A discussion of Recent Developments</u>, (unpublished manuscript 1980), p. 26.

22. Even Components Must Be Brazilianized, <u>Business Week</u>, January 24, 1977, p. 34.

23. Brigagao <u>op.cit.</u> 1980, p. 31.

24. Mattelart <u>op.cit.</u> 1979, pp. 108-111.

25. <u>Arming the Third World</u>. National Action/Research on the Military Industrial Complex (NARMIC), July 1979.

26. For a carefully documented study on repression trade, see Michael T. Klare, <u>Supplying Repression. U.S. Support for Authoritarian Regimes Abroad</u>, Institute for Policy Studies, Washington D.C. 1977.

27. <u>Newsweek</u>, February 26, 1979, p. 47.

28. Ibid. and <u>Newsweek</u>, May 15, 1978. See also SIPRI Yearbook, <u>op.cit.</u>, various years.

29. <u>International Herald Tribune</u>, February 26, 1980; <u>The Economist</u>, January 19, 1980.

30. See Ruth Weiss, The Role of Para-statals in South Africa's Politico-Economic System, in John Suckling et al., <u>Foreign Investment in South Africa. The Economic Factor</u>, Uppsala 1975, pp. 55-91.

31. Kenneth W. Grundy, Intermediary Power and Global Dependency. The Case of South Africa. <u>International Studies Quarterly</u> 4, 1976, pp. 553-580.

32. See, e.g., Philip Ehrensaft, Polarized Accumulation and the Theory of Dependence. The Implications of South African Semi-Industrial Capitalism, in Peter C.W. Gutkind & Immanuel Wallerstein (eds.), <u>The Political Economy of Contemporary Africa</u>, Beverly Hills 1977, pp. 58-85, and Ruth Milkman, Contradictions of Semi-Peripheral Development. The South African Case, in Walter L. Goldfrank (ed.), <u>The World-System of Capitalism: Past and Present</u>, Beverly Hills 1979, pp. 261-284. On South Africa's balance of payments crises see, e.g., Simon Clarke, Changing Patterns of International Investment in South Africa and the Disinvestment Campaign. <u>Foreign Investment in South Africa: A Discussion Series, No. 3</u>, London 1978, pp. 16-20.

33. <u>WMEAT 1968-1977</u>, op.cit., pp. 60 and 146.

34. See Deon Geldenhuys, South Africa's Search for Security since the Second World War. <u>South African Institute of International Affairs</u>, September 1978, pp. 11-12.

35. For a collection of articles analyzing the initial stages of the embargo and its violation, see Peter Wallensteen (ed.), <u>Weapon Against Apartheid? The UN Embargo on South Africa</u>, Uppsala 1979.

36. See Rand Daily Mail, December 18, 1978.

37. The South African nuclear industry, the nuclear bomb and the role of foreign corporate and other interests are analyzed in a considerable number of publications; see, e.g., Raimo Väyrynen, South Africa. The Next Nuclear Weapons Power? Instant Research on Peace and Violence 1, 1977, pp. 33-47, Zdenek Cervenka & Barbara Rogers, The Nuclear Axis, London 1978, Richard K. Betts, A Diplomatic Bomb for South Africa? International Security 2, 1979, pp. 91-115, Kenneth L. Adelman & Albion W. Knight, Can South Africa Go Nuclear? Orbis 3, 1979, pp. 633-647, and Dan Smith, South Africa's Nuclear Capability, London 1980.

38. See Business Week, July 16, 1979, p. 60.

39. This correlation is examined in more detail by Robert S. Jaster, South Africa's Narrowing Security Options, Adelphi Papers, No. 15, 1980.

40. White Paper on Defence and Armaments Supply. Department of Defence, Cape Town 1979, p. 26.

41. See, e.g., Jaster op.cit. 1980, pp. 15-16.

42. See Signe Landgren-Bäckström, Southern Africa. The Escalation of a Conflict, SIPRI, Uppsala 1976, p. 137.

43. Ibid., 129 and 136-138 as well as Moshe Decter, The Arms Traffic with South Africa, Midstream, February 1977.

44. See Michael T. Klare, U.S. Arms Deliveries to South Africa: The Italian Connection. TNI Special Report, Washington D.C. 1977, and SIPRI Yearbook 1976, pp. 246-247.

45. See Landgren-Bäckström op.cit. 1976, pp. 139-141, The Military Balance 1978-1979, IISS, London 1978, pp. 49-50, and The Activities of Transnational Corporations in the Industrial, Mining and Military Sectors of Southern Africa. Report of the Secretariat. United Nations, Commission on Transnational Corporations, E/C.10/51, 22 March 1979, pp. 64-67.

46. NATO's Fifteen Nations, Vol. 23, No. 4, 1978.

47. South Africa 1977. Official Yearbook of the Republic of South Africa, Johannesburg 1977, p. 429.

48. E/C.10/51... op.cit. 1979, pp. 67-68, and Wolf Geisler, Die militärische Zusammenarbeit zwischen BRD und RSA in atomaren und konventionellen Bereich. Blätter für deutsche und internationale Politik, Vol. 23, No. 2, 1978, pp. 166-185.

49. Landgren-Bäckström op.cit. 1976, pp. 131-132.

50. New York Times, October 3, 1971, and SIPRI Yearbook 1978, p. 210.

51.   Defence, Vol. 10, No. 9, 1979.

52.   For general accounts of the role of British and U.S. companies in South Africa see Ruth First, Jonathan Steele & Christabel Gurney, The South African Connection. Western Investments in Apartheid, Harmondsworth 1972, Barbara Rogers, White Wealth and Black Poverty. American Investments in South Africa, Westport, Conn. 1976, and Ann & Neva Seidman, U.S. Multinationals in Southern Africa, Dar-es-Salaam 1977.

53.   The Observer, January 16, 1977. It has been recently claimed that Plessey is transferring a radar system to South Africa and also training in this connection South African military personnel, see UN Chronicle, July-October 1979, p. 35.

54.   The Economist, July 15, 1978, p. 82.

55.   First, Steel & Gurney op.cit. 1972, pp. 186-188, and Financial Mail, July 14, 1978.

56.   Racal Electronics Ltd. CAAT Factsheet, London 1976, and Black South Africa Explodes, Nottingham 1977, p. 49.

57.   See, e.g., Gail-Maryse Cockram, Vorster's Foreign Policy, Pretoria 1970, p. 113.

58.   Decter op.cit. 1977, p. 18, and Philips Violates the Arms Embargo against South Africa, Amsterdam, May 1979 as well as Rand Daily Mail, May 28, 1979.

59.   See, e.g., Ann Seidman & Neva Makgetla, Transnational Corporations and the South African Military-Industrial Complex, Centre Against Apartheid. Notes and Documents 24/1979, pp. 22-27.

60.   See Geisler op.cit. 1978, pp. 179-181, and Jens Klop et al., Verdeckter Rüstungstransfer - Beiträge der BRD zur militärischen Stärkung der Republik Südafrika. Blätter für deutsche und internationale Politik 5, 1976, pp. 505-510.

61.   For further details see Financial Mail, May 5, 1978, and AWST, April 24, 1978, pp. 99-103 and 106.

62.   See, for example, Jaster op.cit. 1980, pp. 27-29, William Cutteridge, South Africa's Defence Posture. The World Today 1, 1980, pp. 26-31, and International Herald Tribune, May 31-June 1, 1980.

63.   See, e.g., Roger Pajak, Soviet Arms and Egypt, Survival 4, 1975, pp. 165-173.

64.   WMEAT 1968-1977, p. 127.

65.   International Herald Tribune, February 25, 1980.

66.   On the Messerschmitt connection see Flight International, September 23, 1978, p. 1148.

67. See Robert Ropelewski, Management: Improvisation Key to Egyptian Growth, AWST, November 13, 1978, pp. 38-42 and 47.

68. See Flight International, January 7, 1978, p. 31. For an analysis of the structure and functioning of the AOI see Raimo Väyrynen, The Arab Organization of Industrialization: A Case Study in the Multinational Production of Arms, Current Research on Peace and Violence 2, 1979, pp. 66-79.

69. Le Monde, October 9, 1974.

70. See, e.g., AWST, December 22, 1975, p. 37, and January 17, 1977, p. 16.

71. See Väyrynen op.cit. 1979 and the litterature mentioned there as well as Michael Moodie, Sovereignty, Security and Arms. The Washington Papers, No. 67, Beverly Hills 1979, pp. 53-59.

72. Le Monde, August 3, 1978.

73. Robert Ropelewski, Arabs Seek Arms Sufficiency, AWST, May 15, 1978, p. 14.

74. See ibid., p. 14 and Flight International, April 10, 1977, pp. 1046-1047, and June 24, 1978, pp. 1939-1940.

75. Flight International, June 10, 1978, p. 1738, Le Monde, September 19, 1978 and September 20, 1978; The Economist, September 23, 1978, p. 80, and Robert Ropelewski, Arabs Push Arms Industry Despite Peace, AWST, November 6, 1978, p. 16.

76. AWST, May 21, 1979, p. 22. See also The Economist, February 11, 1978, pp. 119-120, and February 10, 1979, p. 124.

77. AWST, August 14, 1978 and November 27, 1978 and Le Monde, August 3, 1978.

78. Flight International, January 7, 1978, p. 31.

79. AWST, March 6, 1978.

80. Ropelewski op.cit. 1978, p. 16, and Flight International, December 4, 1976, p. 1626 as well as February 12, 1977, p. 342.

81. AWST, July 3, 1978, p. 24. The Kharj project is only one example of the Saudi policy of rapidly industrializing the country and building several industrial villages, both for the military and civilian technology, in various parts of the country; see, e.g., Business Week, September 4, 1978, pp. 78-79 and March 31, 1980, pp. 52-54 and 59.

82. Le Monde, September 21, 1979.

83. See, e.g., John Whelan, Treaty Leads to Restructuring of Arab Weapons Industry, International Herald Tribune. Special Issue, June

1979, New York Times, May 15, 1979, and AWST, May 21, 1979, p. 22.

84. See, e.g., Le Monde, May 16, 1979, and The Economist, January 12, 1980, p. 88.

85. The Economist, April 7, 1979, p. 18, Washington Post, June 6, 1979, p. A19, and AWST, August 13, 1979, p. 13.

86. International Herald Tribune, January 9, February 14 and March 31, 1980.

87. International Herald Tribune, March 31, 1980 and Special Issue on Egypt, June 1980.

88. See Whelan op.cit. 1979.

89. See, e.g., Ropelewski op.cit. 1978.

90. Foreign Military Sales... op.cit. 1978.

91. Leslie M. Pryor, Arms and the Shah, Foreign Policy, No. 31, 1978, pp. 56-71.

92. The Arms trade with the Third World... op.cit. 1971, p. 578.

93. Ibid., pp. 840-842 and Arms Trade Registers... op.cit. 1975, pp. 46-50.

94. Sampson op.cit. 1977, p. 182.

95. The Arms Trade with the Third World, op.cit. 1971, pp. 574-579.

96. The concept of regional power center is applied to Brazil, India, Iran, Nigeria, South Africa and Venezuela in Raimo Väyrynen, Economic and Military Position of the Regional Power Centers, Journal of Peace Research, Vol. 16, No. 4, 1979, pp. 349-369. For a thorough description of the role of Iran in the U.S. military and economic strategy in the Persian Gulf during the postwar period see, e.g., Richard Falk, Iran and American Geopolitics in the Gulf, Race and Class, Vol. XXI, No. 1, 1979, pp. 41-55.

97. Oil and Turmoil: Western Choices in the Middle East. The Atlantic Council's Special Working Group on the Middle East, Washington D.C. 1979, p. 22.

98. Anne Hessing Cahn and Joseph J. Kruzel, Arms Trade in the 1980's, in Anne Hessing Cahn et al., Controlling Future Arms Trade, New York 1977, p. 31 and SIPRI Yearbook, op.cit., various years.

99. Sampson op.cit. 1977, p. 256.

100. Cf. Michael Klare, Carter's Arms Policy, Business as Usual, NACLA Latin America and Empire Report 6, 1977, pp. 15-23; International Herald Tribune, December 17, 1975 and July 15, 1977 and Flight International, September 17, 1977.

101. Louis Kraar, Grumman Still Flies for the Navy, but it is Selling the World, _Fortune_, February 1976, pp. 78-82.

102. _U.S. Military Sales to Iran_. Staff Report to the Subcommittee on Foreign Assistance, Committee on Foreign Relations, U.S. Senate, July 1976.

103. Interavia 2, 1977; _AWST_, September 13, 1976, December 18, 1978 and January 8, 1979; Lock and Wulf _op.cit._ 1977, p. 75.

104. _Flight International_, January 18, 1973 and _AWST_, June 11, 1979.

105. Lock and Wulf _op.cit._ 1977, p. 74; _SIPRI Yearbook 1979_; _AWST_, May 29, 1978, November 13, 1978, December 11, 1978 and December 10, 1979. There was also a British-Iranian joint venture _Iranian Helicopters, Inc._ which trained pilots at Mehrabab Airport since 1973. See _AWST_, May 28, 1973.

106. _AWST_, July 23, 1979.

107. SIPRI Yearbook _op.cit._, various years; Arms Trade Registers, _op.cit._ 1975, pp. 46-48; _Arms Trade Data Files_, Militarism & Disarmament Project, Institute for Policy Studies, Washington D.C. (no date); _AWST_, February 12, 1979.

108. Lock and Wulf _op.cit._ 1977, p. 75; _British Aerospace_ publications; _SIPRI Yearbook 1979_ and TAPRI data files; Ulrich Albrecht, Militarized Subimperialism: the Case of Iran, in _The World Military Order_, ed. by Mary Kaldor and Asbjörn Eide, London 1979, p. 171.

109. Mattelart _op.cit._ 1979.

110. Baranson _op.cit._ 1979, pp. 74-75 and 92-93.

111. _AWST_, May 28, 1973, January 1, 1979; _Jane's Major Companies of Europe 1980_; _Electronics_, January 4, 1979; Lock and Wulf _op.cit._ 1977, p. 75 and TAPRI data files.

112. A number of Iran's infrastructure projects are discussed in Ulrich Albrecht, Dieter Ernst, Peter Lock and Herbert Wulf, _Rüstung und Unterentwicklung_, Hamburg 1976, pp. 85-99.

113. _Helsingin Sanomat_, July 28, 1975.

114. _AWST_, January 8, 1979.

115. _AWST_, November 13, 1978.

116. _AWST_, November 13, 1978, December 18, 1978 and January 8, 1979.

117. Figures for orders in the beginning of 1979 are from _International Herald Tribune_, February 5, 1979 and _AWST_, February 12, 1979. Quotation from _SIPRI Yearbook 1979_, p. 182.

118. Interavia 6, 1979, p. 47.

119. Helsingin Sanomat, March 30, 1979.

120. On the conception of "failure", see Herman Nickel, The U.S. Failure in Iran. Fortune, March 12, 1979, pp. 94 and 106. The lesson aspect is emphasized by Anthony Sampson in International Herald Tribune, February 7, 1979.

121. For a discussion on the concept of autonomous armament industry, see Herbert Wulf, Indien: Militarisierung und der Aufbau einer autonomen Rüstungsproduktion, Internationales Asienforum, Vol. 6, No. 3, 1975, pp. 272-301, particularly pp. 286-289.

122. Ranjit Peirs, Britain's Order Books Fill Up, Far Eastern Economic Review, May 7, 1976; The Arms Trade with the Third World, op.cit. 1971, p. 474 and Arms Trade Registers, op.cit. 1975, pp. 33-37.

123. Arms Trade with the Third World... op.cit. 1971, p. 474.

124. The International Transfer of Conventional Arms. An Interim Report to the Congress. U.S. Arms Control and Disarmament Agency, January 1973, p. 20. About periods in Indian arms imports, see also Wulf op.cit. 1975, pp. 296-299.

125. SIPRI Yearbook... op.cit., various years; Arms Trade Registers... op.cit. 1975, pp. 33-37. India has also borrowed Soviet arms. In 1971 war with Pakistan India borrowed Soviet airborne warning and control aircraft Moss, thus being able to make deep penetrations in Pakistani airspace. See Steven J. Rosen, The Proliferation of New Land-Based Technologies: Implications for Local Military Balances, in Arms Transfers in the Modern World, ed. by Stephanie G. Neuman and Robert E. Harkavy, New York 1979, p. 123.

126. SIPRI Yearbook 1977, p. 317.

127. SIPRI Yearbook 1978 and 1979; Far Eastern Economic Review, August 1, 1980, pp. 34-35; International Herald Tribune, May 29, 1980.

128. WMEAT... op.cit. 1979, p. 156.

129. Sampson op.cit. 1977, p. 181.

130. SIPRI Yearbook 1979, p. 183.

131. Maharaj K. Chopra, India's Defense Policy and Infrastructure, Military Review, May 1978, pp. 33-44, quotation p. 34.

132. Cf. Wulf op.cit. 1975, pp. 284-287, and Chopra op.cit. 1978, p. 33. See also Far Eastern Economic Review, May 7, 1976.

133. Aerospace Company Profiles... op.cit. 1979, p. 71; Flight International, January 7, 1978; AWST, March 3, 1980, p. 122 and SIPRI Yearbook 1979.

134. SIPRI Yearbook 1979.

135. See, e.g., the statement by the Defence Minister Jagjivan Ram in Indian Express, July 6, 1978.

136. Flight International, October 14, 1978 and November 4, 1978; AWST, October 16, 1978.

137. Aerospace Company Profiles... op.cit. 1979, p. 71.

138. AWST, January 7, 1977.

139. Lock and Wulf op.cit. 1977, p. 98 and Flight International, July 29, 1978.

140. Flight International, November 4, 1978 and December 2, 1978; Far Eastern Economic Review, June 3, 1977.

141. Lock and Wulf op.cit. 1977, p. 103 and Flight International, January 7, 1978.

142. Far Eastern Economic Review, May 7, 1976.

143. Chopra op.cit. 1978, p. 35.

144. SIPRI Yearbook 1979, p. 165, and Lock and Wulf op.cit. 1977, p. 99.

145. Cf. Interavia 4, 1974 and discussion by Ulrich Albrecht and Peter Lock, Multinationale Konzerne und Rüstung in Multinationale Konzerne und Dritte Welt, ed. by Dieter Senghaas and Ulrich Menzel, Frankfurt am Main 1977, p. 135.

146. International Herald Tribune, February 2-3, 1980.

147. Chopra op.cit. 1978, p. 33.

148. Economic and Political Weekly, June 10, 1978.

149. Lock and Wulf op.cit. 1977, p. 100 and AWST, December 10, 1979.

150. AWST, June 11, 1979.

151. AWST, December 10, 1979; The Economist, June 16, 1980, pp. 50-51 and Aamulehti, July 19 and July 20, 1980.

152. Peter Lock and Herbert Wulf, The Economic Consequences of the Transfer of Military-Oriented Technology, in The World Military Order, op.cit. 1979, p. 225, based on Government of India, Ministry of Defence, Annual Report 1975-1976, New Delhi 1975.

153. Wulf op.cit. 1975, pp. 288-289 and The Arms Trade with the Third World... op.cit. 1971, pp. 735-756.

154. For discussion about the economic role of the Soviet armaments in

India, see Jan Öberg, Third World Armament: Domestic Arms Production in Israel, South Africa, Brazil, Argentina and India 1950-1975. Instant Research on Peace and Violence 4, 1975, pp. 222-238, particularly 234-237, and Chils and Kidron, India, the USSR and the MIG-Project, Economic and Political Weekly, September 22, 1973.

155. AWST, January 17, 1977, wrote that a major problem at HAL is a high cost of production which is an obstacle for exports.

156. Bernadette Madeuf and Charles-Albert Michalet, A New Approach to International Economics, International Social Science Journal, Vol. 30, No. 2, 1972, pp. 253-283.

Chapter 6

1. See Juan C. Sanchez Arnau, Debt and Development, IFDA Dossier, December 14, 1979, pp. 60-61. The important role of the military technology in the conquest, not only in military and political but also in economic and technological terms, of the colonies is analyzed in more detailed manner in a thought-provoking article by Daniel R. Headrick, The Tools of Imperialism: Technology and the Expansion of European Colonial Empires in the Nineteenth Century, Journal of Modern History, Vol. 61, No. 2, 1979, pp. 231-263. The validity of this approach is also proved in a case study on South Africa by Asbjörn Eide, South Africa: Repression and the Transfer of Arms and Arms Technology, in The World Military Order... op.cit. 1979, pp. 180-209.

2. On various forms of co-production see, e.g., Claus-Detlef Lehmann, Rüstungsexport und Rüstungskooperation aus der Sicht der Industrie, Wehrtechnik 2, 1978, pp. 14-16.

3. See SIPRI Yearbook 1978, p. 229.

4. The estimate is given by Business Week, March 24, 1980.

5. For an evaluation of standard arms trade sources see Ulrich Albrecht, Asbjörn Eide, Mary Kaldor and Milton Leitenberg, A Short Research Guide on Arms and Armed Forces, London 1978, pp. 49-74. As to the connection between arms trade and other forms of trade, see Jan Öberg, Arms trade with the Third World as an Aspect of Imperialism. Journal of Peace Research, Vol. 12, No. 3, 1975, pp. 213-234.

6. See, e.g., Peter Lock and Herbert Wulf, Consequences of the Transfer of Military-Oriented Technology on the Development Process. Bulletin of Peace Proposals, Vol. 8, No. 2, 1977, pp. 127-136.

7. AWST, June 11, 1979, p. 75.

8. See Legislation on Foreign Relations Through 1978. Current Legislation and Related Executive Orders, Vol. I. U.S. Senate and House of Representatives, Washington D.C. 1979, pp. 264-270.

9. Cf. John Stanley and Maurice Pearton, The International Trade in Arms, London 1972, p. 113.

10. See, e.g., Samuel Lichtensztejn and José M. Quijano, Third World Debt and the International Private Banks, IFDA Dossier, No. 16, 1980, pp. 63-74 (the quotation is from p. 71). It is impossible to show by the available material the precise role of the private banks in the Third World military debt. The sheer logic of things and figures tells, however, that this role is by no means negligible.

11. Anne Hessing Cahn and Joseph J. Kruzel, Arms Trade in the 1980's, in Hessing Cahn et al... op.cit. 1977, p. 36.

12. Öberg op.cit. 1975, pp. 236-237 and the sources used there.

13. The Economist, November 3, 1979, pp. 92-93.

14. See George Philip, The Peruvian Tightrope, The World Today, Vol. 33, No. 12, 1977, p. 468 and James Petras and A. Eugene Havens, Peru: Economic Crises and Class Confrontation. Monthly Review, Vol. 30, No. 9, 1979, pp. 25-41.

15. Financial Times, March 13, 1980.

16. Tuija Meisaari-Polsa, Ingegard Municio and Synnöve Svartvadet, Ut-vecklingsländernas utlandskulder - en data-analys. Institute of Polit-ical Science, University of Stockholm (mimeo), Spring 1978.

17. See Rolf Peikarz, Defense Impacts on International Payments, in Stephen Enke (ed.), Defense Management, Washington D.C. 1967, pp. 294-296.

18. Sanches Arnau op.cit. 1979, pp. 55-66.

19. Göran Ohlin, Debts, Development and Default in A World Divided. The Less Developed Countries in the Intenational Economy, ed. by G.K. Helleiner, Cambridge 1976, pp. 210-213.

20. A/32/88, ... op.cit. 1977, p. 51.

21. Öberg op.cit. 1975, pp. 228-229 and Asbjörn Eide, Arms Transfers and Third World Militarization, Bulletin of Peace Proposals, Vol. 8, No. 2, 1977, pp. 99-102.

22. Michael Klare, Hoist with Our Own Pahlavi. The Nation 4, 1976.

23. There are different groups of poorest countries. The largest groups are the low-income groups by UNCTAD (55 countries) and DAC (52 countries, per capita income up to $ 400 in 1976). The low-income group of IBRD includes 37 countries with per capita income up to $ 300 in 1977, and the UN list of "low-income oil-importing" countries comprises 31 countries with under $ 300 per capita in 1975. Finally the list of least developed (LLDC) countries includes 31 countries at the time of this writing. See Development Cooperation. 1979 Review,

OECD, DAC, Paris 1979, pp. 171-173.

24.   Milton Leitenberg and Nicole Ball, The Military Expenditures of Less Developed Nations as a Proportion of Their State Budgets. A Research Note. Bulletin of Peace Proposals, Vol. 8, No. 4, 1977, pp. 310-315.

25.   It has been suggested that investments in agriculture suffer from high military spending. The following table gives evidence for such a conclusion:

Country	The share of agriculture in GDP, % average 1960-1973	Agriculture as % total current expenditure 1973	Defence as % of total current expenditure 1973
Afghanistan	54.2	1.4	24.3
Bangladesh	58.0	n.a.	11
Brazil	18	2	13
Egypt	29	4	40
Ethiopia	58	3	19
India	50	3	28
Indonesia	46	n.a.	26
Mali	47	5	19
Niger	52	7	9 (1967)
Pakistan	39	3	52
Philippines	35	7	22
Senegal	34	6	11
Upper Volta	49	6	13

Susan George, Feeding the Few. Corporate Control of Food. Institute for Policy Studies, Washington D.C. 1979, p. 18.

26.   WMEAT 1968-1977, op.cit. 1979, pp. 32-69. ACDA estimates the Soviet military spending in dollars by applying U.S. prices to detailed estimates of Soviet military programs - a method which gives high values for the Soviet expenditures. For problems in conversion methods, see ibid., pp. 13-15.

27.   For mechants of death, see Sampson op.cit. 1977 and George Thayer, The War Business, London 1969. For U.S. small arms transfers see the study by Michael Klare 1977 (note 26, Chapter 5).

28.   WMEAT 1968-1977, op.cit., pp. 155-158.

29.   Ibid., p. 152 and SIPRI Yearbook 1979, p. 183.

30.   SIPRI Yearbook 1979, pp. 238-239.

31.   Information is taken from Lock and Wulf op.cit. 1977, SIPRI Yearbook 1979 and International Herald Tribune, May 15, 1980.

32.   Lock and Wulf op.cit. 1977 and SIPRI Yearbook 1979.

33.   Lock and Wulf op.cit. 1977, p. 117.

34.   See, e.g., Christopher Freeman, The Economics of Industrial Inno-
        vation, Harmondsworth 1974, pp. 20-32.

35.   A good account of the impact of military technology on the arms
        race is given by Colonel Richard G. Head, Technology and Military
        Balance. Foreign Affairs, Vol. 56, No. 4, 1978, pp. 544-563. He draws,
        for instance, the following conclusion: 'American R&D style has
        traditionally emphasized qualitative superiority, with smaller num-
        bers, and U.S. military doctrine, while appreciating the value of
        mass, has adjusted accordingly. This preference for high-value multi-
        purpose weapons and the desire to substitute technology for man-
        power can be called an American 'doctrine of quality'. One of the
        results of the doctrine of quality and technological substitution has
        been a certain tendency for technology to drive both strategy and
        doctrine. Soviet military doctrine, until recently, has had no tradition
        of qualitative technological excellence to draw upon, and so it has
        placed great emphasis on quantitative superiority', (the quotation is
        from p. 550).

36.   Cf. David K. Whynes, The Economics of Third World Military
        Expenditure, London 1979, pp. 43-49.

37.   See F.A. Long, Science and Military. Civilization & Science, in
        Conflict or Collaboration? Amsterdam 1972, pp. 126-127, and Emile
        Benoit (ed.), Disarmament and World Economic Interdependence, New
        York 1967, p. 52.

38.   See, e.g., David Holloway, Technology and Political Decision in
        Soviet Armaments Policy. Journal of Peace Research, Vol. 11, No. 3,
        1974, pp. 257-279.

39.   See, e.g., Marion Mushkat, Jr., Defence and Structural Transforma-
        tion of Industry in Israel. Co-existence 2, 1978, pp. 207-218.

40.   David K. Whynes op.cit. 1979, pp. 43-44.

41.   Freeman op.cit. 1974, pp. 219-220.

42.   See Michael Moodie, Sovereignty, Security and Arms.. The
        Washington Papers, No. 67, Beverly Hills 1979, pp. 23-30.

43.   Herbert Wulf et al., Transnational Transfers of Arms Production
        Technology. Institut für Friedensforschung und Sicherheitspolitik an
        der Universität Hamburg, Hamburg 1980, pp. 33-36.

44.   M.R. Bhagavan, Technological Transformation of Developing Coun-
        tries. Economic Research Institute. Stockholm School of Economics.
        Research Paper 6186, Stockholm 1980, esp. pp. 25-27 and 59-62.

45.   Taiwan is here placed in the group of semi-industrialized countries in

spite of the fact that Bhagavan, possibly by mistake, places it in the non-industrial category.

46. For further information see Wulf et al. op.cit. 1980, pp. 37-44.

47. On Indonesia's industrialization see, e.g., John Wong, ASEAN Economic Perspectives. A Comparative Study of Indonesia, Malaysia, the Philippines, Singapore and Thailand, Hong Kong 1979, pp. 57-61. Wulf et al. (op.cit. 1980, p. 42) come to the conclusion that in addition to Indonesia also Israel, Pakistan and the Philippines have stretched their military production beyond their actual industrial capacities.

48. David Jenkins, The Military's Secret Cache. Far Eastern Economic Review, February 8, 1980, pp. 70-72.

49. See Wulf et al. op.cit. 1980, pp. 51-70.

50. For a summary of these studies see, e.g., Whynes op.cit. 1979, pp. 69-73.

51. Gernot Köhler, Structural-Dynamic Arms Control. Journal of Peace Research, Vol. 14, No. 4, 1977, pp. 315-326.

52. See Dieter Senghaas, Elemente einer Theorie des peripheren Kapitalismus, in Dieter Senghaas (ed.), Periphere Kapitalismus. Analysen über Abhängigkeit und Unterentwicklung, Frankfurt am Main 1974, pp. 7-36.

53. For further consideration see Robin Luckham, Militarism: Force, Class and International Conflict. IDS Bulletin, Vol. 9, No. 1, 1977, pp. 15-27.

54. See Bernadette Madeuf & Charles-Albert Michalet, A New Approach to International Economics. International Social Science Journal, Vol. 30, No. 2, 1978, pp. 275-279.

55. See Bhagavan op.cit. 1980, pp. 53-56.

56. Herbert Wulf, Dependent Militarism in the Periphery and Possible Alternative Security Concept, in Stephanie G. Neuman & Robert Harkavy (eds.), Arms Transfers in the Modern World, New York 1979, p. 248.

57. See Geoffrey Kemp, Arms Transfers and the 'Back-End' Problem in Developing Countries, in Stephanie G. Neuman & Robert Harkavy (eds.), Arms Transfers in the Modern World, New York 1979, pp. 264-275.

58. See Hannu Kyröläinen, An Analysis of New Trends in the U.S. Military Training and Technical Assistance in the Third World. Instant Research on Peace and Violence 3-4, 1977, pp. 167-183, and the documentation presented there.

59. A publication by British Aerospace, UK.

60. Summarized from International Herald Tribune, February 27, 1980.

61. This problem is analyzed, for instance, in Walter J. Levy, Oil and the Decline of the West. Foreign Affairs, Vol. 58, No. 5, 1980, pp. 999-1015. See also Valerie Yorke, Security in the Gulf: A Strategy of Pre-Emption. The World Today, July 1980, pp. 239-250.

62. Constantine Vaitsos, World Industrial Development and the Transnational Corporations: The Lima Target as Viewed by Economic Actors. Industry and Development, No. 3, 1979, pp. 37-39.

63. Wulf et al. op.cit. 1980, pp. 44-49.

64. ECOWAS: Defence Pact Fears. Africa, No. 107, July 1980, pp. 35-36.

65. See World Military Expenditures and Arms Transfers, 1968-1977, ACDA, Washington D.C. 1979, p. 159.

66. Michael Moodie, Sovereignty, Security and Arms. The Washington Papers, No. 67, Beverly Hills 1979, pp. 41-42.

67. See Javed Ansari & Mary Kaldor, Military Technology and Conflict Dynamics: the Bangladesh Crisis of 1971, in Mary Kaldor & Asbjörn Eide (eds.), The World Military Order. The Impact of Military Technology on the Third World, London 1979, pp. 136-156.

68. Geoffrey Kemp & Robert L. Pfaltzgraff, Jr., New Technologies and the Emerging Geo-Strategic Environment, in Geoffrey Kemp et al. (eds.), The Other Arms Race. New Technologies and Non-Nuclear Conflict, Lexington, Mass. 1975, pp. 136-137.

69. Ibid., pp. 137-138, and Malvern Lumsden, New Military Technologies and the Security of Small and Medium-Sized Countries in Europe. Current Research on Peace and Violence 1, 1980, pp. 26-27. For a useful technical account see also Jorma K. Miettinen, Sotateknologian kehityksen vaikutus taktiikkaan. Sotilasaikakauslehti 11, 1979, pp. 794-807.

70. See Herbert Wulf, Dependent Militarism in the Periphery and Possible Alternative Concepts, in Stephanie G. Neuman & Robert Harkavy (eds.), Arms Transfers in the Modern World, New York 1980, pp. 253-261. The table is a summary of a more comprehensive presentation by Wulf.

71. The implications of economic self-reliance for the military doctrines and establishments are explored by Johan Galtung, Self-Reliance: Concept, Practice and Rationale, Chair in Conflict and Peace Research, University of Oslo, Papers, No. 35, Oslo 1976.

72. See, e.g., Bernard Brodie, War and Politics, London 1973, pp. 452-453.

73. This point is made by Daniel R. Headrick, The Tools of Imperialism: Technology and the Expansion of European Colonial Empires in the Nineteenth Century. Journal of Modern History 2, 1979, pp. 260-261.

74.   See Hartmut Elsenhans, Counter-Insurgency: The French War in Algeria, in Mary Kaldor & Asbjörn Eide (eds.), The World Military Order. The Impact of Military Technology on the Third World, London 1979, pp. 110-135. The same questions are treated more fully in Hartmut Elsenhans, Materialien zum Algerienkrieg, 1954-62, Berlin 1974.

75.   This point is generalized in Andrew Mack, Why Big Nations Lose Small Wars. World Politics 2, 1975, pp. 175-200.

76.   For more details see Strategic Survey 1979, London 1979, pp. 93-98.

77.   These points are summarized from the following works: Guy Brossolet, Essai sur la non-bataille, Paris 1975, and Horst Afheldt, Verteidigung und Frieden. Politik mit militärischen Mitteln, Frankfurt am Main 1976. See also Horst Afheldt, The End of the Tank Battle. Atomic War on Area Defense. Bulletin of Peace Proposals 4, 1977, pp. 328-331.

78.   Bert V.A. Röling, Feasibility of Inoffensive Deterrence. Bulletin of Peace Proposals 4, 1978, pp. 339-347.

79.   For more details see, e.g., Alvin J. Cottrell & Frank Bray, Military Forces in the Persian Gulf. The Wanshington Papers, No. 60, Beverly Hills 1978, pp. 27-46.

80.   See Ulrich Albrecht & Mary Kaldor, Introduction, in Mary Kaldor & Asbjörn Eide (eds.), The World Military Order. The Impact of Military Technology on the Third World, London 1979, pp. 7-15 (the quotation is from p. 9).

81.   See ibid., pp. 12-14.

82.   The existence of a number of distinct layers in the world military order is empirically shown by Randall Forsberg, Resources Devoted to Military Research and Development, SIPRI, Uppsala 1972.

83.   See Mary Kaldor, The Role of Arms in Capitalist Economies: The Process of Overdevelopment and Underdevelopment, in Arms Control and Technological Innovation, ed. by David Carlton and Carlo Schaerf, London 1977, pp. 322-341.

84.   See James Kurth, The Political Consequences of the Product Cycle: Industrial History and Political Outcomes. International Organization 1, 1979, pp. 32-34. The relevant weapons technologies are discussed in Richard Burt, New Weapons Technologies: Debate and Directions, Adelphi Papers, No. 126, London 1976, pp. 2-10.

85.   On the control of military R&D see, e.g., Harvey Brooks, The Military Innovation System and the Qualitative Arms Race, Daedalus 3, 1975, pp. 75-97.

86.   Peter Lock & Herbert Wulf, Rüstung und Unterentwicklung, Aus Politik und Zeitgeschichte B 18/79, May 5, 1979, pp. 22-23 and 25.

87.   See The United Nations and Disarmament, 1945-1970, United Na-
       tions, New York 1971, pp. 25-125 passim.

88.   This is seen conspicuously in the fact that in no arms-control
       agreements concluded since 1868 the economic and industrial aspects
       have been touched in any detail, see Arms Control: A Survey and
       Appraisal of Multilateral Agreements, SIPRI, London 1978.

89.   Economic and Social Consequences of the Arms Race and of Military
       Expenditures, United Nations publication, sales no. E.78.IX.1, New
       York 1978. This report is in fact an updated, although substantially
       much improved and lengthened version of the UN document with the
       same title which came out in 1971.

90.   Ibid., pp. 42-43.

91.   It has also been argued that the general verbal linking of arms
       control/disarmament measures and development issues to each other
       is a rather meaningless exercise. If some concrete results have to be
       achieved much more concrete proposals on the transformation of
       military 'bads' to the development 'goods' should be made. This in turn
       requires more careful analysis of the economic and other consequ-
       ences of various alternatives; see, e.g., Göran Lindgren, Nedrustning
       och utveckling. Institutionen för freds- och konfliktforskning. Uppsala
       universitet, Uppsala 1980.

92.   For an analysis of various approaches see Ulrich Albrecht, Research-
       ing Conversion: A Review of the State of the Art, in Peter Wallen-
       steen (ed.), Experiences in Disarmament. On Conversion of Military
       Industry and Closing of Military Bases, Uppsala University. Depart-
       ment of Peace and Conflict Research, Report No. 19, 1978, pp. 11-
       43. It has been shown, for instance that in the United States the most
       important direct suppliers, other than personnel, to $ 1 billion of
       typical military budget outlays include: aircraft, aircraft engines, and
       parts ($ 132 million), radio and tv apparatus ($ 82 million), ordnance
       ($ 79 million), construction and construction repair ($ 52 million),
       business and professional services ($ 32 million), transportation ($ 23
       million), industrial chemicals ($ 17 million) and petroleum refining ($
       13 million); see Controlling the Conventional Arms Race, United
       Nations Association of the United States, New York 1976, pp. 71-72.

Annexes

ANNEX A   AEROSPACE SALES, BY SELECTED COUNTRY AND SUB-SECTOR (1976) (in million current US $)

Country	Airframe		Engines		Equipment		Space		Total	
USA	11 243	46.8 %	3 532	14.7 %	3 820	15.9 %	5 429*	22.6 %	24 024	100.0 %
France	3 031	71.5	787	18.6	326	7.7	94	2.2	4 238	100.0
United Kingdom	1 554	44.8	1 038	29.9	831	23.9	49	1.5	3 472	100.0
FR Germany	1 123	65.6	197	11.5	274	16.0	118	6.9	1 712	100.0
Italy	350	63.9	86	15.7	69	12.6	43	7.8	548	100.0
Netherlands	287	91.7	-	-	18	5.8	8	2.5	313	100.0
Belgium	69	55.2	22	17.6	20	16.0	14	11.2	125	100.0
Total of 6 European countries	6 414	61.6	2 130	20.5	1 538	14.8	326	3.1	10 408	100.0

*Including missiles.

Source: EC. Here taken from The World Aerospace Industry Today. IMF World Aerospace Conference, Report 3. Seattle, Washington, USA, May 22-24, 1979, p. 15.

ANNEX B   CIVIL AND MILITARY AEROSPACE SALES IN PRINCIPAL WESTERN COUNTRIES (1976) (in million US dollars, %)

	Civil		Military		Total	
USA	8 664	35 %	16 035	65 %	24 669	100 %
France	911	23	2 997	77	3 908	100
United Kingdom	944	33	1 905	67	2 849	100
FR Germany	236	18	1 084	82	1 320	100
Italy	111	22	388	78	499	100
Netherlands	250	90	28	10	278	100
Belgium	16	32	34	68	50	100
Total of 6 European countries	2 468	28	6 346	72	8 904	100
Japan	93	11	741	89	834	100
Total	11 225	33	23 122	67	34 317	100

Source: EC

Note: Transactions between manufacturers in 6 European countries are subtracted from the sum of the national sales.

ANNEX C   VALUE ON WORLD MARKET OF MILITARY AIRCRAFT AND HELICOPTERS IN SERVICE BY DESIGN ORIGIN (1976)

(in million US dollars)

Designed in	USA				EEC				USSR				Other	
	Aircraft	Helicopter	Total	%	Aircraft	Helicopter	Total	%	Aircraft	Helicopter	Total	%	Aircraft	%
USA	53 999	8 181	62 180	99.4	406	–	406	0.6	–	–	–	0.0	2	0.0
Canada	353	78	431	88.9	17	–	17	3.6	–	–	–	0.0	36	7.5
Latin America	1 028	176	1 204	58.1	526	59	585	28.3	–	4	4	0.2	278	13.4
EEC	5 597	790	6 387	39.3	8 659	1 082	9 741	59.9	–	–	–	0.0	128	0.8
Non-EEC Europe[1]	1 879	964	2 843	45.9	815	97	912	14.7	429	15	444	0.7	1 999	38.7
Middle East + [2] North Africa	4 682	757	5 439	48.3	1 171	276	1 387	12.8	3 655	204	3 859	34.3	466	4.6
Africa South[3] of the Sahara + Madagascar	157	42	199	24.3	175	58	233	28.4	353	8	361	44.1	26	3.2
South Africa + Rhodesia	186	–	186	17.3	767	118	885	82.7	–	–	–	0.0	0	0.0
Asia	2 737	668	3 405	45.0	631	111	742	9.8	2 184	63	2 247	29.7	1 168	15.5
Australia	513	47	560	67.3	195	33	228	27.5	–	–	–	0.0	43	5.2
Oceania	137	35	172	74.1	42	3	45	19.4	–	–	–	0.0	15	6.5
World total	71 268	11 738	83 006	75.9	13 404	1 837	15 241	13.9	6 621	294	6 915	7.5	4 161	2.7

Source: EC.

Notes:

[1] Austria, Finland, Greece, Norway, Portugal, Spain, Switzerland, Turkey, Yugoslavia.

[2] Abu Dhabi, Algeria, Dubai, Egypt, Iran, Iraq, Israel, Jordan, Kuwait, Lebanon, Morocco, Oman, Saudi Arabia, South Yemen, Sudan, Syria, Tunisia.

[3] Cameroon, The Central African Empire, Chad, Ethiopia, Gabon, Ghana, Ivory Coast, Kenya, Madagascar, Niger, Nigeria, Somalia, Tanzania, Uganda, Zaire, Zambia.

ANNEX D   PATTERN OF ENGINE SUPPLIES IN WORLD AIRCRAFT PRODUCTION BY MAJOR PRODUCING REGIONS

Engine company	U.S. military aircraft	U.S. civil aircraft a)	French aircraft	British aircraft	Aircraft in other ICs b)	LDC-produced aircraft c)
			Number of models powered			
Pratt & Whitney d) USA	35	60	3	3	9	11
General Electric USA	22	5	1	0	10	3
Detroit Diesel Allison e) USA	7	3	0	0	4	0
Continental USA	6	5	2	0	2	2
Avco Lycoming USA	6	6	20	11	34	16
Garrett f) USA	2	1	3	3	8	1
Rolls Royce UK	2	17	2	24	17	7
Snecma France	0	0	10	0	0	0
Volvo Sweden	0	0	0	0	10	0
Other	2	6 g)	2	1	13	8
Total no. of aircraft models	82	103	43	42	107	48

Source: Calculated from lists of U.S. military aircraft, U.S. transport aircraft and leading international aircraft models, provided by Aviation Week & Space Technology, March 3, 1980.

Notes: a) Excluding business and personalaircraft; b) Includes leading civil and military models built in Australia, Canada, Czecho-slovakia, Federal Republic of Germany, Finland, Italy, Japan, Netherlands, Spain, Sweden, Switzerland and Yugoslavia; c) Includes leading civil and military models built in Argentina, Brazil, India, Israel, South Africa and Taiwan; d) Belongs to United Technologies Corporation; e) A division of General Motors; f) A subsidiary of Signal Companies; g) Six passenger and cargo models of McDonnell Douglas, powered by CFM-engines, built by General Electric, USA and Snecma, France.

Company	Aerospace production profile													
	Attack aircraft	Bombers	Fighters	Reconnaissance	Observation	Marine patrol	Anti-submarine	Early warning	Transport	Training	Utility	Helicopters	Missiles	RPV
General Dynamics		x	x						x	x			x	
McDonnell Douglas	x		x	x					x				x	
United Technologies/Sikorsky												x		
Lockheed				x		x	x		x				x	x
Boeing		x						x	x				x	x
Hughes												x	x	
Raytheon													x	
Grumman	x		x		x			x						
Rockwell			x		x					x	x		x	x
Textron/Bell												x		
Northrop	x		x	x						x				x
Martin Marietta													x	
Fairchild Industries	x		x											
Ford Aerospace & Communications													x	
Vougt/LTV	x												x	
Cessna	x				x					x	x			
Beech									x	x	x		x	
Kaman												x		

Source: Aviation Week & Space Technology, March 3, 1980.

Note: Aviation parts and equipment producers excluded. RPV = remotedly piloted vehicle.

THE MISSILE INDUSTRY IN THE UNITED STATES

Company	Mission category					
	Air-to-Air	Air-to-Surface	Anti-submarine	SAM	SSM	Battlefield support
General Dynamics	x	x		x	x	
McDonnell Douglas	x	x				
Lockheed					x	
Boeing		x		x	x	
Hughes	x	x		x		x
Raytheon	x			x		x
Rockwell		x				x
Martin Marietta	x	x			x	x
Ford Aerospace & Communications	x			x		x
Vougt/LTV						x
Goodyear Aerospace			x			
Texas Instruments		x				
Bendix Aerospace				x		

Source: *Aviation Week & Space Technology*, March 3, 1980, pp. 104 and 150.

Note: SAM = surface-to-air missile.
SSM = surface-to-surface missile.

PRODUCTION PROFILES OF NON-U.S. MILITARY AERO-SPACE COMPANIES

Company	Country	Aircraft mission											
		Attack, strike	Bombers	Fighters	Surveillance, reconnaissance	Maritime functions	Transport	Training	Utility	Early warning	Ground support	Amphibian	Interceptor
GAF	Australia						x		x				
Canadair	Canada											x	
De Havilland	Canada						x						
Dornier	FRG						x		x				
Valmet	Finland							x					
SNIAS	France				x	x	x	x					
Dassault	France	x	x	x	x	x	x	x			x		x
Reims[b]	France							x	x				
British Aerospace	UK	x	x		x		x	x		x	x		x
Pilatus-Britten-Norman	UK				x		x						
Short Brothers	UK						x						
Aeronautica Macchi	Italy	x						x					
Aeritalia	Italy	x		x			x	x					x
Rinaldo Piaggio	Italy								x				
SIAI Marchetti	Italy	x				x		x			x		
Kawasaki	Japan					x	x						
Mitsubishi	Japan			x	x	x	x	x			x		x
Shin Meiva	Japan					x			x			x	
Fuji	Japan							x					
Fokker-VFW[a]	Netherlands				x	x	x	x					
CASA	Spain	x		x			x	x					
Saab Scania	Sweden	x		x	x		x	x					x
FAA	Switzerland							x					
Pilatus Aircraft	Switzerland						x	x					

Sources: Aviation Week & Space Technology, March 3, 1980, pp. 120-123, World Armaments and Disarmament. SIRPI Yearbook 1979, London 1979, pp. 72-139.

Notes: [a] Including Rhein-Flugzeugbau, FRG, a subsidiary of VFW.

[b] An affiliate of Cessna Aircraft, USA.

ANNEX H   MISSILE PRODUCERS IN WESTERN EUROPE, JAPAN AND AUSTRALIA

Company	Home Country	Air-to-surface	Air-to-air	Surface-to-air	Surface-to-surface	IRBM	SLBM	Anti-submarine	Anti-tank	Anti-aircraft (low level)	Anti-missile	Anti-ship	Air-to-ship
Dept. of Productivity	Australia							x					
Matra [b]	France	x	x	x	x								
SNIAS	France	x			x	x	x						
Euromissile [c]	France/FRG			x					x			x	x
MBB	FRG								x		x		
British Aerospace	Great Britain	x	x	x					x	x	x	x	x
Short Brothers	Great Britain			x	x								
Oto Melara	Italy				x								
Sistel	Italy	x		x	x								
Selenia	Italy			x	x								
Kawasaki	Japan							x					
Mitsubishi Electric [d]	Japan			x	x								
Mitsubishi Heavy Industr.	Japan			x								x	
Toshiba/ Kawasaki	Japan			x									
Kongsberg Vaapenfabrikk	Norway											x	
Bofors	Sweden	x		x	x				x				
Saab Scania	Sweden	x			x							x	

Sources: Aviation Week & Space Technology, March 3, 1980, pp. 110-111; SIPRI Yearbook 1979, op.cit., p. 140 and TAPRI data files.

Notes: a) Production or development; b) Mostly together with Thomson-CSF; c) A joint venture of MBB and SNIAS; d) With a licence from Raytheon, USA.

ANNEX I   THE LEADING WEAPONS INDUSTRIES IN FOREIGN MILITARY SALES OF THE U.S.

- Top 25 Companies Ranked According to Net Value of Military Prime Contract Awards in Fiscal Years 1976-1978

Company	Sales 1976 $ 000	Rank	Sales 1977 $ 000	Rank	Sales 1978 $ 000	Rank	Total sales 1976-78 $ 000	Rank based on total
General Dynamics	45 841	18	303 322	4	1 475 524	1	1 394 687	2
Litton Industries	258 454	4	120 941	10	523 620	2	903 015	4
Textron	115 470	10	73 540	15	441 456	3	630 466	8
Lockheed	139 111	9	305 226	3	297 292	4	741 629	5
McDonnell Douglas	480 460	2	446 134	2	273 857	5	926 594	3
Raytheon	218 555	6	149 028	8	271 046	6	638 629	7
Northrop	292 502	1	853 022	1	266 978	7	2 145 524	1
General Electric	248 134	5	220 958	6	175 657	8	644 749	6
Ret Ser Engineering					167 791	9	167 791	15
Hughes Aircraft	174 256	8	156 092	7	156 188	10	486 536	10
United Technologies	104 198	11	87 102	12	115 302	11	306 602	11
Vinnell Corp.					103 726	12	103 726	20
FMC	201 141	7			70 683	13	271 133	12
Grumman	303 662	3	252 814	5	69 992	14	626 468	9
Ford Motor			42 260	17	65 642	15	107 902	18
Harsco	61 428	15	39 698	18	63 648	16	164 810	16
Westinghouse Electric	43 862	20	70 986	16	56 403	17	171 251	14
Mi Rung Construction			137 710	9	56 323	18	194 043	13
Hyundia Construction					41 193	19	41 193	32
Chamberlain Mfg.			26 099	21	37 761	20	63 860	29
Honeywell	55 161	17			32 879	21	88 040	22
General Motors	44 714	19			31 969	22	76 683	26
Hercules			19 879	25	30 519	23	50 398	31
American Telephone & Telegrapf	24 596	23	26 773	20	28 176	24	79 545	24
Teledyne	27 024	22	21 241	24	26 871	25	75 136	27

Source: Foreign Military Sales, Top 25 Companies and Their Subsidiaries Ranked According to Net Value of Military Prime Contract Awards, Fiscal Years 1976, 1977, 1978. Department of Defense, Washington Headquarters Services, Directorate for Information Operations and Reports, May 15, 1978 (mimeo).